One
Woman's
West

Introductory

In the fall of 1838, a Virginia Planter with his Kentucky wife and family of six children, emigrated to Southwestern Missouria and settled on a piece of land in Green County, near the village of Springfield.

Missouria was then a wild region thinly inhabited, Indians were occasionly seen wandering through the Country, the Prairie wolf and other wild animals, were often started from their lair Prairie Chickens and wild Turkys were distributed all over.

The family were delighted with the Grand Prairie in which they had found

*The first page of Martha Gay Masterson's remarkable handwritten account of life on the Western frontier.*

# One Woman's West

Recollections of the Oregon Trail
and Settling the Northwest Country
by Martha Gay Masterson
1838-1916

### Edited by LOIS BARTON

Spencer Butte Press
Eugene, Oregon
1986

Copyright © 1990 by Lois Barton
ISBN 0-9609420-2-5
Library of Congress Catalog Number 86-15570

Book Design: *Gwen Rhoads*

Cover photography courtesy of the Oregon Historical Society,
ORHI 4626, File #188

First printing: *September 1986*
Second printing: *August 1989*
Third printing: *September 1990*
Fourth Printing: *September 1991*
Fifth printing: *October 1992*
Sixth printing: *March 1995*
Seventh printing: *October 1997*

**Other books by Lois Barton:**
*Howard & Edith Holloway Family History,* 1978, 1993
*Spencer Butte Pioneers,* 1982
*Lane County Historian Index,* 1984
*Daughter of the Soil,* 1985
*A Quaker Promise Kept,* 1990

Published by:
**Spencer Butte Press**
84889 Harry Taylor Road
Eugene, OR 97405
(541) 345-3962

This book is printed on acid-free, recycled paper.

# Dedication

To those courageous women
whose dependable competence and
compassionate outlook tempered
the cultural development of the
Pacific Northwest.

# Acknowledgments

The fascination of discovering details of a life lived out a century ago on the ground where I have walked for thirty years has provided many hours of enjoyment. Every picture of the place where Martha Gay walked has added another thrill to my search. She seems very vital and familiar, like a well-known family member. I am delighted to offer you this account.

As is always the case, the search could only be completed through the willing and skillful cooperation of many people and organizations. I am particularly indebted to Martha's great niece, Claire O'Callaghan and her cousin Ann, to June Stewart who allowed me to copy the transcript of Martha's story, and to Ken and Jim Mortensen, Alfred's great, great grandsons who did extensive research on the Masterson family. Hazel Vorhis and researchers of the Ozark Genealogical Society provided a wealth of information about the Gay holdings in Missouri. Ed Nolan and Glenn Mason, formerly at the Lane County Museum, sent vital tidbits from Spokane and Helena. Marty West, Ed Thatcher, and Charlotte Mills of Eugene held the key to vital clues. Iver Masterson of La Grande, Tom Stephens of Mitchell, and Ethel Briggs of West Virginia all responded out of personal interest in persons and places of the text. The Oliver Museum staff in Canyon City knew where to look in their picture files for the scenes appropriate to the story. Special collections personnel at Washington State University in Pullman, and University of Idaho in Moscow were most helpful. Vicki Davis, Susan Koentopp, and John Wood went out of their way to be helpful. Volunteers at the Clark County (Washington) Historical Museum, the Dayton (Washington) Historical Depot Society as well as Donna Nelson of Silverton (Oregon) and Douglas Olson of the Eastern Washington State Historical Society, were all most kind. The Springfield, Missouri Art Museum provided a picture of Springfield circa 1850 with no charge.

To all of you and others not mentioned, I offer my heartfelt thanks.

# Table of Contents

# Foreword

*"Too many interpretations have been built on the records men have left of their experiences in the West. It is time to let women speak for themselves and to examine what they can show us of the society they lived in."*—Let Them Speak For Themselves. *Women in the American West, 1849-1900, Christiane Fischer. New York: Dutton, 1978*

THIRTY-FOUR YEARS AGO I moved onto a farm in the foothills of the coast range at the head of the Willamette Valley in Oregon. Soon after I settled there, I became acquainted with a long-time resident named Harry Taylor whose stories of the preceding fifty years whetted my appetite for discovering more about the early settlers of this area. When the last of our eight children entered school, it became possible to begin the five-year search which culminated in the publication of *Spencer Butte Pioneers,* a book about those hardy souls who crossed the Oregon Trail in the 1850s and made their homes in this place. That book told of their experiences in crossing the long trail, their resourcefulness, and optimism in a new land where native Americans still roamed, and food and shelter were hard to come by.

Among those early settlers who homesteaded within "shouting distance" of our place, I was particularly drawn to Martha Ann Gay because of the plainspoken but poignant tales she told about her trail trip and her life in the Northwest. Only a portion of her story was found during the research for *Spencer Butte Pioneers.* After publication of that book, a nearly complete transcript of her life story came into my possession.

As I eagerly read through this more complete version, I found a page missing from the story wherein her father offered—in jest—to bargain with some Indian braves for horses in exchange for his daughters. What a terrible place to be left in suspense! It took me several months to locate the original manuscript and find out how they got out of that predicament.

In her story, Martha made an effort to conceal actual names of early playmates and later acquaintances as she recorded her memories. There is an original draft of material, which she later copied as she made the final version of her story, on which this book of recollections is based. In both the original draft and the later copy, names have been erased and other names written into the erased spaces. Also, names in the two versions did not always agree. Those names she included cannot be found in the 1840 and 1850 census records of Springfield and Greene County, Missouri. For some unknown reason the author chose not to identify most persons by their actual names in this history. In one case, she actually erased her brother-in-law's name as originally written and substituted "Mr. Jackwell" for John Cogswell. It is not clear whether protecting identities was a writing scruple of the 1890s, or an attempt by the author to respect the personal privacy of her friends, relatives and difficult characters.

Martha's story is a remarkable account of life on the Western frontier between the 1850s and the turn of the century. She begins by describing life in Greene County, Missouri in the 1840s and her family's preparation for their trip West over the Oregon Trail. Martha's telling of that 1851 trip across the plains, the Rockies and Cascades provides a graphic, first-hand account of one of America's most stirring historical movements as witnessed through the eyes of a thirteen year old girl with a gift for detail and writing.

The story continues with Martha's description of the family's homesteading in the Willamette Valley. Then in 1875, she married widower James Alfred Masterson, a blacksmith and survivor of the Ward Massacre, and took on the raising of his children. She packed up and moved the family 20 times in 20 years following her husband into gold rush towns, railroad construction camps and all over the Northwest. She operated hotels, boarding houses, grocery stores and dry goods shops. She traveled from The Dalles to Canyon City over the stage route by team and wagon in the dead of winter with two small children suffering from whooping cough. She offered to adopt an eager young Chinese boy who was working as a "tea carrier" on the Cascade Locks construction crew. And during the nomadic years, Martha's own two small sons died and were left buried in lonely graves when she had to pack up and move on to new "opportunities" in new locations picked out by husband Alfred—who turned out to be a dreamer and lifelong drifter.

The bulk of this book is told in Martha's own words. I have added a few historical notes, pictures and details about the family researched from private and public archives in an attempt to help the reader see and understand more clearly what Martha describes. To avoid confusion and assist the reader, I also have corrected punctuation and misspelled words.

How fortunate we are that Martha recorded her memories. Her stories are told from a different perspective than those of the well-known male historians, past and present, whose emphasis has been more on logistics and conflict with the Indians. Martha provides us with an authentic version of what an ordinary girl from an ordinary Missouri family experienced on their wagon trip West; she gives us an eye-witness glimpse of how pioneer women saw the beauty and bleakness of the frontier wilderness; and she also provides an insight on how some women, who were tied to itinerant homesteaders, maintained their dignity and good cheer by creating comforts and civility while having very little to work with. Historical manuscripts of this kind—that is, of such length and perspicacity—are rare indeed.

In describing her forebear, a great niece of Martha's said, "Aunt Mattie was a pert little woman who was fond of children and a wonderful storyteller. She lived with her daughter Frances when she got old. Frances never had any children of her own, and she had a beautiful house which she kept very tidy. When we went to visit, Aunt Mattie would take us out under a tree and tell us stories about crossing the plains and about Indians in her effort to help protect Frances' tidy house."

A brief picture of the situation on the Missouri frontier prior to the Gay family arrival will help the reader better understand prevailing conditions as Martha recalls those early days. Her story begins in Greene County, Missouri in 1838. Before 1800, this area was inhabited by Indians, mostly the Osage who were related to the Sioux. According to Harris and Phyllis Dark in *Springfield of the Ozarks*, Henry Schoolcraft, a leading geologist, made camp in 1818 where the village of Springfield was later established. Schoolcraft described abandoned Osage hunting village huts as "looking like inverted birds nests; long green poles, sharpened at both ends, were bent and stuck into the ground, the top ends crossing at the center to make a

*"Osage hunting village huts looked like inverted birds' nests; long green poles, sharpened at both ends, were bent and stuck into the ground, the top ends crossing at the center to make a circle. Twigs, leaves, moss and grass woven in between the poles made them habitable against the weather."*

circle. Twigs, leaves, moss and grass woven in between the poles made them habitable against the weather."

As the Osages moved west, settlers began to work their way up into the area. Schoolcraft encountered a few hunters and their families in 1818-1819 living in log houses along the White River. Schoolcraft's companion, William Pettijohn, came back from a hunting expedition and reported that he had discovered "the country which floweth with milk and honey, bear's oil and buffalo marrow—a settler's dream come true."

According to the Darks, "Those early settlers didn't realize they were trespassing on Indian lands. When the Delawares began to arrive, Thomas Patterson went to St. Louis to inquire about the validity of the settlers' claims. The Indian agent said that the Delawares owned the land. Most of the settlers moved, but about ten years later, when the Indians were sent to their final reservation in Kansas territory, many of the original families returned to their early claims."

It was in the late 1820s and early 1830s that the Indian claims to the area were finally withdrawn through treaties and the land became open for settlement. The Darks state that early settlers cleared the forests at the edge of the prairie for their farms because they distrusted the prairie grass land which didn't grow trees. Martha's father, on the other hand, chose to settle on the prairie.

Greene County was established by the Missouri legislature in 1833. An unusually severe winter in 1835 was hard on settlers and their livestock. Then, in June of 1836, a cholera epidemic broke out in town, resulting in the death of at least seven people. The official incorporation of Springfield took place in February 1838. At this time, the population of the town was about 300, nearly one-third slaves. A few months later, Martin Gay brought his family to Greene County from Arkansas.

It is at this point that Martha's detailed and colorful reminiscences pick up the story of the Gay family and continue through the events of the next 78 years. The editor reminds the reader to keep in mind the social and cultural circumstances of the era between 1838 and 1916. You need to understand that Martha Gay Masterson was a woman of her time and her writings about the racial groups who peopled the West along with the Caucasian pioneers express an ambiguity of attitudes prevalent in her time.

When Martha wrote about Indians as "savages," Negroes as "darkies" and "pickaninnies," and Chinese as "Chinamen," she was expressing the racial biases and language of her day—and for days to come. What the discerning reader will discover, however, is that Martha also wrote with understanding and compassion about the native people, the blacks and the Chinese she met in the frontier outposts of her life. In passages which refer to these groups, she sometimes voices the stereotypical prejudices of the times, but also writes with kindness and recognition of their intelligence, dignity and plight.

She seems to have instinctively realized the contradictions in her own attitude. Although she used racial terms we find offensive today, she also wrote about playing with children who were black, offering to adopt a bright Chinese boy, sending Alfred to rescue an Indian girl being tortured, giving shelter to a native family in the dead of winter and hiring an Indian girl as companion to her children.

Perhaps one of the most important revelations in Martha's manuscript—along with other frontier manuscripts written by women which are currently coming to light—is the difference in how men and women viewed the indigenous peoples, the blacks and the Asian workers. Martha seems to have been an accurate reporter of what she witnessed, often distinguishing one tribal group from another. In some of her stories, the Indians were peaceful and honest, and in others were not. There is some recognition on her part of why the Indians had grievances toward the settlers—particularly concerning the slaughter of the buffalo and the betrayal of treaties.

In her writing Martha has caught some of the ambiguity of the American character which we are still dealing with today. She was a real woman very much a product of her social and cultural world. She tells us real stories seen from the perspective of her rather unsophisticated, rural background. She lived with contradictions and to her credit, attempted to honestly say what actually took place in her frontier village life. We learn a lot from Martha about the ambivalent points-of-view held by the settlers, and it becomes a challenge to the discriminating reader to unravel the puzzle of what caused the tragic conflict and violence that so characterizes this period of American history.

# Chronology

1838   Martha born in Arkansas.

1851   Left Missouri for Oregon April 10.

1871   Married J.A. Masterson August 27. At home in Waconda, Oregon.

1873   John Balf born March 12 in Silverton, Oregon.

1874   Moved to Canyon City. Martha's mother died.

1875   Balf died. Moved to The Dalles, then Lane County. Freddie born May 23 at Creswell.

1876   Moved to Eugene in spring. Spent summer up the McKenzie. J.A. to eastern Oregon in the fall.

1877   Frances born at Cogswell place February 11. To Prineville and Ochoco for three months. Winter at Bridge Creek.

1878   To The Dalles for the summer. In fall moved to Lower Cascades.

1879   To Upper Cascades. Had grocery and dry goods store. Ship canal under construction. Freddie died.

1880   J.A. working with "the company". Martha ran boarding house.

1881   Closed out boarding house due to ill health.

1882   Moved out on line of N.P.R.R., camping for the summer. Had supply store and traded with settlers and workmen. In October to Vancouver, Washington.

1883   To Dayton in eastern Washington.

1884   To Coeur d'Alene, Idaho. On to Delta in the spring of 1885.

1886   Moved to Spokane.

1887   Mamie died.

1888   Bess married in Spokane.

1889   To Pend Orielle in the spring.

1889   Martha and Hortense to Coeur d'Alene so Hortense could go to school.

1890   To Gray's Harbor in May. To Centralia in fall.

1892   To Eugene for last move.

1898   Frances married June 8.

1916   Martha died in Eugene December 12.

*[These dates are approximate and based on Martha's account of their movements. A few dates can be confirmed by reference to ages of the children or some similar notation in her writings.]*

# Part I
# The Road West

"*Life in the wilderness challenged every woman to become her essentially ingenious and resourceful self, that inventive and persistent creature who made civilization in the domestic sense possible.*"
—Westward the Women. Nancy Wilson Ross. San Francisco, California: North Point Press, 1985. p. 173

IN 1892, 41 years after she actually traveled the Oregon Trail, Martha Masterson decided to record the story of her life. She wrote on the lined pages of three writing tablets. In her firm handwriting she covered every page completely, both front and back. She apparently had access to her brother James' diary, kept by him as they crossed the plains, because her recollection of events coincides very closely with his report of daily happenings.

In her account she frequently referred to times when the family got together and talked of earlier days and of their trip from Missouri to Oregon. Such repetition of family memories would have established these experiences indelibly in her mind. Because of the family story-telling tradition, writing seems to have come rather easily to Martha as she faithfully chronicled tales of their past.

In 23 years time, Martha's father, Martin Gay moved his family from Kentucky to Tennessee to Missouri to Arkansas and back to Missouri before leaving for Oregon. His wife, Ann, was very reluctant to undertake the long and dangerous trip to Oregon with 11 children to look after while expecting a twelfth. She eventually consented and cooperated in preparations for the trek with a good heart. Her example was probably an important reason why her daughter Martha went along as amiably as she did in her 20 moves with husband Alfred.

1

After the Gay family reached Oregon, they established a home near Albany, but Martin decided within a year to relocate in Lane County where there was more unfenced land available for pasture and ranching. He promised Ann they would never move again, and they didn't.

Martin Gay was opposed to slavery. Martha refers to her father's black helpers as tenants. But there were slaves in her family who belonged to her grandmother and other relatives when the Gay family lived in Missouri. Martha's childhood playmates were black as well as white. She was critical of owners who were cruel to their slaves and wrote about the loyalty of freed Negroes who had been treated kindly.

Martha's family sometimes called her Amanda. Her youngest sister was named Sarah Julia, but all through the account she was called Pink. Her other sister, Mary Ann, was known as Mamie, and some of her brothers were occasionally referred to by nicknames. Since Martha wrote freely about her sisters, naming them without reservation, one wonders why she was so cautious when it came to accounts involving her brothers, her husband and Alfred's sons from his first marriage. When she noted that a "brother" was to be married, I was able to identify which brother because of previous research on *Spencer Butte Pioneers* and I've indicated this in editorial notes. Perhaps Martha's pattern of not identifying male family members by name was indicative of the distance which existed between women and the affairs of the men in their lives.

Chapter 1

# Childhood Memories
# Of a Missouri Farm

IN THE FALL OF 1838 a Virginia Planter with his Kentucky wife
and six children emigrated to southwestern Missouri and settled
on a tract of land in Greene County near the village of Springfield.
With the help of neighbors a large log house was built, and they rejoiced to be in a good warm shelter when the winter storms set in.

My father was born in 1803. His foreparents were English and
had settled near Jamestown in 1630. He often related his family
history as handed down from one generation to another, telling us
about the early settlements and Captain Smith and the pretty story
of Pocahontas, an ancestor, and about Mount Vernon, the home of
General Washington. He was proud to say they lived in the same
county.

Mother was born in Kentucky near the home of Abe Lincoln and
was about the same age. Her parents were Southern people of
Scotch descent. Grandmother claimed to be a lineal descendant of
Mary Stuart of Scotland.

I was born in Arkansas in November 1837, two thousand miles
from my present home. *[Martha was the only one of the Martin
Gay family who was born in Arkansas. A neighbor of the Gay's,
Joseph Gott, who had emigrated from Kentucky to southwest
Arkansas, once described Arkansas at that time as "the best poor
man's country in the world; i.e., if a man went there poor he was
sure to remain so." Did the Gays also live only briefly in Arkansas
for similar reasons? Ed.]*

We had been living on the *[Missouri]* farm two years in 1840
when the first incident of my life of which I have any recollection
was indelibly stamped on my mind.

My brothers and sister Mamie were playing with me in the door
yard late one evening. We were having a nice time, but stopped our

3

*"A great shaggy prairie wolf leaped over the fence almost in our midst."*

play when we heard the greyhounds chasing some wild animal which seemed to be coming directly toward our playground. Imagine our terror when a great shaggy prairie wolf leaped over the fence almost in our midst. We all screamed with fright and ran toward the house and met mother coming out to look after us as she had seen the wolf coming our way. I was so frightened that I fell limp in my brother's arms and he thought I was dead.

I have no remembrance of anything more till the next summer when I was three and a half years old.

Mother had left me with Mamie and gone to visit our neighbor. One of the boys brought a pretty butterfly and laid it in my lap as I sat on the floor playing. I put out my hand to take it up and it flew in my face, frightening me into a spasm. In memory, I can see that butterfly yet.

From my fourth year I can recall many events of my childhood days. I often look back to those days. My young mind was filled with wonder as the events of life unfolded. Life on the farm was happy; rambling through the groves after wild plums and grapes, hunting berries and birds' nests, picking strawberries and wild flowers, tramping through the snow in winter setting traps for prairie chickens and snares for rabbits. I always followed where my brother Martin, Jr. led the way. He was two years older. His sports and plays were mine too. Mamie had to help Mother. I was not yet old enough to work and I did not mind to be called a tomboy. We set our traps and caught our birds and rabbits and carried them proudly home.

Father, being a thrifty business man, soon had a large farm all fenced and in cultivation. Also an orchard of fruit trees set out. Barns and shops and houses for tenants were added to the improvements, and when I was seven years old there was quite a village on our farm. Many new settlers had come to make their homes in the grand prairie, and we now had good schools.

My brothers and Mamie attended school and I assisted mother about the work and looked after the little children. I often wished I could go to school as I felt that would really be an important event in my life. At last I was permitted to go if I would promise to be good and quiet, for Mamie said the teacher was very cross. I remember him as an old-style man wearing a long swallowtail coat, said coat being very black and slick. He was a cross, surly-looking individual and carried a rod of correction in his hand. He had a long nose and a sharp chin. I was of the opinion that all school teachers looked just like him. He marched around occasionally and if he discovered any fun or idleness going on, down would come that switch causing the juveniles to draw themselves into small parcels to evade

*Murray school*

the rod. How we disliked him! He usually sat stark and stiff in a chair and we all had to go to him to ask how to pronounce a word or do a sum. We dared not ask "Work an example" as children do now.

One morning as we were going to school Mamie found a little white lamb in the fence corner. Its mother had deserted it. We carried it back to the house and I stayed at home to care for it during the day. We were pleased when mother said we could have it for a pet. We taught it to play with us. It soon wanted to follow us all about the farm and also wanted to go to school with us. We taught it to bunt and we had many a romp with our lamb. However, it got to be a dangerous playfellow for the little children. We always had a baby in the house and we older children had to take care of the baby as mother had to work.

My first experience at caring for a baby was a sad one. Mother told me to take baby brother out in the yard and walk with him to keep him quiet till she dressed to go to Meeting. We did not say *church* then. I had been walking with him till I was tired and was going in when I fell with him in my arms and his head struck a stone doorstep. I raised up and tried to lift him, but when I saw blood on his forehead and he did not move, I thought I had killed him. I then screamed to mother. She ran out and got the dear little one and carried him in and called father. In a little while they revived him and dressed the bleeding wound. The little sufferer was some days recovering. A load was removed from my mind when little Dave was well again.

I was afraid to carry him ever after this mishap and was glad when he could walk. But walking also brought him into trouble as he persisted in following me everywhere over the farm. One day I asked mother to let me go to the shop to get blocks to play with and see father make a table. He was a cabinet maker and I liked to watch him while at work. I had left Dave playing in the dooryard and did not think he saw me go.

I was on my way back to the house when I saw him coming up the road near the fence to meet me. I saw Billy, the pet sheep, running toward the child. I ran as fast as I could to protect him, but Billy got to Dave first and hurt him quite badly. He then tried to attack me, but I climbed on the fence after I got Dave over. Father had to sell that sheep and we were not sorry to see him go.

My grandparents came to live with us when I was quite small, and also an uncle and aunt and their children came on the farm. They were all from Tennessee and had their servants with them. My father was opposed to slavery and we had no slaves. Grandmother's old colored woman was a curiosity to us little folks. We were shy of her at first and kept very quiet when she came near us. She was a kind motherly old negress and we soon became very fond of her and received many little tokens from her hand, sweetmeats and candy balls. We really loved dear old Chaney.

While my uncle and aunt lived with us their little Sarah died. We had never seen a dead person before, and we could not realize what death meant. We did not know why little Sarah was so cold and still and why she slept all the while. But when they put her in a little casket which father made and buried her away off in the farther corner of the orchard under a peach tree we realized she had gone and would be with us no more.

Grandmother told us she was an angel. Then we wanted to know where angels lived and why we could not see them. We did wonder and talk about that dear dead baby. We could not understand why she had to be buried. We wanted to keep her. We were taught to care for the little grave and to know that it was a sacred place. We would step softly and speak in subdued tones when we were near it. When playing in that part of the orchard, we were pleasant and kind toward each other.

Grandmother was a great Bible student. She was rather a tall old lady dressed in the style of that day. She wore a Martha Washington kerchief pinned firmly across her bosom. Her glasses were of goggle size and her cap was white. She had a kindly face and I always picture her as sitting in a large armchair with a Bible open on her lap and a crowd of children about her listening to Bible stories. She would read to us till she would droop her head and go to sleep. Then we would move quietly away and leave her to rest. When she awoke and we were gone she would say, "Why, bless me, did I go to sleep?" We thought her very old.

Grandfather was nearly one hundred years old. He was small and very much stooped. He was fond of children and we had many a romp with him. Born about 1750, he was a young officer in the Revolutionary Army, a captain of a company. In 1812, during the battle, his company ran out of powder. He had a powder mill at home and Great Mother *[great grandmother?]* stirred off the powder and sent it to him to carry on the fight against the British. During his absence she managed the mill for she understood the work, having often helped him make powder. We were very fond of our grandparents.

When I was little there was a call for a company of volunteers in our part of the country. The men were often mustered near our house and we could hear the fife and drum. My brothers were not old enough to go, but one of my cousins went and an uncle. They went to Mexico and never came back. Grandmother was sorry, but she said it was right for them to help defend their country. They were descendants of soldiers and wanted to go and help fight for their rights. The soldiers were gone a long time and when they came home many were missing from their ranks. When they were mustered out of service there was a great dinner given to them and then they went home.

One of my uncles was an officer in the Mexican War and was in some severe engagements and never received a wound, but had several horses killed under him.

Grandmother moved away from us when I was quite young. She would come and see us and we were always glad to have her. Grandfather seldom came as he was so old.

Time wore on. The boys were a great help to father in many ways. Four of them were now old enough to assist in farm work. Our tenants were good and industrious people, but father thought it right for his sons to learn farming.

In the spring when the men were plowing the fields and planting the corn, it was my delight to go out and follow after them, tripping along the fresh turned furrow and watching for snakes. But my greatest pleasure was to be permitted to drop the grains of corn in the hills. I would tramp around after my brothers planting the corn and think it was just fine sport. Then later on gather roasting ears for dinner. And the husking bees were jolly times.

I thought the cotton fields were pretty, but I did not like to pick cotton. It was slow work for me. I thought it better suited for darkies and left it for them.

I liked to help about pailing the cows and churning the cream in the great wooden churn. It was my special work to go after old Pink and Cherry and drive them home. Then I opened the gate and let the cute little calves run to them, then Mamie, my older sister, gave me a little cup and taught me how to milk.

We had a nice dairy built over the spring where we kept the milk and butter and cream jars. Mamie was in the dairy one day churning. A crowd of us little folks were playing nearby. One of the little boys thought to play a joke on her, and he fastened the door on the outside. Then we all forgot about it and wandered off to another part of the yard. Soon a baby brother came from the house toward the spring. Not seeing us about, he went to play in the water and dropped his cap in. In trying to get the cap he fell in. Mamie heard the splash and called to us to open the door. We had gone away and didn't hear her. She yelled for help, knowing it was surely the baby. At last she got the door open and ran to the spring and found baby there drowning. She snatched him from the water and called for mother who came running and got the child into the house. She did all she could to resuscitate him. At last he gasped, and she quickly undressed him and rolled him in hot blankets. When we came in mother asked who had fastened the door so Mamie could not get out, saying it nearly caused baby brother's death. We were very sorry and tried to be good a long time after that accident.

I had been sent on an errand one day and was told to hurry back. The shortest road home was through the pasture. I was running along all right till I spied a drove of little pigs lying asleep in a fence corner. I thought it would be fine sport to rouse them and get a better view of them. I did so by stirring them about with a stick. This caused them to squeal out, and the mother who was nearby came charging toward me. I ran from her in great alarm and fell headlong, rolling into a small creek. I scrambled out and ran home crying, all wet and muddy. After that I was willing to leave little pigs asleep.

There was a large grove about a mile from our house where wild grapes, plums and berries grew. I wished very much to go with my brothers and Mamie to see a cave there which they told me about and also to get plums, but mother said I was too small to walk so far. I begged until I got permission to go. How I enjoyed that walk, the wonder and amazement I felt when I stood on the brink of the precipice peering down into the dark crater of that cave. The boys led us around to a path by which we could descend into the cavern. We found some special shells and stones and saw the den where the wolf lived—the one which had jumped over the fence and scared us. We hunted birds' nests, gathered some plums and went home to tell mother of our adventures. How children magnify things! That cave was about ten feet deep and about twenty across.

The most wonderful cave near us was at the old schoolhouse. It was very large and opened out from the foot of a hill at the root of some large walnut trees. A spring of cold water came rushing down from it. The cavern extended back under the hill some distance.

There was a plum orchard and wild grapevines on that hill where the boys made grapevine swings for their sweethearts fifty years ago. The old schoolhouse was a log structure with a big fireplace, long narrow windows, wooden benches devoid of backs and no desks. There we learned our abc's. Some of the big boys and girls studied Rukham's grammar.

When I was seven years old I went home with one of my cousins to stay all night. I had never been away from home to spend a night before. I was very well pleased till the shades of evening descended. Then I wished I was at home with mother. My aunt and cousins were very kind to me, but I wanted to be at home in my own little trundle bed.

Mamie was out playing one evening with our brothers when two neighborhood boys came to play with them. Presently, Frank and one of the visitors got into a fight, as boys usually do, and began throwing stones at each other. Of course their brothers had to help them in the fight. Mamie was in danger of getting hurt, and her brothers stood in front of her to shield her from the stones. She peeped around at the boys and a stone struck her on the forehead and cut a gash. She cried out and fell to the ground. The stormy battle ceased and the angry boys all ran to her. When they saw the blood running over her face, they were frightened and got her into the house as quickly as they could. The visitors ran home and told their mother, insisting that she go quick to see Mamie. My sister often told me what caused the cute little scar over her right eye and said she received it in her first battle. She carried that scar to her grave fifty years after.

Mamie went to school alone one day in early autumn. The boys had to stay home to help pull corn. The road led down by the big spring, up by the shop and orchard, then across the bleak prairie. She was well acquainted with the way and no danger was thought of in permitting her to go and come alone. If she wished, she could return with neighbor children.

The afternoons were short and even before time for her arrival Mother was anxious about her and often looked out to see if she might be coming. Night was fast approaching. A dark cloud was rising. Mother was too distressed to stay indoors. She went out and called to father, telling him Mamie had not come home. Then she started out to search for her. She saw Mamie coming quite fast with her dinner bucket in her hand and her hood blown back showing her excited face. Following her was a large prairie wolf. Father at once called his greyhounds. Old Remus came quickly and chased the wolf to its den. Father carried Mamie home in his arms, thankful for her timely rescue. The prairie wolves, when hungry, were very ferocious and would attack people.

Father went next morning and found the wolf den and killed the

*"I turned and saw a big wolf coming after me, but it stopped when I had my face toward it."*

old wolf and captured its whelps and gave them to Mamie for pets. Mamie was not permitted to go alone any more till the wolves were all killed off.

## The Story as Mamie Told It

I left the schoolhouse when the teacher and the other children did. When we got to Nellie Lair's home, she asked me to stop and play a little while and I stayed too long. Nellie's mother said if I was going home I had best run along as it would be dark in a little while. Anna and John had gone ahead of me. I had asked them to walk slow, but they lived so far away they had to hurry. I ran as fast as I could but I could not see them. When I was coming up the long lane, I got afraid of wolves. Then I climbed over the fence and ran faster. When I heard a noise, I looked back and saw a big wolf standing with its front feet upon the fence trying to get over to come follow me. I was so scared I did not know what to do. I did wish father would come. I ran on and I heard the wolf growl. I turned around and saw it coming after me, but it stopped when I had my face toward it. So I walked backwards to keep it from following me till I got some distance away. Then I would turn around and run from it. When it would come near me again, I would face it and walk backwards. I had turned from it and was running when father came to me and then old Remus came and chased it away. I was so tired when father met me. I think the old wolf would have got me very soon.

I went next morning and showed where the wolf got over the fence and father soon found its den and killed it and got the little baby wolves and gave them to me for pets. They were very cunning little creatures and grew nicely, but brother Frank teased them so much that one of them snapped his hand and we had it killed for fear it would bite me. One choked to death on a cob. Then the other one pined for its little playmates and wandered away on the prairie. Frank was sorry he had tormented them so much, but then boys always like to tease little girls and their pets. Frank did at any rate. I was provoked at him for I missed them as playthings. I will never forget my wolf chase anyway.

*Mary Francis (Mamie)*

I liked to go to the schoolhouse by the cave. When we went to school in the summer time we would put our bottles of milk in the cave to keep cool. Then at noon we would have such nice little dinner parties, then go on the hill above the spring and gather red plums and berries.

We had great kilns to dry peaches near the orchard. It was sport for we girls and boys to gather the peaches and cut them ready for the dry kilns. In the evenings we would stay out and keep the fires burning in the kilns and play on the greensward chasing fireflies and listening to the whippoorwill songs. Often the tenant's children would come and join in our sport.

I remember one family of tenants as being very nice people. We liked their little boy and girl very much. We were all out playing one day near the shop, and we wanted an ax to chop a stick. Little Jim said he would go to their house and get one. We saw him coming with it, carrying it on his shoulder. When he got nearly to us he fell down and the ax struck his hand and cut off two of his fingers. How frightened we were! We thought Jim would die, sure. We got him home to his mother and then ran after our father and he dressed the poor bleeding hand. After Jim was made comfortable, someone asked what we did with his fingers. We had not seen the severed fingers and we went to hunt for them, but could not find them. We searched as long as it was light, then went again the next day and many times we looked but never found them. Jim's hand got well but it was a crippled hand. We were sad to hear him lament about his fingers. He said he was afraid something had carried them away. Mother said she thought so too, but did not wish to tell him so.

We had ducks on the farm and Jim and Amelia would go with us to hunt their nests. We were out searching for nests one day when we found a guinea hen's nest. Who ever saw so many eggs in one nest? We could not carry them all in our hands and had to get a basket. When we counted them, we found there were sixty. Mother told us that was five dozen eggs. Guinea hens all claim one nest. Mother said that was their habit unless chased away. When we went back a week later to get more eggs there was not one there. We searched awhile and found a new nest and also found a thief taking the eggs. A huge blacksnake was helping himself. He had swallowed several and was still by the nest. We ran away and left that nest and the eggs to the snake.

As time wore on father enlarged his farm. He had tenants to manage the farm work and he worked at his trade, making furniture for the neighbors. But he thought to better his condition by speculating and accordingly went in the pork business. He needed a partner to carry on the work properly. The partner thought a third man was needed to run such as business as they anticipated having. The company was organized. Men were sent out to buy and collect fat hogs. Hundreds were at last ready to be driven to St. Louis. Father and the men started with a fine drove of nice fat hogs. They were some time going the long distance because they had to travel slowly. At last they arrived at their destination. They could not sell their hogs at the price they expected and could not afford to take any less. So they concluded to build a flat boat, kill the hogs, make pork of them and send them down to New Orleans. This all caused a great expense and great delay. After seeing one of the partners start on his way down the Mississippi River, father and the other one came home and waited patiently to hear from him and the boat load of pork. But they never heard. All the debts and great expense arising from the enterprise fell to father to settle. The other man was a bilk.

Mother had opposed the project from the start. Father had to sell off all the horses and cattle, sheep, corn and farming implements to settle up the partnership business. When he had done this, he found he was financially ruined and felt very much discouraged. We had been on the farm eight years. We hated to see our gentle horses and pet cows driven away.

Father got a nice seven-acre lot in the edge of town and built a house and then came and moved us to it. He did not sell the farm. We all hoped to go back to it some day. I did not like our town home very well at first, but when I got acquainted with some children and accustomed to the place, I became very fond of life there. Mother was well pleased. We soon had friends about us and were happy in our new home.

Chapter 2

# Life in Springfield, 1846-1851

I WAS NINE YEARS OLD NOW. Father built shops and went into the cabinet business very extensively in the fall of 1846 and soon had all he could do. Our lot was a stony piece of ground but well situated. He had the stones all picked up and built into a stone fence around the garden, making a fine wall which served as breast works *[a low barrier to protect gunners]* for soldiers in a battle fought there during the Civil War. There were some very large forest trees on the lot which bore nuts. Father left those standing. Our place was like a country home. There were great shade trees in the little pasture and immense elm and walnut trees in the back yard. Father had a well dug near an old oak tree. While the men were digging the well, they found an ax and a musket ball. It was a mystery how they ever got there, away down under the ground, for Missouri was then a new country. We added one convenience after another till we were very comfortable.

My two oldest brothers *[James and Frank]* helped father in the shops and three others, Mamie and I went to school. *[Martha refers here to her other brothers John, Baker and Evans.]* Small boys were permitted to attend if they were very pleasant and nice. No bad boys or large boys could go. We had a model school. Professor Beck and his cultured wife were from New York, and that alone was in those days proof of its standing as a superior institution of learning. Their able assistant was a sweet young lady. We were students of the Seminary in Springfield. The rules were very strict and we did not dare break them.

Everyone was to go in at the ringing of the first bell and stand by their own desk ready to be seated as the second bell rang. Then not a whisper till recess. Out on the playground not an unpleasant or bad word to be spoken. No quarreling and no unkind remarks to be

15

made at school. If our lessons were not perfect we had to stay in and study or get three black marks and a scolding and stand behind the blackboard with our names on the board telling who was in disgrace for imperfect lessons. I recall being behind the board once when a little friend was also sent there. We were forbidden to speak or even look at each other. Maggie told me at recess that she did want to cry but feared the teacher might know if she did. So she only sighed.

The playgrounds were near an old graveyard. We would go there and look at the cold marble slabs and read the names on them and memorize the inscriptions. Some of the girls had friends and relatives buried there. The place was in a shady grove and the trees were well trimmed and the grass cared for.

One day on the playground a group of girls were playing housekeeping. We made calls like grown young ladies and were happy for a time till someone made a remark about a certain lady staying too long. Then a few hasty words. Then a quarrel followed. Maggie Dolan called Felia Randell a fool and said she was too contrary to live in either heaven or hell. We all knew instantly that someone would tell the teacher of that speech for that was very unladylike. Maggie was a great favorite with most of the girls. Ting-a-ling went the bell. We walked to our seats and as we faced the teacher's desk we saw Felia's little sister telling her teacher something. We knew she heard what Maggie said to Felia and we knew the professor would hear of the quarrel. Then the bell rang and the professor said all who heard the expression which Maggie made to Felia please come down near the desk. Then we had to tell on Maggie. She was found guilty and had to stay after school and commit to memory three pages in history. Maggie told me the next day that two pages and a scolding paid the penalty, as she was a favorite. We were all soon friends again.

At the close of each term we would have an examination and exercises. Then prizes awarded. They were given for the greatest number of perfect lessons and the best behavior. I received the prize once in my class and I proudly wore the white wreath and was envied by my classmates till I wished I had not received it.

There were two Indian girls attending our school. They were very bright pupils. One was a fine artist and the other liked music. The Eastern Indians are a more intelligent race than those out West.*

---

*This statement of Martha's was probably based on her personal observations, and doesn't take into account the longer association with Caucasian culture which Eastern Indians had.

*Springfield, Missouri, circa 1850. Note slave quarters in foreground. Springfield was incorporated in February, 1838, at which time nearly one-third of the population was slaves.*

One day we saw some men riding up the street and when they drew near we noticed they were Indians. They were in town on business in connection with the press. One of them was an editor and was well educated.

### The Skeleton in the Closet

Sister and I went home with the doctor's daughter to spend the night. They lived in the country near town. They had a regular Southern mansion, a large family and a small army of darkies of all ages from a little pickaninny to an old white-haired mammy. Some were black as midnight and some were not so black, but all were slaves. We were having a good time playing games and telling stories. Someone proposed making a hobgoblin scarecrow. This we thought would be a fine thing to frighten the colored population. The hob was accordingly made and when we got him all made up to our notion and placed on a cousin of the doctor's, we got frightened of him ourselves. Then we went quietly out to the negros' quarters and had goblin rattle on their windows and peep in at them. They were very superstitious people, easily frightened. They ran screaming for their master. We got back into the house as quickly as we could and hid the scarecrow and when they came in we seemed as much excited as they did. Poor darkies, they were too scared to sleep that night and did not want to go back to their cabins.

Sister and I occupied a large room downstairs with the doctor's daughters. After we had put out the candles, one of the girls whispered over to us and said, "Did you ever see a skeleton?" We said no. Then said one, "Are you afraid of a skeleton?" Sister said no. I said, "Yes, I am."

"Well, then," said the little girl, "you had better cover your head for there is one over there in the closet and it's all bones. Dry rattling bones they are too. It's just an awful looking thing."

"Why do you keep such an article?" I asked.

"It is the doctor's and has to stay there so he will know how to cut off people's arms."

I was too scared to sleep. I listened all that long night to hear the skeleton shake his bones. I never went into that room again.

There was a very old man living in our neighborhood. I think he was ninety years old. Father liked to talk with him. He was well informed and had much to say on political questions. He had been a soldier in the Revolution and I think an officer in the War of 1812. His hair was white but he retained all his faculties. He was bright and cheerful and fond of children. He always reminded me of the prophets we read about in the Bible. When I knew him he was very much stooped.

He came to see us when we were starting West. He had much to say about the war cloud which was gathering in connection with the slavery question. He said there would soon be a fearful war in the United States. We asked him where and he said, "Right here and everywhere. You will live to see it, but I will not. This beautiful land will be a battlefield." And sure enough it was. A fierce battle was fought through Springfield and on Wilson Creek.

Maggie Dolan and I went home with a schoolmate to stay all night. She had a lovely home on Wilson Creek. She had often told me about their peacocks and silkworms. I was delighted to see the peacocks strutting about, spreading their gaudy tails in the sunlight. The cocoonery was a busy place. There seemed to be thousands of the silkworms. The little ticking noises they made were like so many little watches ticking away. The ladies who had charge of them were very kind to show us how the thread was drawn from the cocoons.

They also showed us some silk thread they were spinning on a little wheel and gave us some cocoons for mementos. We then walked over the lawn down to Wilson Creek and then to a large spring to see the milk house where Aunt Linda kept her milk and butter. She was a kind old darky and let us carry the cream mug and butter platter to the house. We went to some peach trees and got peaches for dinner, then walked about until we were called in.

The meal was a very quiet one. The father was dead, the mother very old. There were two maiden sisters and two brothers and my friend who was the youngest of the family. She was twelve years old.

After dinner we played and looked at Jennie's pets. She had rabbits, birds and cats and a gentle pony. When the shades of night came down, I got homesick and felt like crying. Maggie and I had a large room and she told me there had been a ghost seen in that room once and it walked right down the wall. I was very timid and asked her to please not tell about ghosts. I soon fell asleep and when I awoke the sun was shining. We heard Aunt Linda calling us for breakfast and found the family awaiting us in the breakfast room.

I had another friend who lived out of town on another road. I often went to see her. She was my classmate and my own age. I scarcely ever stayed very long at her house. Their servants were very cross.

I was staying with her one Christmas night and her father told her to go to the servants' house and get him some tobacco. Anna was afraid to go alone in the dark and asked me to go with her. It was only a short distance. We started out across the yard and were scared when we heard low voices near us. We ran back into the house not knowing who it could be out there.

One of the slaves had run away a few days before and we were afraid it was him talking to some of the house servants. We waited till we thought they had gone then we started again. We ran quickly to old Ned's house, Anna got the tobacco and we ran home. She would not tell her father about hearing the talking. She thought he was too cruel to his slaves. He had whipped Tom before he ran away. Anna did hope Tom got a supper from old Cinda, the cook.

Anna's father was the only man I knew who was cruel to his slaves. Anna was sorry for the slaves and tried to have him treat them kindly. He had been brought up to treat them harshly and no coaxing from Anna would convince him that it was wrong. When the slaves were set free, his all left him. There were many who stayed with their masters after they were free. My aunt told her women they were free and asked them if they wanted to go away. They cried and begged to stay saying, "How would you get along without us? We do not want to go. We have no other home." Then aunt assured them they could have a home and plenty as long as she lived.

Our nearest neighbors lived just across the street. They were from Tennessee, a family of four. Father, mother and two children, a girl of eight and a boy of five. They were wealthy Southern people and engaged in the mercantile business. Mr. Larmer was a proud aristocratic man of overbearing disposition and not very well liked by his neighbors, while his wife was a sweet lovable little woman admired by all. Bessie, their little daughter, and I were often together. We attended the same school, going and coming together.

The Larmers had four servants—Dan the coachman and gardener, Aunt Emly the cook, Mandor the house girl, and Molly the maid. We often played on their lawn near a fountain. Molly, being Bessie's maid, was usually with us. She was a trim, neat little negress and we liked to have her in our plays. She had a little sister too who would come out to watch us.

One day Bessie said she would make a good little girl of Molly's sister and dipped her in the fountain. The little one screamed out. Aunt Emly ran out to see what harm had come to her blessed little chile and found her almost drowned. She told her mistress what Miss Bessie had done and we all had to go in and receive a lecture from Mrs. Larmer. She told Bessie it was very naughty to treat the child so. Bessie said she didn't mean to be unkind. She had only baptized her like the preachers did. We let that be the last baptizing except for a few cats and pigs, but we usually played preaching once a week and had all the children on the street in attendance. Bessie sang nicely.

Bessie got the fever one cold winter. She was very sick for a long while and I was not allowed to go near her till she could sit up. Then I would go and read to her and amuse her. It was a long, long time before she was well enough to leave the room. She had lost her long brown ringlets. She never looked like her former self to me again because we came West the next spring before her hair grew long again.

## The Lizard

On the next street back of our home lived an old couple with their granddaughter and a train of servants. Little Mattie was a motherless child and a pet of her grandparents and nurse. She was a fair girl with laughing blues eyes and flaxen curls. They were from Mississippi. The old gentleman had been a reverend and was stately and trim in long coat and tall hat. The old lady was too aristocratic for that small town and often went to some city for pleasure.

She had had a long sickness and after her doctors pronounced her well, she imagined she could not walk. No one could convince her to try. She did not walk and was a helpless burden.

One day they all started on a journey off to some city in their own conveyance to visit friends. At noon they stopped by the roadside to rest under some shade trees and eat their dinner. Some cushions were placed under an oak and grandma was carried to them. She was resting nicely and all were enjoying their dinner when they were amazed to see her jump up and run to the coach and climb in without any help. They all looked after her in astonishment. They did not know what possessed her to do such a thing. Thought she was demented. The darkies were afraid to go near her, thinking an evil spirit had seized her. She could not speak for some moments, then she cried out, "Lizard!" Then louder, "Lizard!" They looked and near her cushions they saw a large lizard basking in the sun. It had been disturbed and had run directly across the old lady's lap. She unconsciously jumped up and ran and ever after that fright she walked as lively as she ever had. She often laughingly told about her scare and said she did not wait to think whether she could walk or not. She just tried to get away from that pesky lizard.

## The Singing School

Sister came home one evening from a friend's house and told me we were to attend a singing school. Now I had never even heard of a singing school and I wanted to know what it was like, how it was conducted and what was required of a singing pupil. I wondered about the singing part of it and how a scholar could learn a singing lesson. I finally told Mamie I did not want to go. She tried to explain how the class was taught. When she got ready to go she insisted I go with her. Mother said if I did not like it I need not go again. So I went and was delighted with it. I met so many of my friends there. I was eager to go all the time and became so interested in it that the teacher selected me to sing in a chorus at his concert. We went to practice quite often. There were ten little misses near the same size. We would stand around the melodeon [*a small reed organ*] singing while the instructor played for us. We felt quite proud of our accomplishment the night of the concert and a little superior to those girls who did not sing. I learned what a singing school was, if nothing more, and was glad I had attended.

A school friend came in one day and told me she had a little baby sister at her home and asked me to go with her and see it. Mother said I could go, so off we scampered to see the cute baby girl. It was a cunning baby and I did so wish it was my own sister. I had eight brothers and only one sister. Nelly said I could call her sister my own and come every day to see it. She let me hold it too, but I wanted a wee baby sister in my own home to love and pet like other little girls had. I told mother so. She said I could pet my little brother, but I was tired of boys.

Grandmother came to see us in our new home. We had not seen her for a long time and we were glad to show her about. She liked our situation very much. We were very near a church and she could sit in our window and hear the sermon. She said it was very convenient and stayed with us a long time. We had many nice talks with her and she would go walking with us in the pastures and listen to our stories about the squirrels and bobwhite quails. She was a dear, patient grandmother, never tiring of our ceaseless chatter.

One day when I came home from school she told me to come into the nursery. Then she showed me a nice little baby. I asked her whose baby it was. When she told me it was my little brother, this was just too much. I turned away and left the room saying I did not want it in my home and they could send it away if it was another boy. I was disgusted. Nine brothers and one sister. It was just awful. *[Lodowick Wadlow Gay was born 8-28-1848.]* It was several days before I became reconciled and then I made a great pet of him. I was sorry I had given him such a cool greeting on his arrival. Grandmother went home soon after and we missed her so much. That was her last visit to us.

## Chapter 3

# Oregon Fever

W E HAD LIVED IN SPRINGFIELD THREE YEARS and were very happy and prosperous and the future looked bright. But father got the Western fever. He had talked about Oregon and the Columbia River for many years and wanted to go there. He wanted to take his nine sons where they could get land. The government promised to give homes to all who would go to Oregon. Mother was not willing to go. She did not want to undertake the long and dangerous journey with a large family of small children. To cross the plains in those days with ox teams was a fearful undertaking and a tiresome one too. She begged father to give up the notion but he could not. He received a letter from an old neighbor who had been in Oregon two years. He insisted on father coming West, telling him what a lovely land it was and about the many resources, the genial climate and the rich mines in California.

Mother finally reluctantly consented to go. Father at once set about making arrangements for the journey. He told us of his intention and said he wanted us all to go with him to the new country. He told us about the great Pacific Ocean, the Columbia River, the beautiful Willamette Valley, the great forests and the snowcapped mountains. He then explained the hardships and dangers, the sufferings and the dreary long days we would journey on and on before we would reach Oregon. He then asked if we wanted to go. We rather thought we wanted to stay with our school friends and our societies. But children were expected to do as their parents said in those days and father said we must come. Lovers, sweethearts and associates were all left behind and we came with our father and mother to Oregon.

My oldest brother, James, was about to be married. He told his intended bride he expected to go West the next spring and she promised to go with him. With such an understanding, they were married.

The wedding was a very pleasant event. The bride *[Frances Gott]* and her maid were lovely in pure white with bare neck and arms. Two little girls also in white with bare arms and baby waists stood as candle bearers. The groom and his best man wore cutaway coats of black. The large parlor where the wedding took place was artistically decorated and crowded with friends and relatives of both families.

The ceremony was impressive. After many congratulations, all repaired to the dining hall where an elaborate wedding dinner was waiting. The afternoon and evening had been calm and pleasant, a lovely autumn day *[October 10, 1850]*. Friends clustered around the bridal pair wishing joy and talking of the long journey on which they would embark and of the journey across the plains. Many protests were put in against the last mentioned. Someone said, "They won't go. It's too far and we don't want them to go. We'll talk them out of that notion."

We were playing games, merry as larks, but hark that deep rolling sound. Everyone listened to another booming, then nearer the next one came. A thunder storm! Peal after peal and flash after flash of vivid lightning. The storm was tearing down toward us. Everyone was excited now. Many were in light evening dress and bare-headed except for a wreath of flowers. Many who lived nearby rushed out hoping to reach home before the rain descended. Mother called to me and we started out, but oh how dark it was. Instantly an electric flash marked our route, then another so that our path home was lighted all the way. The steeples were aglow with light during that storm. We had barely reached our door when the rain came down in torrents.

The next day was a lovely one and the bridal party with many friends dined at our house. The Groom's Day it was called, or the infare dinner. Much mirth and puns and jokes filled the hours. Late in the night the friends bade adieu, some wishing us all a safe journey across the plains. Some begging us to stay.

As brother intended going West in a few months they did not set up housekeeping but lived with us and visited relatives during the winter. Father had been very busy for some months selling off his property and settling up his extensive business. He sold the dear old farm we had left three years before.

He soon made up his mind that it would be quite an undertaking to prepare for such a long journey across the plains with a large family. Everything to be used must be serviceable and of the very best. The clothing for such a journey for such a family was no small matter. The provisions were enough to stock a small grocery store. We had to start out with enough to last five months. The wagons were ordered. They were to be strong and the boxes made deep and well ironed off so they could be used, if necessary, as boats for crossing swollen streams. The oxen were selected. None of inferior quality were of any use, so we got only the best. Few horses were needed. The firearms were chosen and plenty of ammunition stored away in waterproof boxes, for we all expected to fight our way if need be. Side arms were procured for all who were able to carry them, and when equipped in belt and guns, the men and boys reminded one of Don Quixote land pirates.

Those side arms created quite an excitement one day just before we started on our way. Two of the little boys who were delighted with the bright guns had seen where they were secreted, and when the family was at dinner one night, they stole into the room and armed themselves with guns and started to Oregon. When we called the children to dinner they were no where to be found. No one had seen them leave the house. We could not find them anywhere in our neighborhood. An old lady passing by on her way to market, seeing the excitement, inquired. On being told, she said she saw two little boys out on the road toward Wilson Creek carrying something very bright in their hands. She was not near enough to see what it was. A brother was sent in haste to overtake them. He was alarmed when he saw they had the pistols. Meantime, we had also discovered at home that the pistols were gone. So we were glad to see them come home uninjured. They were very crestfallen when they had to lay down their arms and surrender to parental authority.

Friends and relatives who had heard of our intended journey came from far and near to persuade father to give up the wild notion. They said the family would be slain by Indians or perish on the deserts. They told him it was an injustice to his family to be thus exposed. But father had made up his mind. He said others had made the journey and we could too. He knew it was a fearful undertaking but he felt equal to it. Our foreparents had been pioneers of Virginia and Kentucky and were Indian fighters. Father told people he was not as much alarmed about the Indians as many other obstacles we might encounter: the swollen streams, the cyclones and dangerous roads, the snow in the mountains, sickness, suffering for water, shortage of fuel and other privations. He thought if we were kind to the Indians they would not molest us.

I was thirteen years old now and I had many school friends who were dear to me. They came to see me often and watch the preparations which were being made. Bolts of heavy canvas were in the house being measured off for the four immense wagon covers. Also the great tent was cut out and a dozen or more working on it. Dozens of garments of all sizes and colors were in progress. For more than a year the sewing was being done, all by hand. Many neighbors came to the sewing bees. How they would talk and cry over their sewing, saying we would all surely be lost crossing the plains.

When the time drew near for us to be off, our home was sold and the household furniture disposed of. Many family relics which we could not take along were given to friends. Farewell sermons were preached and prayers offered for our safety. Friends came from afar to say goodbye. The great white tent stood in the yard, a wonder to old and young. The four covered wagons were loaded with the supplies ready to roll out on the long journey.

# Chapter 4

# On The Trail

T HE TENTH OF APRIL was the day set for starting *[1851]*. All the town and part of the county had surely heard of it. In the morning the tent was folded and put carefully in a place assigned to it and looked upon with much interest as that was to be our home for five months. We had a light folding table and a light stove and hoped to be quite comfortable. The sleeping berths were in the wagons as father thought it more healthful than sleeping on the ground and less danger from snakes and Indians.

Some friends had spent the night with us and others arrived at daylight. All places of business and the schools were closed during the forenoon, and everybody came to say goodbye to us. From early morning till ten o'clock they came. The house and yard and streets were crowded with people. Friends and schoolmates were crying all around us. One neighbor became so enthused by the deep expressions of sorrow that he leaped upon a goods box and made a speech, speaking for the crowd. He wished us a safe and pleasant journey and a prosperous and healthy life in the far West. The sad farewells were all spoken. We took a long last look at all, then closed our eyes on the scene and moved forward. Their wails reached us as we moved away.

The first day we arrived in our old neighborhood and stopped with a family of old friends near the schoolhouse. We had a happy time looking over the old playground and searching for wild flowers. But time was precious to us now. We took leave of them next morning and went to our aunt's. After a short stay with them, we went on to grandmother's who lived in the next county. We had to stay one night with an old farmer before arriving at her home. He had a big house and a large family. He also had an apiary. I never saw so many bees at work as that old man had. He said if we wanted some honey all we had to do was to furnish a man to rob the bees, for he never liked to rob them and was afraid of them anyway. A cousin of mine was along with us and he agreed to take their honey. He soon had a large quantity of it ready for us. We had a feast on milk and honey.

The next day we arrived at dear grandmother's. She was glad to see us and looked upon our wonderful outfit with amazement. She said we were well prepared but she was sorry to have us go so far away.

We waited here for our sister-in-law. She had not come with us. Her parents and kin folks had coaxed her to stay, telling her if she would not go her husband would stay with her. But when they saw him take his whip and start his team out, they gave up the idea. They then consented for her to come with her husband as she had promised to do. She told us to go on and wait three days at grandmother's for her and she would come. Father said we would wait, but if she was not there at the time specified we would go on, as his son was going to Oregon. We had a nice visit with our relatives and late in the evening on the third day we saw the coach coming with Frances accompanied by her father and brother and sister. They had to call in help after we left to complete her wardrobe for the trip. The next day her father asked that we all try to protect her from the dangers. Father assured him she would fare just as his own family did, and they parted.

The saddest parting of all was when my mother took leave of her aged and sorrowing mother, knowing full well that they would never meet again on earth.

We started out on our journey across the plains, each day leaving civilization farther behind. We were nearing the point designated for organizing the company. All who were going were to meet there on a certain day.

We found many there and others soon arrived. We visited around the camps to see the young girls who were to be our company. We found several who became our friends, but often thought of those we left behind.

After the evening meals were over, all the men and some of the women assembled around a great campfire. The business of the evening was to organize for protection and assistance. A captain was elected, sentries appointed, the rules of action and movement made known to all concerned. There were twenty-seven wagons, about seventy-five persons, and several hundred cattle and horses. A different leader was appointed for each day. In this way no one had

*Covered wagons in Manhattan, Kansas in the early 1860's.*

the advantage—for the leading team is the best position in a long train on account of the dust which can be almost suffocating.

We were soon getting accustomed to the daily routine of moving onward. The country was rolling with lively little rivulets rippling on their way. One morning, soon after the long train of white coaches had got straightened out and in motion with the herd of cattle and horses following after, I was aroused from my reveries by a roaring noise like a tornado. It was approaching from behind us and the next moment the herd came rushing by, causing the teams to suddenly start up and give us passengers an unexpected ride. No serious damage was done. This was our first stampede and an introduction to what we might expect later.

One day we met some Santa Fe traders. They were on their way to St. Louis with Mexican silver to exchange for dry goods. They had a fierce bold guard with them who looked like land pirates. They were armed like warriors and looked ready to strike death to friend or foe.

We arrived at Fort Kearney. It was a curiosity to us all with the strong old fort looming up, its tall palisades set deep in the ground, the great heavy gates creaking on their strong hinges and the armed sentries marching to and fro.

We had now got well out into the Indian nation. We scarcely ever saw an Indian. Those we did see were very friendly and we hoped we had been mistaken about them as we originally thought they would all want to fight us.

One morning in May we entered an Indian village of some note. There were good houses and nice gardens near each and a church and schoolhouse beyond on a hill. This was a pleasant sight as it had been weeks since we had left civilization. As we were quietly passing through the place, we were greeted by the booming of cannon which alarmed us. Suddenly there sprang into our sight a band of five hundred Indian warriors in paint and feathers, all on horseback and armed with guns, bows and arrows, tomahawks and scalping knives. Our captain called a halt and he and father went forward to ascertain the meaning of this battle array. They had not attempted to molest us, but the place was alive with Indians. A white man assured our leaders that there was no occasion for alarm. We could proceed on our way. Those were friendly Indians who belong at that mission. They had been out fighting the Pawnees and had been victorious. They were returning with their trophies of war and a lot of prisoners and this display was only to welcome them back. They were a ferocious looking band in their black and red paint. Some who had lost relatives in battle were painted black and others were black with red stripes and spots over their faces and bodies. They were yelling and gesticulating furiously. We were glad to get away alive. The agent told father they would not torture their prisoners but would make slaves of them.

Soon after leaving the village we encountered a swollen stream and had trouble crossing it. We came near losing one man. His team became unmanageable and he was thrown out into the river in some way. He got a cold bath but succeeded in saving his life. We consumed several hours in getting all the wagons and stock across, then pitched camp for the night as it was raining. There was plenty of wood and grass and we were happy to be comfortable and warm after such a drenching.

The next morning we rolled out early. All went well for a few days, then we had an accident. The captain's little two-year-old Tommy fell out of the wagon and before the team could be stopped a wheel had passed over his body and nearly crushed him to death. He suffered terribly for days but finally recovered.*

Some days after this, we camped near another Indian village.

---

* Children on the overland trail were subject to a form of benign neglect as adults carried more than their normal share of care and work. Accidents involving children became one of the hallmarks of the road. Children fell out of wagons . . . from *Women's Diaries of the Westward Journey* by Lillian Schlissel, p 49

There was a nice church and schoolhouse, good dwellings, orchards, gardens and fields of corn. There were some white families at this mission. The agent and teacher was the brother of an old friend of father's and he said the Indians learned to be farmers very easily. He said they were doing well in school and he also said they would not steal. Our captain thought if they were so honest he would not put out sentries for the night. Next morning, when the cattle were driven into camp, a fine pair of oxen, a calf and cow were missing. After searching for them and not finding any trace of them, the agent was informed. He sent an Indian to help hunt for them. The Indian did not find them. At last one of my brothers tracked them to a lot in the woods some distance away. They had been put in there and the bars laid up to keep them in. Brother went in and drove them toward the bars to let them out when an Indian interfered, saying they belonged to him. At that moment our captain, who was also looking for them, rode up and ordered the Indian away, helped get the cattle out and hurried them toward the camp. We had been detained several hours by the agent saying the Indians were honest.

We were now well out on the wide spreading plains. As far as the eye could see in every direction was a valley stretching off, seemingly endless. Occasionally a tree could be seen in the distance and here and there droves of buffalo.

We encountered some heavy storms on this wild moor. I recall one evening, about three o'clock, we were moving slowly along. The day had been warm but now a dark cloud appeared. It soon obscured the sun. A breeze began to fan hot cheeks and parched lips. This was pleasant but in a few more moments was followed by the crash of thunder and streaks of lightning. By now the wind was a fearful tornado. The train ascended a bank to get on higher ground as the place where a halt was first called had been down in a stream bed. We did not dare unhitch the teams there, fearing a deluge and no means of getting out if the teams should stampede during the storm. After getting on higher ground and turning the wagons as best we could against the storm, every team and all the horses but one black bobtail pony were turned loose to try to find shelter for themselves. All the men got into and under the wagons away from the rain which came down in torrents. When the rain was over the men rushed out after their teams and were shocked to find they had run across the plains ahead of the storm. What to do? They couldn't overtake them on foot and the horses had followed after the cattle. Then someone remembered the bobtail pony. He quickly mounted him and went off after the stock which had got several miles from us. They were all recovered. I had often seen that pony following after the wagon day after day and never knew what use he was till the storm scared our teams away. We all petted Jack after that. He lived to reach Oregon and many years after.

After the storm, we looked over the bank to where we had first halted and saw a rushing river. The water was five or six feet deep. That taught us to keep out of the ditches. We moved on a few miles, camped for the night and had some troublesome times trying to get fires going as everything was so wet by the storm.

We reached the ford on South Platte the first day of June, this being the first very large stream we had encountered. It was wide, deep and muddy. We either had to ford the nearly two miles or make boats out of the wagon boxes and ferry across. This would be a slow business. After consultation with two men who had been across the plains and were somewhat acquainted with the river, we decided to ford. We dreaded it. My sister-in-law was badly frightened. She asked to come into the family wagon with mother.

All things being made secure, a young man who had crossed before rolled up his pants and waded into the stream with his hand

*"We consumed several hours in getting all the wagons and the stock across."*

on the head of his lead ox. How we trembled as we watched the long train starting in. Then it was our turn. Father was with us to encourage us. Another man helped our team to keep on the right line, for if we got off the ford we could go down into quicksand. We looked far ahead and saw the leader near the farther shore. Then another one reached the bank and soon we would. The ford is in rainbow shape. We started in and went downstream in a half-circle and came out on the other shore almost opposite where we started in. At last we all reached the shore safely.

And now a misunderstanding arose, the first since we had started on the journey. Some wanted to lay by the remainder of the day and others wanted to go on. Hot words passed. One man drew his gun to shoot another. The company disbanded and formed two separate companies. The captain rolled out on the road and said all who wished could follow him. Several others went. Father did not go. Four families stayed with him. Those who had gone on insisted on traveling faster. Father and some others did not wish to rush along and wear out their teams on the beginning of the journey.

The fast travelers got to Oregon first but lost nearly all their stock. They had a great deal of trouble in many ways. Some of their company were rather quarrelsome and we were glad to be rid of them. We now had the company we at first intended coming with. A good man was elected captain of our new company with father as able assistant and counselor. The families were all good people, mostly farmers and used to hard work. We were all from the same county and had known of each other before starting out. We were like one great family. Father had four wagons. The four other families each had one wagon, eight in all and eleven men who were able to carry arms and fight if necessary. We usually camped near some other company for protection when we were in a dangerous part of the wild way. We also protected others when we could do so.

After getting out on the plains, Indians often came to us to sell beads and moccasins. A squaw came one day and she soon sold all but one pair. When a young man asked to buy a pair, he tried to put those on but could not. She thought she could if he would let her. She was very anxious to sell them. She insisted on trying to put them on him, but he did not want her to do so. The boys begged him to let her try. At last, he said she might try if she thought she could. She quickly understood him and ran to him and snatched one foot up and put on a moccasin and then the other one. Then she laughed at him and said, "Lazy man." He had to buy them as they were on his feet.

The face of the country changed somewhat and we saw a few mountain peaks in the distance. The road up the North Platte is rough in many places. Game was more plentiful. Antelope and sage hens were often seen. Buffalo, too, were running around. We dreaded them and did not care to encounter them. They were dangerous when wounded or crossed in their headlong career. A hunter's well-aimed shot would sometimes bring one down, but more often he would be chased by it. Sometimes great herds of them would come snorting by us and go rushing away.

One morning very early, we heard buffalo lowing some distance away. The captain noted that the lowing came nearer and nearer. He had everybody get ready to start out as quickly as possible as he had observed that we were camped in a buffalo trail which led to a watering place at the river. All was rush to get off. We heard them coming beyond the hills which were near us. The men hurried with the stock for, if they get into the buffalo herd, they will stampede with the buffalo and we can never get them. At last we started. Everybody was on the lookout. We heard the leaders bellowing furiously. They discovered us just as we saw them. There they came thundering down toward us. Nothing would turn them. Their heads were down and on they came. What to do? They seemed to be coming directly across our wagons. The captain on horseback watched them. We waited for him to say what to do. We were moving slowly along. He called a halt. Every team was staked, then there were the buffalo. They passed just in front of our foremost wagon. We heard their heavy puffing and could almost feel their breath as they passed. The earth trembled under their weight as off they went. We all looked after them as they disappeared over the hills, then moved on, thankful to escape being trampled.

Father was a good marksman and had little else to do. As hunting was his chief delight, he kept our little company well supplied with fresh meat most of the time. One day we needed fresh meat for a sick person and, after the camp was reached, the men began looking about for game of some kind. Someone spied an antelope across the river and pointed it out to father. Everyone thought it was too far away to hit. Father thought he could kill it from the river bank. He picked up his best gun. All the men and boys were out watching to see if he could hit it at such a long distance, estimated by some as a mile. Father stepped off toward the river to be more alone. A sharp report rang out and the antelope fell. When he saw the shot had brought the game down, father walked back to camp and said, "I've done my part. Go after it." Two men went over very easily and got it. We divided with the company and all feasted on sweet tender meat. It was a beautiful camp with a wide valley, deep flowing river and tall mountains.

There are many objects of wonder on the plains. We camped near Chimney Rock one night, as we thought. Next morning a man who was at leisure said he would walk out to it and meet the train at noon. He walked till he was tired and did not appear to be any nearer than when he started. He came to camp saying he thought it was only two or three miles away, but he really believed it must be twenty. Things seemed to enlarge and draw near us on the plains. One morning just as we left camp, father saw some black objects in the road ahead some distance he thought were Indians. We moved on and kept an eye on the supposed Indians. We were very much surprised to see those Indians arise and fly away. They proved to be crows magnified by the fine air and elevation.

The Steamboat Spring on Bear River boils and puffs like a steamboat. When we drew near, the train was called to a halt and we all made a visit to the spring. It was in the river near the bank then, but we learned that when the river was low it was on shore.

The great banks of soda were a wonderful sight and seemed a pity to be wasted on the dreary wild. But the mirage was really the most magnificent of all to those who were fortunate enough to witness it. Lovely lakes would appear, green groves and shady vales. Splendid scenes were looked upon with wonder and awe, then they would slowly float away, leaving the plains spreading out as far as eye could see.

Our long journey was not altogether devoid of pleasures. We spent many happy hours visiting our neighbors in camp, talking and singing, telling stories, guessing conundrums. There were some very amusing incidents. Everything was made much of that was amusing or interesting as we had no news or word from home. So we originated our own news and mirth.

An Indian came to camp with a lot of buckskin pants for sale. They were smoked a lovely cream color. One of the teamsters bought a pair *[using flour in trade, according to brother James' diary entry July 16, Ed.]*. Next day he looked all dressed up in cream pants and red blouse. The road during the day often led across a muddy stream. The water being low, one ford was a mud hole. So many wagons crossing had mixed a good thick mud. The man in the new suit drove into the ford with his team and they got stuck in the mud. He could not get them to pull the wagon through. He had to get out in the mud and urge them on. Each step carried them into the mire deeper and deeper. He came safely out, but those cream pants were a thing of the past. When he arrived safely on the bank, a cheer rent the air. All the company was watching him. He needed no help as he could manage his own team best alone. He was a most comical sight to behold. In the days to follow, he often heard about those cream pants and that mud hole.

When we were in camp one Sabbath Day, an Indian came to us and asked for food. We fed him and then told him to go. He was not inclined to do so at all, but wandered from camp to camp. He was a surly savage-looking fellow.

One of the men was chewing a piece of ginger root and he gave the savage a bite. The Indian thought to eat it as the white man seemed to do. When it burnt his mouth, he instantly became warlike and drew his gun to shoot the man. He thought he was poisoned and his anger knew no bounds. He lurked around till nearly dark, then crept away. We feared he had gone after his clan and would come back during the night and try to get at the man. We kept our man closely concealed and a guard out all night to give warning if the foe was heard. They didn't come. The next morning after we had started out, we saw the same Indian following along near the train off to one side of the road. When we camped for the night he also stopped. The next day when we stopped near a river the men drove the cattle down to water. Across the river, the Indian was watching for the man. Some of the company wanted to shoot him, but the captain did not approve of such an act. So they let him alone. We never saw him again, but we kept out a guard and were ready for battle.

Some days after this a squaw and a papoose traveled along near us for several days. She rode a good pony and kept about a hundred yards from the train. She never came near enough to speak. Seemed to be going to some other tribe. Always toward night, she would ride quickly away. Then next day, we would see her again. Some thought she had been a prisoner and was making her escape and staying near us for protection.

One pleasant evening some Indian boys wanted to display their skill with bow and arrow. When we gave them a biscuit they would set it up, step off some distance and pierce it with an arrow. Father got a pan of biscuits and he would measure off a distance, set up one and tell them to shoot at it. The one who struck it first got it for his own. They had considerable sport over the biscuits. The old braves enjoyed the sport extremely and wanted father to let them shoot too. He set up a dime for their target. I think only one of them hit the dime.

W now felt at home in the wagons and had settled down into a contented state and looked forward to the land of promise which we were slowly but surely approaching.

Early on the morning of June 14 I was awakened from a nervous sleep by the wailing of an infant. I asked mother whose baby was crying so. She said it was hers. I said not a word for some time, fearing I might have to welcome another brother. I already had nine brothers. I was so anxious to know I asked, "Is it a little brother?" Imagine my joy when she said it was a little sister. Then I hastily dressed and wanted to see it. I thought it surely was the cutest and sweetest little sister in all the wide world. What name could we find that was appropriate for such an angel? We welcomed her with love [*and named her Sarah Julia, Ed.*]. She was so precious we hovered around her to ward off danger. Her eyes were like the blue sky after an April shower. She was soon the pet of the company. Everyone came around to see "Pink," saying it was a joy after a long day's journey. I thought she should be called Angelia. I did not want to call her after anything earthly.

My greatest fear was Indians. I asked the captain to set out more than one sentry every night for fear the savages would steal her. I always tried to keep her out of sight when they came around. Sometimes they would see her. Then they would jabber about her being so small and say, "No good papoose." I was so glad when they would leave.

Some braves came to our camp one evening to sell ponies. Father asked them in a jesting way how many ponies they would give for Mamie or I. They were at once eager to trade and offered a number of their best. Father then said, "No, I do not want to sell the girls at all." They got angry and we got alarmed and ran and hid in the wagons. Father could not make them understand it was a joke. He fed them and tried to talk them into a better humor. He never asked another Indian how many ponies he would give for one of us. He saw how we felt about it and he feared they might try to steal us, as they do not understand joking at all in a business way.

When we got to Ash Hollow, our band of trusty men were ordered to keep their guns in good shape and loaded ready for use. Our party was quite weak and we were in danger just now—passing through a wild region where thousands of warlike savages prowled around. There was a large emigration and we tried to camp near some other train, yet we were often alone at a camp. On such occasions the men stood guard all night.

We were now at Fort Laramie and hoped to be more secure while we were near the soldiers. We camped there one night. The post was located on Laramie Creek near its junction with the Platte. We were glad to see the abode of white men once more. Some of the soldiers came to our camp and talked to us about the country through which we were passing and told us about the different Indian tribes we would encounter and advised us to treat them kindly.

We crossed the North Platte on the twenty-first day of June on a good ferry boat at the rate of three dollars per wagon, but were glad to get across so easily and did not mind the price. We would willingly have paid more rather than tried the fording.

Here we met with a large train of emigrants known as the Illinois Company with whom we traveled a great deal the remainder of the journey.

Wood and water were very scarce many times. We had casks to carry water along with us but wood suitable to take with us was hard to procure. Willow bush occupied too much space. Sometimes we had no wood at all. Then we would collect grass and twist it into coils and burn it in our little stove to cook with, and we would pull grass the night before to get breakfast with next morning. Thus we managed to get along, the weather being warm. We only needed fuel for cooking purposes. We had a guide book which informed us of all good camping places. Otherwise, we would have fared much worse. Sometimes we had to travel after night to reach water and grass for the stock. It was considered a dangerous thing to do. The Indians would secrete themselves in a ravine or near the road and await us, then frighten the teams and cause great trouble.

One night we were moving slowly along. Father and the captain had gone ahead of us to find the camp. Suddenly, just as we were crossing a ravine, every team seemingly started at the same moment. They ran a short distance when my brother, whose team was in the lead, managed to stop them and the next wagon locked wheels with his. In this way they were all stopped, excepting the hindmost one which struck out over the country. The tent which was tied on the rear of that wagon broke its moorings, yet attached to the wagon went sailing in the breeze. In the dim starlight it presented the appearance of a company of white ghosts running after the wagon. The herd of cattle and horses came dashing up too and all together raised quite a dust and turmoil, and we momentarily expected to hear a war whoop. We were agreeably disappointed.

After getting the stock quieted and back in the road, and the runaway wagon in line, we found no one hurt. So we went on to camp where we found our captain and father waiting for us, and fearing we had got lost because we were so long in arriving. When they heard of our stampede they advised all to be as quiet as possible, make no fires or lights. They set out sentries and the remainder of the night was spent in fear as there was no other company near us and we had little hope of assistance if attacked.

Next morning, while we were preparing breakfast, we were alarmed to see Indians skulking along through the sage brush, coming toward our camp. Our men stood near their guns. The Indians came up to us wanting to sell fish. They were the most degraded looking of any we had met. They could not speak a word of English but made known they wanted food. We fed them and they quickly disappeared. We were satisfied they had caused our trouble the night before and had come to our camp to find out our number if possible. We hurried forward and soon overtook a company. There were many war-like tribes in this section of the country, and we were kept in dread suspense for days.

We arrived at a large stream. Its banks were thickly set with trees and underbrush which gave the savages every advantage. The road led up the bank through the woods some distance after crossing the stream. The captain and father went ahead of the train and noted every indication of danger. They were alarmed to see red paint in some water they passed, then were suddenly confronted by five Indian braves bedecked in emblems of war. Their chief grabbed the bridle of the captain's horse and said in good English, "Stop, white man. Stop, white man." The captain replied, "No stop," and quietly signalled to the train to move up faster. He had been across the plains once, understood considerable about Indians, and he knew these were warriors and would have killed them on sight if the train hadn't been near by. They didn't know our strength. They knew, if we would stop, they could entrap us there in the thick brush as there were Indians behind almost every tree just waiting for a signal from their chief. The captain led the train to higher ground, expecting a battle right then and there.

When we got out of the woods and on high ground the train was called to a halt, the Indians still with us. While the teams were resting after their hurry up the hill, and the Indians were more quiet, we ate our lunch of cold bread and meat and offered them a part. They accepted the food but remained on their fine horses. They were on the war path. One of them was wounded in the arm. Their chief rode from one wagon to another, peering in to see if he could lay his hand on anything to steal. They were surly and not disposed to talk to us. They would speak among themselves and look toward the river and down a deep ravine.

The captain said they were talking about their company and some of them wanted to call a recruit. They were really parleying about attacking us, but our men looked resolute. They kept trying to steal. The chief rode right up to the wagon where mother was sitting with my baby sister in her arms. He made a grab for the child, but his horse jumped and mother had clasped her arms tightly around the babe when she saw him approaching as she feared him. He looked so desperate as though he meant to strike her. She cried out in alarm and father ran to her. She told him what the Indian had done. He informed the captain who was just trying to settle a disturbance between one of the boys and another Indian. The boy had a pocket mirror and, for sport, gave it to the Indian and told him to look at his war paint. This made the Indian mad and he wanted to fight. The captain quickly got hold of the glass and looked at himself and showed the Indian that no harm was intended and got his wrath somewhat appeased. We prepared for battle. The chief was mad and his men were mad. He gave a signal to his band and dashed off toward the river, his retainers quickly following, yelling as they went. We were rather astonished at their abrupt departure until we saw a large train of emigrants following after us. Their timely arrival had no doubt saved us.

We heard a few days later that there were three hundred warriors near by, and they they had attacked a train at the same place and ran off all their horses.

My oldest brother was keeping a diary, and one day just after he had crossed a river the road lay up a hill. He had his diary laying on the wagon seat by him and it fell out. We had gone a mile or more before he missed it. He got permission and rode quickly back to where he supposed he had lost it and there it lay. He jumped down to pick it up and saw fresh Indian tracks in the sand where we had just crossed the river. They had obviously been made since we were there. He raced back to the train on his pony that always walked behind the wagon tied with a halter. This was the second time Jack had proved his usefulness, even if he was a small pony. Brother had not seen an Indian, but we suspected their presence and hurried forward, soon catching up with the Illinois train which we had not seen for several days.

As soon as we got to camp we all scampered out to see what we could find. All the young folks together felt able to defend ourselves from snakes or Indians. If there were any graves near camp we would visit them and read the inscriptions. Sometimes we would see where wolves had dug into the graves after the dead bodies, and we saw long braids of golden hair telling of some young girl's burying place. We often saw human skulls bleached by sun and storms lying scattered around. The first ones we saw were shunned by us. We did not dare go near them. Later on, after becoming accustomed to seeing so many of them, we would pick them up and read the verses which some passerby had written on them, then perhaps add a line or two and set them up to attract someone else as they passed by.

We were out playing about camp one evening. The little children were with us. We did not dare go far as the hostiles were near us. The men had all gone to the river with the stock. We were camped near a precipice. It was a dangerous place, about two hundred feet perpendicular. The sage brush was high and thick. We were playing hide and seek. A three-year-old girl had her rag doll out too. We missed her and could not find her. We kept running about calling for her. At last we heard her answer in her baby way. Her mother called again as we could not see her. She was toward the precipice. We found her standing on the brink shaking her rag dolly over the fearful abyss, all unconscious of the danger.

We looked down and saw the men and stock near the river. The men looked like children and the cattle and horses like dogs. They all soon came back to camp and said we were in a dangerous place. Indian tracks were thick and not an Indian to be seen. The captain decided to move on although it was late in the evening. We soon reached another camp ground and found other emigrants there for the night. We willingly gave them a recruit in numbers and felt more safe ourselves. The experience our captain had received in crossing the plains before was of great benefit to us in many ways and many times. We placed great confidence in his judgment and always came out victorious. He was a noble-hearted man.

We crossed Green River the 4th of July. It is a broad deep river bordered by stately trees reflected in its waters, a beautiful dark green—hence its name. There was a good ferry there and we crossed over so quickly we hardly realized it. We then camped and prepared to celebrate the 4th in an appropriate manner as all true-hearted Americans should do. The ferry man had a violin and he favored us with some music. The juveniles marched about, raising a red handkerchief for a flag. The boys fired a salute and mother said we must have a good dinner, which she then prepared. She even graced our table with a cake which caused the boys to throw up their caps and shout hurrah.

Then a Mormon who was there told us about Salt Lake and the city they intended building there. We thought we would like to go there and see the place, but it was too far off our road. We were not very favorably impressed with his description of Mormon life. He told us he had seen a widow and her two daughters married to one man by the same ceremony. We thought that was too many sweethearts in one family. He also said the Mormons were growing rich there by raising stock. The Indians in this part of the country were great thieves and caused us much trouble. They would steal horses and cattle continuously and run them off and sell them to the Mormons.

The face of the country had now changed. The great mountains reared their heads on every side. Our road wound around through the valleys. We saw some nice country and the streams abounded in fish. We had great sport catching them. Game was plentiful. Sage hens in abundance. Mountain goats and antelope too. The Indians lived well on game which nature provided for them.

The men went out to hunt mountain goats. They found several and followed them some distance from place to place, from crag to crag, the goats keeping out of range. At last they came near an old monarch of the mountains. They thought they would bag him sure, and almost smelt his savory fat joints roasting before the camp fire, but he sprang from one steep crag to the brink of a chasm. Now, they thought, he cannot jump that. We will get him. He surprised them by springing lightly across and ran off up the mountain side. They could follow no farther and came to camp with a lot of sage hens for supper.

They were walking along a trail on a hillside and imagined the earth moved under their feet as though it would sink. They dug down and found ice. They brought a lot of it and melted for drinking water. Our guide book told us of this wonder. We also found snow near camp and picked flowers beside it. The grass was luxuriant at this camp.

We met with fur traders near the Rocky Mountains. Their great strong wagons, loaded with furs and drawn by six mules, were regular land schooners, sure enough. They carried immense loads. The men with those schooners were a rough looking set of customers. They were dressed in leather suits trimmed with fringe and wore fur caps. Their long shaggy hair and beards made them look as though they had never seen civilization. Some of them would stop and talk. Others gave us a wild look and passed on.

An old trapper stopped and talked with father some time and told about the buffalos, their habits and a good mode of hunting them. He said they were more dangerous than a grizzly bear when wounded. He gave father a pocket compass and a flint and steel for striking fire.

Sometimes we would see great herds of buffalo, thousands of head in a drove. They would not turn aside for anything, but put their noses down near the ground and go rushing along, their great bodies swaying and heaving. We were told not to try to turn them in their course.

One of our company rather flattered himself that he was not afraid of a buffalo and got permission to leave the train for a few hours to try his luck. He soon found a small herd and selected one and shot it, thinking that if he did not kill it, he was safe behind a knoll where he had secreted himself before firing his shot. The buffalo fell when shot and the hunter thought he would take a closer look at his game, as the others had scampered away. He was about to leave his hiding place where he was just peeping over the knoll, when to his great astonishment the beast arose and ran directly toward him. He had just time to escape to a ravine and thus elude its attack till he could reload his gun. The second shot finished the job and he brought some of the meat to camp to prove his success. Once home, he excitedly related his experience in buffalo hunting.

The old trapper talked to father about the Indians. He said they were warlike tribes now around us, and we would not see them till they were in our immediate presence. They had great herds of ponies but took delight in stealing horses from the emigrants. They always wanted to swap ponies for good horses. Said their ponies were away, but they would go fetch them. Then if they got an opportunity, they would mount a horse and off they would go. No use to search for a horse after they once got it.

In the afternoon of one of those dusty sultry days we were moving cautiously and slowly along, hoping for some train to overtake us. We reached camp just before sunset. We had to stop there for wood and water. It was a dangerous place, being near a willow swamp. We felt satisfied that Indians were in that brush. We camped out of gun range and made our post as secure as possible. Still, we felt insecure for the night as no other train had arrived. We rushed about and made as much noise as we could to make believe there was quite a company of us. The stock were allowed to graze near camp and, after supper, the team cattle were put in a corral which was made by running the wagons around in a circle. Then the orders were to let the fires die out and all keep quiet. Sentries were stationed and we were ready for the night.

Father and the captain kept guard near the wagons to protect the families which were in them. There was little thought of sleeping except by little children and innocent babes during that night of terror. Often during the watch father would come to the wagon and whisper to mother telling her to keep awake. If the Indians did charge upon us, we would have a better chance to escape them if we were up and ready to fight. Father came again and said they heard them and the cattle had given signs of their presence and tried to run away, but had been quieted down. Every moment was now dread suspense. We almost feared to move or breathe. All was quiet again, and father left us and went toward the guard. It was now three o'clock. Hope began to rise. We waited, listened, prayed. A little bird sang, then another. Was it a token of deliverance? Father came again and said the Indians were leaving. They knew we were up. They heard us calling the cattle. Streaks of morning light could be seen in the east. Was ever morn more welcome?

Soon the sentries came in and said they were gone. Fires were built, and in a short time the camp was all astir. The cattle were out to graze with men guarding them to keep them away from the willow swamp. Someone noticed arrows sticking in the oxen's backs, several of them. They had been shot from some distance. That was to frighten the cattle away. I was aroused from my morning nap by my sister calling to me to waken and see what was over my head. I opened my eyes and there right over my head was an arrow, and near my side was another sticking in the wagon cover. I could reach up my hand and touch them. Moccasin tracks were in the road near our wagons. One or two Indians had crept in there during the night, and from some cause best known to them, had gone away. After we were all ready to leave camp, some of the men wanted to stay there concealed, and wait for the Indians to come into camp, and then fight them. The captain and father concluded it was better policy to leave them alone, since they had not harmed us very much.

Then the boys said they would put breakfast to cook for them. They had about a dozen jackrabbits which had been killed the day before, and they were put on the fires to broil for the Indians. We rolled out very thankful to be alive and able to go. The road led up a hill, and we could look back and see the Indians take possession of our late camp ground. We tried to travel near some train after that fearful night.

There were trading posts occasionally, near the roads. And sometimes we could purchase a few beans or potatoes or some article which we needed, but prices were exorbitant and the articles inferior. French and Indians were usually in charge of these posts.

Chapter 5

# Fellow Travelers on the
# Western Slope

M ANY FAMILIES HAD STARTED ACROSS THE PLAINS
very poorly prepared for such a journey. Their wagons and
teams were not at all suitable; somewhat light wagons or hacks and
small horses for teams. They were dressed in their fine city clothes.
One family came to us and wanted permission to camp near us for
protection. They wished to run an independent train with our
defense. They had started with one wagon carrying all their provisions, their bedding and a large cook stove, their trunk containing
all their fine clothes, hats and bonnets, none of which were fit to
wear on the trail. We gladly allowed them to travel with us.

The family consisted of man and wife and two children. The
daughter was near my own age. We were soon chums. The boy was
younger. They were anxious to get to Oregon, but there were many
hardships for them. Soon their team weakened. We got them to
leave their stove, but still the load was too heavy. Then a feather bed
was laid out by the roadside. Later a trunk of fine clothes and band
boxes were left, and yet we feared they could not get through.
Many times we would get to camp and they would be very late arriving. Then our men would go back and help them along. Father's
people would always help them up the hills and over hard places. In
this way they finally reached the land of promise.

An aristocratic family came and stayed with us for some time.
They were traveling alone. Had one wagon and a pair of oxen for a
team. The man and his wife and their two servants constituted this
family. Jehu, their man servant, rode a pony and drove their two
cows after their wagon which always followed ours. Margery, the
maid, sat in the back of the wagon, which position was very nice,
for Jehu liked to talk with Margery as she was his sweetheart and he
was deeply in love. He drove the cows day after day. Sometimes

they would stop to eat and he would not notice it and would go on and leave them. Our men would see them and knowing how they happened to go astray would drive them into camp, as they were very much amused over Jehu's love affair. One evening they thought they would teach him a lesson, that business was before pleasure, and they left his cows back a distance. He was greatly excited when he could not find them in the herd. When told they were left he cried, and said he was afraid to go back after them. One of the men went with him and soon brought them into camp. He was more careful after that.

The lady was very handsome and was seldom seen. She dressed as if she were in her city home. She did not seem to realize that she was surrounded by thousands of hostile savages. What trinkets those diamonds would have been for the painted braves.

The gentleman dressed in broadcloth and silk hat, and had charge of the team. It was really amusing to see them. They came West forty years too soon. They should have waited for the palace cars and Pullman sleepers.

We stopped at Fort Bridger and camped overnight. The buildings were mostly composed of stone and were low, dark and desolate looking, built mostly for defense. The place seemed poorly garrisoned. We only saw two or three soldiers and the commander. We heard chickens crowing the next morning, the first since leaving civilization.

A Frenchman and his family were living there and trading with the emigrants. Sister and I went to see the French lady while we were camped near the post. We asked her if she was afraid of the Indians, and she said they would not hurt her while she stayed in the fort. She said she got very lonely there, and would like to go home.

We at last reached the Western slope. The great Rocky Mountains were between us and other days and old friends and home. We now directed our thoughts toward the setting sun, realizing there was a line between us and the past. The trees were different. The animals and fowl also and we saw no more buffalo. But we saw the great mountain peaks capped in snow. There was something inspiring about those great Rockies looming up in grandeur.

We were rolling down toward the great Pacific Ocean, but there were days and weeks to plod along yet. In imagination we could see the lovely Willamette Valley spread out around us bordered by the green forests, fanned by passing breezes, and dotted over with happy homes, waving grain fields and orchards loaded with luscious fruits.

We saw many new graves and heard of sickness and sorrow on every hand. Teams fell by the wayside. Provisions gave out. Hired hands became tired of the slow gait, lost interest, cruelly deserted their employers and struck out on foot, or took a horse and went forward, in their haste to reach the new country. There was much suffering. Those who had food to spare willingly divided. Fathers and mothers died and left little children to the mercy of strangers. Some families lost all their cattle and had to depend on others as they struggled on, hoping to reach the promised land. Many gave up all hope. The weak and timid fell.

Our oxen were very poor and weak. Teams were doubled to enable them to get over bad roads and up hills. We cast out everything we could spare. We gave away any oversupply of provisions we had on hand and lightened the loads all we possibly could. All who were able walked most of the time as we could easily keep pace with the train. The old people and the little tots rode. We had jolly times. Crowds of us would get out together from different trains. We would climb mountains and pick wild flowers and hunt for pretty stones, but always near the trains and always watching for Indians.

My mother, who had endured the hardships and privations as only a mother can on such a journey, at last had to submit. She took to her bed where she lingered for days and weeks between life and death. In her feverish delirium she would see her children carried off by the foe, or tortured by her side. Again she would be wandering amid scenes of her past. We begged her to let us stop so she could rest and regain strength. But she urged us on fearing we would all perish in the mountains. So we made her as comfortable as we could and kept going day by day. Friends came to help. The women of the Illinois train did all they could to rouse her from the lethargy into which she had sunk. When she could take food dainty morsels were brought to tempt her appetite, and cheering words encouraged her. They would take baby sister and keep her for hours. Then one evening mother was stronger. She asked to be allowed to sit by the camp fire. When she tried to stand she would have fallen, but for strong arms to support her. After some time she recovered and we rejoiced to have her with us.

Soon after mother recovered Mrs. Ross, one of our company, was taken down with a fever. We had little hope of her recovery as she was usually feeble, but good care brought her back to health. Those two cases were the only serious illness we had during the journey. There were some cases of alkali poison and some accidents but none very serious. The young people were usually all well and ready to defend themselves. We had many talks about how we would manage to escape if the Indians should take us prisoners. We told each other what marks we would leave to guide those who would search for us. We often almost imagined we really were in captivity and then we were frightened.

We often asked father to let us go fishing, but he said girls did not know how to fish. When we reached Bear River, a stream abounding in fish, father told us girls we could go and fish near the camp. We were delighted. And, oh, the fish! The fish! We caught loads of them, so many we could not keep them, as warm as the weather was. Finally, we took what we could use and put the rest back in the river. The water was black with great schools of fish, and this is no fish story either.

When we reached the Snake River, a treacherous looking stream twisting along between high rugged banks which hid it from view, we looked at the American Falls from an eminence. Then we moved on and some distance below were able to ford the stream and traveled down the north bank till we reached Fort Boise. The river was much larger here than when we first crossed it.

We found a commander and a few companies of soldiers at the fort. They told us the ford there was dangerous and advised us to use a large canoe. They would ferry our loads and the families across, and the Indians would help in getting the wagons and stock across at a ford below the fort. We decided to take their advice.

Father got mother and all we children in the canoe and told us to sit very still and he would take us across safe. The river was wide and deep but not very swift. The other families all crossed in the great canoe. The provisions and bedding all being at last across, the dangerous part began. There were droves of Indians there to help with the wagons. We only needed about a dozen. They all wanted to help and then all wanted pay. They failed to comprehend we did not want them all, and would not pay those we did not need. Then they tried to steal. We were able to drive them away without fear as the soldiers were nearby.

After leaving the Fort, we traveled over a high sagebrush country, going slowly but steadily, tramp, tramp day after day, the same old routine. It would be very monotonous but for the ever-changing scenery. We traveled over some lava beds which were a curiosity. We saw a boiling hot spring.

We now found bunch grass and our stock fared better. On Powder River the fine bunch grass was very plentiful. The coarse bunch grass is not as good, but grows larger. It looks like wheat or oats but is not so tall.

When we were in camp on Butter Creek, an Indian came to us and said he was a "close tibicum." We did not know what a "close tibicum" was. He then began singing and dancing around and striking his hand on his heart saying, "Close tum tum, close tum tum hine close tibicum." As he jumped around and charged here and there we thought he was perhaps a Shaker, or of some such clan. He impressed us with the idea that he really was one good Injun. When he said, "Close Walla Walla," we thought he might be one of Doctor Whitman's pupils and was as good as he represented himself.

We had some very rough, steep and rugged road as we approached the Blue Mountains. Our weak and jaded teams made the ascent with much difficulty. Descending a very steep hill into the Grand Ronde Valley we had to fasten trees with long brushy tops behind the wagon, detach the team and let the wagons down with long ropes or chains.

The valley with no fields or houses seemed a veritable paradise. Near the hill and the river were Indian wigwams, and all around over the valley were thousands of Indian ponies. This looked more like home than the sage brush country.

One day after leaving Grand Ronde Mamie said she would get out and walk a while. She made a misstep some way and fell so her arm was run over by the wagon wheel. Luckily no bones were broken. We never needed to stop the wagon to let us in or out. The teams were very gentle, and we could get out and walk a while, then get into the wagon again and not trouble the teamster.

When we came down into the Umatilla Valley we bought potatoes from a Frenchman who had gardens there, and beef from a trader. It seemed such a promising place we wondered if we would find another so magnificent. Our journey's end was nearer as we traveled down the Columbia having left the Snake some days before.

We walked up on a high hill to look down over a valley and saw the Indian ponies. There were great herds of them. One chief of the Umatillas came to our camp, bringing his squaw and papoose with him. He could speak English. Father asked him to stay and have supper with us. He was very kind to emigrants and thought we must be wonderful people to come so far. Father gave him sugar for potatoes. He asked father to go home with him and see his house and was pleased when he went. We could see his cabin and did not feel afraid to have father go. He was invited to stay and see the papoose strapped to his board and put to sleep—a novel perform-ance. The baby was strapped securely to the board, his arms down by his side. His head was kept in place by a leather band around his forehead being fastened to the board. He was then stood up against the wall where he cooed as happy as any baby till he got sleepy. Then his mother crooned a wailing baby song and he dropped off to sleep. Father said the chief's house was a very good log hut.

There had been whites in this part of Oregon for some years, and the Indians were more civilized and not so war-like as the tribes of the plains and about the Rockies and Snake River. The Nez Perce are a tall fine-looking tribe of Indians.

When we got to the Deschutes River we camped, and consulted about which route to take across the Cascade mountains. Some decided to cross by the Barlow route, and others thought it better to go by The Dalles and down the river by flat boats. Here the com-pany separated as we were now in Oregon and safe to travel alone. Father and the Captain concluded to take their families across the mountains, feeling it was safer than a flat boat on a rough river in a rain storm.

While we were camped on Deschutes River, it being September, the weather was quite cool. The first night was clear and frosty and here we witnessed a grand display of the Aurora Borealis or North-ern Lights. It was a very brilliant display, and some, who had never seen or even heard of such a thing, were very much alarmed. Father, who was something of an astronomer, explained that they were Northern Lights and often appeared on cold nights in the fall of the year. They loomed up in grand broad red and white stripes.

We rested a few days then went to Barlow's gate where we started across the Cascades. We found many others near the gate ready to start across. We passed the gate and approached the first steep hill. There we were met by a storm, a sad greeting and a poor introduc-tion for worse was to come.

For days we had been meeting persons from the valley who were going with strong teams to assist friends across the mountains. Some met fathers and mothers, others met children. Some were hunting friends whom they expected. We asked them many ques-tions about Oregon. We were glad to see them and feel that we were approaching the homes of white men once more. They welcomed us, but gave a doleful account of the road through the mountains.

With brave hearts and jaded teams we slowly ascended the eastern slope. Old and young were out in the rainstorm footing it up that rugged mountain, over rocks, fallen trees, and through mud and water. There was a great deal of crowding and confusion. There was only one narrow road and no way to pass with great trees thick on either side. Some had to move slowly and others wanted to go faster but could not pass. Then they complained. There could be no hurry with the poor jaded oxen. Sometimes they would fall in the mire to rise no more. Others were put in their places and thus we struggled on.

One day the great train of us only moved one mile. At last we reached the summit in a snow storm. Next was down hill. We descended all right until we came to Laurel Hill. To get down it in a storm was a fearful task. Again we must tie trees on the back of the wagons and remove the teams while the wagons were lowered with long ropes.

After we got down Laurel Hill, we had a good camp ground a short distance from the road in a place where the timber was not so thick. All who wished could pass on, and thus we got rid of the brawlers.

We camped in the road one night on Zig Zag River. The children were fishing from the bank of the rapid little stream with pin hooks and thread lines. I went down the trail to get a bucket of water and was standing on the root of a large tree, holding to a swinging limb with one hand and dipping water with the other from a great whirlpool. The children were almost directly over my head. One of my brothers fell over the bank into the deep water at my side. I instantly dropped the bucket and caught the boy as he rose to the surface. Someone helped me pull him out of the river and get him up the trail to the camp fire. He nearly drowned and was badly frightened. As mother was getting his wet clothes off he tried to tell her how he fell, saying, "I di-di-didn't fall in feet first. I fe-fe-fell in head first." He always claimed I saved his life. I think I did too.

We were ascending a long tiresome hill and all who were able to walk had to do so as the wagon was a load for the poor oxen. We really didn't mind the walking, as there was no hurry and no danger of Indians now.

We were about half way up the road and someone said, "See that big stove." We went to look at the stove which had been left by an emigrant who was almost in sight of the valley. Mamie was standing in front of the stove with her foot on the hearth, resting and waiting for our wagons to come up the hill. While we were looking and remarking about its size, two men came riding along and also noticed it. The gentlemen spoke to us and then rode on after their stock. They had a band of cattle they had brought across the plains.

The older man said to the other, "Did you notice the pretty black-eyed girl that had her foot on the stove? She is to be my wife." His partner asked who she was. The man said he did not know, but when he got settled he would find out. We looked after them and spoke about them. They were strangers to us, and we thought they were from the valley and had been out to meet friends. They were weary emigrants like ourselves and were driving their own cattle. When we got up the hill they were gone. Their wagons were ahead of us. They had left their cattle to bring the wagons up and had gone back for them. We met those two men many times in after years.

After six distressing days of hardships and suffering we got to Foster's, and camped at this haven of rest for weary emigrants. We rejoiced to know we had at last arrived in Oregon settlements after five long months. We got vegetables from Mr. Foster and had a regular feast. When we were all seated around enjoying our evening meal father looked over the group and said to mother,"We must thank God, Ann, that we are all here. Yes, all. Father, mother, twelve children, one daughter-in-law and one young man who came all the long way with us."

# Chapter 6

# A Home in the Valley

W E RESTED ONE DAY, then moved to the home of an old friend who came out here some years before. What a joyous meeting that was. They asked many questions about friends back home and about our journey.

After a day or two we went on to another old neighbor's place who had sent for us to come and stay in their home till we had selected a homesite of our own. They were expecting us and were all out in the yard to meet us. There was a large family of them. We had played together when we were little children. Father and his old neighbor were so moved by this meeting that they lost their power of speech.

There was a young lady Mamie's age and one of my own. How they did chatter. We were almost carried into the house. They danced around us making quite a scene.

We were non-plussed when they spoke jargon to us. They had been accustomed to talking with the Indians so long they had learned their language and used it about as much as they did English. I asked one of the girls if she was afraid of the Indians and she said, "Wake six." I thought she asked me to waken from sleep, and turned from her knowing I was awake. Then I said, "What do you want me to wake for?" She explained that was Indian talk. Then I wanted to learn and she taught me two words before dinner—no and yes.

I was surprised to see the children so wild, but thought it was because they were so much alone. They said they never went to school. I asked them if they went to church or Sunday School. They shocked me by saying they didn't want to go. The children played with us and looked at our great wagons and our clothes which were of a different style than their own.

53

Their house was a large log structure built for protection from Indians. It had large fireplaces. We gazed with wonder over the great farm. We went with the children from one object of interest to another. Then we went in to dinner. The table was loaded with luxuries, but we were so anxious to talk we could hardly eat. We wanted to see this new country and find us a home and build a house before winter.

Father and the old neighbor went out to see the piece of land he had selected for us. Father was pleased with it and decided to build at once. We spent a few happy days with them, and then went to our valley near Albany and erected our tent. We had neighbors near us and we felt at home at once. We were also near a sawmill. Father ordered lumber for the house, and selected a tree for shingles. With the help of two boys he made the shingles while two other boys hauled lumber. In a few days material was on the ground for our house.

One Sunday afternoon, soon after we camped, we saw a man riding at breakneck speed toward our tent. We could not imagine why he came so fast, or who he was. As he approached, we saw he rode a fine horse, and had a long rope dragging after him like a Spaniard or an Indian. He was well dressed and fine looking. When he arrived he dismounted, and caught the rope in his hand to let the horse walk away to the extent of the rope to feed.

Father stepped over to meet him, thinking he was some old friend who had heard of our arrival and come to see us. He was rather surprised when the man asked him if his daughter was in. He wished to speak to her. He was a single man, he said, in search of a wife, and he handed father a note of introduction. It was from an old friend stating that Mr. Galloway was a very nice gentleman and financially well-to-do. He was in great haste to marry to save a half section of land, as the law stated that all married men were entitled to a certain amount of land if married before a set date. If not, they lost the land. Hence his haste. He only had a few more days to find a land partner. He insisted on seeing Mamie.

Father said, "No, sir. I have no daughter to barter for land. You had best go as you came, in haste." While they were talking sister passed near them, and the man said, "Is that your daughter? I like her appearance." Father clenched his fist to knock him down, but thought better of the case. As it had become very stormy he loaned the gentleman a cloak, and advised him to search farther. He told him of the emigrants near by and laughingly sent him on his way with the comment, "Well, this land is worth saving." We later heard that he found a lady who was willing to marry him. He went after a parson and they were married in the emigrant camp and so he saved his land.

Father and the boys were all carpenters. They soon built the main part of our house and shingled the roof. Then we moved in, and they put up partitions and built the chimney afterwards. The rainy season had now set in, but we were all right for the winter in a house of our own. One convenience after another was added till we were quite comfortable.

As soon as we got into the house, some of the boys went to work in the woods mauling rails, and others went to hauling them home to build pens for the cows and calves. They also planned to fence in the farm and garden to be ready for use in the early spring. One boy was set to work plowing. At odd times one brother built parks *[shelters in fenced yards]* for chickens, and went all around and bought chickens. In five months we had considerable work done on our new place. Father built a shop and made some nice furniture of Oregon maple.

Our house was near a small stream but we wanted a well. Father said he would ask the oldest settler how deep he would likely have to dig before he would get water fit for use, because it was several miles to the river. Father thought he would have to dig down as low as the river bed at any rate. The oldest settler, with a twinkle in his eye said, "I guess you won't have to go very deep." A spot near the kitchen door was selected as a handy place for a well, and the boys began with a will to dig a well in Oregon. Mother told them not to work too fast as they might get tired long before they got deep enough. I think they had dug about five feet when they had to quit on account of the great rush of water into the well. We were pleased to see water so plentiful, but how could it be walled while there was so much water? In a few days we had a hard rain, and were surprised one morning to see our well running over. We were more surprised one morning to see our well all caved in and full of mud and gravel. We filled it up, packed it down, covered it over and carried water from the creek again. Later on we dug a well on higher ground.

The oldest settler asked father if he had to dig very deep to find water. Father answered, "No. I find wells very near the surface during the rainy season in this country." We asked the oldest settler how long he thought the rain storm we were then experiencing would last. He said, "Why, it's the equinoxial storm." When we saw him three months later we questioned him again about the rain, and he said, "Oh, this is the equinoxial." We wanted to know how long the equinoxial storm lasted on the Pacific coast, and he said from October till June. We found out by waiting that he was a truthful old man.

We had brought flour from Marion County to last, we thought, till the new mill, which was being built in Albany, was ready for business. However, the slow transportation of that day caused a delay in the arrival of the mill stone. The whole community ran out of flour. It was so far to mill and the roads were so bad, that with hopes of getting a mill nearby very soon people deferred going to Salem. We had everything in plenty except bread, and because it was the staff of life, we felt awkward trying to eat without it. The children cried for bread, and mother cried because she had none for them. Brother Jack came in one day and said that the new mill was at work. Our grain was there and would be ground when its turn came. A neighbor called the next day to tell us that the miller had decided to grind only a few bushels for each till all had bread. I think we were without bread about two weeks.

My oldest brother had stopped in Salem to work at carpentering when we got to Oregon. Not liking it there he moved to Albany, three miles from our home. As the Christmas holidays approached we made preparations to keep the day as we had done in Missouri. My brother and his wife came to that first Christmas. My second brother and our friend who had crossed the plains with us were on hand too. We had quite a talk about the new country and its resources. After several days with us they all returned to their homes and employment.

Many families of our emigration had settled in our neighborhood and had small farms fenced and houses built. Spring was nearly here. Our forty acres were fenced, plowed and sown to grain. The wild flowers were blooming. They were all new varieties to us so different from those in our old home, and the birds which greeted us on their return were nearly all strangers. The meadowlark appeared to be the same. The blackbird was different, having red wings.

We lived near a large butte and often went walking on it. Brother and his wife were visiting us, and we climbed to the highest point to look around. We were admiring the scenery when someone spied a large boulder and thought it would be fine sport to start it off, and see it roll down into a flat below us. We started it off bounding down the hill, and were very much alarmed to see it spin across the flat and mount the next bank. Surely it would stop before it reached the top, but it didn't. We all ran to see where it would stop, and held our breath as we heard a crash. We feared it had struck our neighbor's house at the bottom of the hill. We expected to see the pretty white cottage in ruins, but were relieved to see the stone had only crashed through a fence and gone tearing on to demolish a pig pen and set a fat porker free. That stone gave us a good fright. We went to the house to apologize, but found no one at home. Later, brother met a son of the family and explained and wanted to make amends, but the young man said it was a joke on the pig and of no consequence.

A gentleman called one day in early spring. He was a stranger to us, but had crossed the plains when we did and told us he had seen us in the mountains. He was very sociable and inquired about the oldest daughter, saying he remembered seeing her by an abandoned stove along the trail and had met her once since at an old friend's house where she had been on a visit during the winter.

After talking quite a while he asked if Miss Mamie was at home. Mother, not thinking he was a beau, told him she was calling at a neighbor's down the road. He then departed and went to the neighbor's. Mamie saw him coming and asked her hostess to tell him she had gone. He knew better, because he saw her dodge behind the door. She was not inclined to make his acquaintance and hoped to evade him. He insisted on seeing her. They had a short conversation and parted. He went to Lane County to look for a stock ranch. She came home and told us she had seen the man who passed us in the mountains while we were looking at the big stove, and that he wanted to make her acquaintance.* She had a love in the East whom she hoped to see some day and did not care for an Oregon beau. She was not fickle and thought it best to be off with the old love first.

*The man who declared his intention of marrying Mamie Gay was John Cogswell. John left home in Michigan at the age of sixteen. He first found work on the Erie Canal. Later, while working in Missouri, he decided to take the trail to the "far west." He started on foot, but met a man taking a herd of horses across the plains who offered John a horse to ride for his assistance. John first reached California in 1845.

He made a trip to Oregon in the spring of 1846, worked a while near the mouth of the Columbia River sawing lumber for ship building, and returned to California in 1849.

By 1850 he had mined enough gold for his needs and returned to Missouri. He outfitted himself with stock, then returned to the Willamette Valley.

He took a claim on the north side of the McKenzie River, four miles east of the Coburg Bridge. When he was established there and had a house ready he started out on horseback to find the Gay family who had come to Oregon in 1851. From *Lane County Historian*, Vol. VI, p. 27-31.

*Martha, Sarah Julia (Pink) and Mary Frances (Mamie) Gay.*

*Pink died of tuberculosis at age 19.*

Chapter 7

# On Father's Homestead
# In Lane County

A BOUT THIS TIME father made up his mind to go farther
south and secure a stock ranch near the hills as the valley land
would soon all be fenced. Our friend, the captain, father and my
oldest brother went to Umpqua and to Lane County. They returned
well pleased with the latter place. They all sold their homes and
moved up the valley and settled near where Eugene is now located.

We found some families of the Illinois Company living there. Our
ranch was near the hills. We did not like the place very well. We had
come West to live in the Willamette Valley and we were not ready to
leave it and live so isolated.

But here we were in Lane County. Father put up a camp, tem-
porarily, for a kitchen by standing four posts in the ground to support the roof. The wagon boxes with their covers were set off the
wagons and served as bedrooms. In this way we could get off the
ground and did not fear the snakes, as father had the boxes placed
on blocks of wood. We fixed up our cooking utensils around our
camp kitchen and made things quite convenient.

One afternoon just as we had finished our dishwashing, and had
all the milk pans set up on a shelf and the buckets and cups hung
about on the eaves of the roof, we were surprised to see a man
riding directly toward our camp. He spoke and alighted, and as the
posts of the kitchen were handy, he tied his horse to one of them.
We recognized him as Mamie's would-be beau. He said he had
located on the McKenzie River. While he was busy talking with
sister his horse became frightened and tried to pull loose. To our
dismay his horse pulled down our kitchen. Pots, kettles and pans all
fell in a crash under the roof. He was very much chagrined, of
course, and tried to assist in rebuilding our temporary shelter. We
could not help laughing at the catastrophe. Mamie had given up her

59

old lover and was becoming very fond of her new beau. We often reminded her of our demolished kitchen.

We had only been in camp a short time when we discovered we were in a rattlesnake district. We would see them all about us. There were hundreds of them, everywhere. Father felt bad to see the pesky things. He advised us to use the greatest precautions. He, at once, prepared to build us a log house, as there was no sawmill near and logs were plentiful. We saw small bands of Indians occasionally and thought a log house would be a better defense if they should molest us. They were displeased about whites settling in that place as game was plentiful in the hills.

Summer time was best for our work of building. We were very comfortable in camp and didn't need to hurry. When our house was all finished we moved into it, and felt proud to have such a house. Five large rooms and an extra nice stone fireplace. We built near a large spring and did not meet with such an experience about a well as at the first home. We had one neighbor about a mile from us. The next one was five miles away. Brother James and his wife came and built near us. Our captain settled several miles away in Siuslaw Valley.

Our house was near a hill and in the edge of a little vale. We could look over the valley, a nice view. We were trying to like the place. I think we should have but for the snakes. They were everywhere. Mamie and I were walking one morning when she spotted a rattler. I jumped back and saw another. Just then she saw a whole nest of them. We feared to move. We had walked right to the mouth of a snake den. We killed five and as many more got away. We got away too and told the boys. They searched and killed several large ones, then watched the den but found no more there.

## A Wedding

Mamie told me one day, soon after we had moved into our new house, that she was intending to leave us and go to a home of her own. I suspected as much as her beau had been very attentive of late.

Preparations for the wedding were even now in progress. Father, not wishing to purchase his supplies retail, went to Portland and bought his groceries and dry goods wholesale. Portland was then a village of 1,000 inhabitants. Mamie sent her order for the wedding outfit by him when he set out with two wagons and a boy. Father gave her order to the merchant with instructions to fill it just as ordered. After the merchant looked it over he said, "Well, old man,

*John and Mamie Cogswell were married October 28, 1852 (the second marriage in Lane County marriage records as recorded at the courthouse). "The wedding march was the steady patter of an autumn rain."*

you are to lose your daughter." Father said, "I think I am gaining a son." He was gone on that trip about ten days. We were just as proud as we could be of the nice things he brought us from the city. Mamie's wedding dress and all her articles were very nice. I thought they were just beautiful, but I had to cry over them for I began to realize now that she was to go from us. I had always had her with me. I had no other one for company. How could I live without her?

Many families had moved into our neighborhood during the last two or three months. New houses were all over the country. Three families of our old company and my sister-in-law's parents [the Gotts] had all settled very near us. The rainy season was here again. Storm clouds gathered, wild geese were going south, the wind sighed among the fir trees and matched the sadness in my heart. For the day of the wedding was near and Mamie would soon leave us.

Some old friends came fifty miles on horseback to attend the wedding. They, (including a young lady who was to be bridesmaid) were with us several days.

The date rolled around [October 28, 1852]. The guests arrived in a rainstorm. Some came in wagons, others on horseback and a few on foot. The groom and his attendants were late. Also the parson. At last, everyone was there. The room was crowded, everyone expectant. The bridal party entered from a side door. The wedding march was the steady patter of an autumn rain. Mamie and her maid were charming in white. The ceremony was short and impressive.

Father could not bear to witness the scene, Mamie being his pet from infancy. With my baby sister hugged close in his arms he walked in the dooryard till after the ceremony. He was sorry to give his daughter to another, but trusting it was for her happiness, he had consented to the union.

Their friends clustered around wishing joy. The congratulations over, we repaired to the dining room for an old-fashioned wedding supper. Old time games were played through the evening till the rafters rang with the fun. It was midnight when the party broke up. Then mothers bundled up their children and themselves while the men hitched up the ox teams and all went home. The wedding march was still sounding on the roof.

The next day being fair, Mamie and John asked us young people to go on a "bridle tour" with them—that is to say, horseback riding to see the country. We came home late, tired and hungry and did ample justice to a bountiful supper.

The next day Mamie went to her new home, also on horseback, as there was no such thing as a buggy or coach in this part of the country at that time. She came to see us in a week or two and told us how well she liked her cozy little white cottage under some great oak trees on the banks of the McKenzie River.

During her absence the friends from a distance had gone home. We had settled down to our daily routine and were very lonely without her. I turned my attention more toward my baby sister who was now one-and-a-half years old. She was very interesting. She talked and tried to sing. We made much of her. When Mamie came home for holiday, she asked to take Pink home with her for company. Mother said, "No, we can't spare baby."

Father and the boys again fenced land for grain and gardens, plowed, sowed, reaped and mowed with a will. Father promised that he would never move again. The next summer we had a fine crop of wheat, oats, corn and potatoes and a good garden. We liked our home now and felt reconciled. More emigrants arrived and settled around us. We seldom saw Indians now, but those who did come were rather saucy and considered dangerous.

One day mother had gone to a neighbors and I was left to get dinner and look after the children. Father and the boys were down in the field half a mile from the house. I had dinner on the stove cooking and felt proud to be left to prepare the meal alone. I was busy about the table when one of the little boys ran in and said, "Shut the doors quick. I see three Indians coming into the yard." I ran to the door and told them to stay out. I closed the door and barred it. In the meantime, they ran around to the kitchen door and walked in before I could get to it. I told them to go away. They said, "No, give us dinner." I refused. They went to the stove and raised the lids from the kettles, then to the cupboard and looked around over the shelves. They saw I was afraid and told me so. I got the children into the front room and left the Indians in possession of the kitchen. One of the little boys was looking out at the window and said, "I see father coming." The Indians heard him and got out quickly and went to their ponies. Father followed after them. He had a long flail he had picked up, and he flourished it defiantly and scolded them for entering the house when I told them to stay out. He had seen them coming toward the house and realized they knew he was away. He feared they would frighten us and take a lot of provisions. He told them to go and not come back there again. They were glad to get away without a whipping. As they rode off one of them said in good English, "The old man is mad." Father replied, "Yes, I am mad, and if you ever come here again I will thrash the ground with you." They were decked out in paint and feathers and dressed in Indian costumes. We always treated Indians kindly when they came around in a quiet way.

Our horses had all been driven away a short time earlier before those three came, and we laid it to those Indians as we had seen them pass the evening before. They had called out loudly to us. We had all retired and father would not answer them. They rode around the horses and looked at them, while father watched them in the dim twilight. They then waited till later and ran them off. The next morning we were sorry to find the horses all gone. One of the boys followed after their trail and fortunately overtook them about twenty miles away. The Indians saw they were being followed and ran off and left the horses. Brother was glad they did as he felt like fighting them. They were armed and he was alone, so it would have been a losing fight. He was gone so long we feared they had harmed him, or gone into the mountains with the horses, and we would not get them back. So we were very glad to see him come home with them all. Father thought they ran the horses off for pure meanness, not really wanting to steal them, but wanting to give us trouble for being on their hunting grounds.

Our first crop of wheat was cut by hand with an old style scythe, and then stacked in the field around a level spot of ground which had been scraped off smooth for a threshing floor. The sheaves of wheat were untied and scattered over the floor evenly. Then several pairs of oxen were driven around over it to tramp out the grain. We thought the flour made from that grain was of an extra quality. It was a rare variety of wheat, rather expensive in those days. Father made one sale of five bushels of seed for twenty-five dollars. He said it seemed like robbing the man to take five dollars per bushel, but he didn't want to cut the customary price.

Before another crop was ripe father had a barn ready to store it in, with a good threshing floor and bins for the grain. He also had a park for chickens. We raised them in great numbers. It was my work to look after the poultry. I enjoyed this work and was delighted with my success. I often got up before the sun to feed them in their coops. To see the hundreds of cute little chicks come running at my whistle was more fun than work. Gathering eggs was also fun. I would often send Pink to where I knew she could find eggs and watch her excitement when she found a full nest hidden away in a corner of the hay loft.

[Martha's oldest brother, James, had homesteaded near his father's place, and although Martha makes only passing references to this, James' diary details frequent visits back and forth by many of the family members. He had been settled long enough to be planting an orchard. In his diary he listed the number and variety of fruit trees and the order in which they were set "in the northwest corner of my garden."

James had a cabinet shop. He wrote about finishing "four doors and 60 light of sash" for Mr. Killingsworth some time

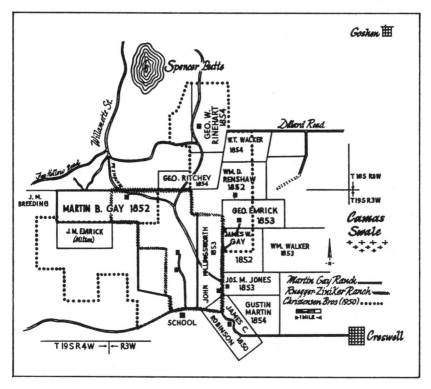

Homestead map. "Father bought land from time to time till he had 2,000 acres under fence."

after he helped Mr. Killingsworth stake off his claim, which lay between James' and his father's farms.

Typical diary entries read as follows:

• Father was here today and Mr. Richie to borrow a saddle.
• I went to father's to get the wagon to hawl [sic] wood but could not find the oxen.
• Mr. Killingsworth was here. Br. John was here and stayed all night.
• Sister Mary and Martha was here and stayed all night.
• Mr. Jones son was hear. [sic] Mr. Killingsworth, Mr. Read, Brother Green, Mr. Ward, Brother John and Baker.
• I went on the swale to kill geese.
• Mother was hear [sic] today and Kelly was here.
• I was at Mr. Emricks.
• I was at fathers to get help to kill a hog. Brother John was here and helped me kill it.

• Mr. Emrick was here. Father was here to make a saddle.

From these entries it is clear that the family members were
back and forth frequently, helping each other as well as
visiting. Occasionally Martha identified a family member in
connection with some incident, as in the following story.]

Brother Mark *[Martin, Jr.?]* went to the hills after stock. His
horse got frightened at a snake and jumped and threw him off. His
foot hung in the stirrup and he was dragged some distance. Eventually the saddle girth gave way and the saddle fell from the horse,
and that ended his being dragged over the rocks and stumps.

He met with several accidents which came near disfiguring him
for life. One day he was hauling rails. His team was a yoke of old
oxen. The large wagon was loaded with rails. He had hauled several
loads with no trouble. But this time the wagon broke and dropped
the rails and the back wheels while the front wheels were still attached to the team. Brother was thrown off to the front. His foot
caught in the tongue, holding him there. The team ran into a
yellowjacket's nest. The bees swarmed around stinging the oxen
and causing a runaway. Martin was dragged along, almost under
the oxen's feet. We heard the racket and saw the team and piece of
wagon racing down toward the house. Not thinking he was there
we went out to look for him, and found him in the road just behind
the wagon where he had been left a moment before. He was bloody
and his clothes had been torn from him. Father carried him into the
house. His hands and face were badly skinned. His head was cut
and his arms bruised and scratched. When he could speak he asked
if his eyes were gone. They were so swollen and full of dirt he
couldn't open them. It was some days before he could see and a long
time before he got entirely well. He said the oxen had often been
stung before. This time when the wagon broke and gave them a
fright, they ran away. They were an old yoke we had worked across
the plains. Living in Oregon had put new life in their old heels.

Mother came home one evening and told us we had a niece over
at brother James' home. John and Mamie had a daughter the same
year. Father said he felt quite old now to have two little girls to call
him Grandpa.

Brother Frank made us a visit. He lived in Albany. While he was
with us we all went to the woods after hazelnuts. Frank said he
would drive old Dick and Bob to one of the big wagons so we could
all go together. He filled the wagon box half full of straw and drove

up to the gate and called us to hurry as his team wanted to go. Mamie and her little girl, now a year old, were visiting us. The baby stayed with mother and Mamie went with us. We called at James' home and got Frances and her Susie. Away we went down the long fence towards the woods, all shouting and laughing at our outfit and glad to be out together. The little boys and Pink thought it great sport. Frank urged his team till they almost ran. It made us think of a stampede on the plains.

While we were having our fun mother was having a serious time. Soon after we started she missed the baby, and immediately searched all through the house, upstairs and down, out in the yard, in the barn and orchard. Then down to the spring. Where was the child? She called and listened. No answer. No one to help her look. She ran back into the house and the child called to her in its baby way. There in the middle of the bed, the little one sat very quietly pulling the needles out of grandma's knitting. She had no doubt been there all the while, very quiet because she was in mischief.

Time went on and we were to have a school. The neighbors all gathered and talked the matter over. A log house was built on the site chosen. A committee called on a man who was considered suitable for a teacher and engaged him to teach a term of five months. How glad we were. We tripped off that mile to the first day of school. There were about twenty boys and as many girls. Father sent eight scholars and we had two girls boarding with us, making one-fourth of the school going from our house. Pink was quite small but she wanted to go, and the big brothers would carry her on their shoulders when she got tired.

We had fine times. Friday afternoons we usually had spelling matches. On such occasions, it was easy to see who were the favorites. It was not always the best spellers who were chosen by the leaders of the two teams. The teacher's oldest son and daughter were considered about the best spellers in school. Some of my brothers were also very good. We had several terms of school in the old log schoolhouse.

In 1854, the Indians were quite savage and made threats against the whites. One came when father was absent and demanded pay for the land. He said if we did not pay him he would burn our barn. We got him to leave by telling him to come when the Boston man was at home. He never came back.

Sometimes they would watch to see the men go off to the fields, or to the woods to work. They would then silently walk in and help themselves to provisions, take the bread out of the oven and order more. They were armed with guns and knives. The squaws seldom came about.

I was spending a few days with Mamie, and we were aroused one morning before daylight from our sleep by someone calling to us to get up and make our escape as the Indians were on the warpath. While sister and I were preparing to leave, my brother-in-law went to the pasture after the horses. We had everything packed we needed and were anxious to go, but he didn't come. He came at last without the horses. The fog was so dense he could not find them. He feared too that the Indians had stolen them. He went to look again, this time more successfully. He got them in the harness in double quick time, and we hurried to Eugene, which was then a village of a half dozen families. It seemed everybody in the country had come to town. Runners had been sent all over to rouse people for action. Such a diversified lot of soldiers were seldom to be seen. All were armed and all had some frightful story of outbreak to relate. Some had seen the smoke of burning buildings. Others had really heard shrieks of terror. There was great excitement. The men were ready to fight, but where was the foe?

When we got to father's they had already heard of the reign of terror. Runners had been sent to all outside settlers. People rushed to strongholds with their families and prepared for defense. A party of well-armed men were sent out to investigate—sent to where the smoke had been seen and the screaming heard.

After a few days the reconnoitering party returned and reported at headquarters. They had found no hostiles. They found two white men camped out who were hunting deer, hence the great smoke. One of their dogs had caught a hog and it squealed. That squeal was mistaken for screaming. The whole scare was pronounced a false alarm. The army disbanded and families returned to their homes. That was the only Indian scare we ever had in Lane County, and it was a false one.

A ferocious old ex-chief named Jumbo came and asked father to keep his gun for him while he went to Oregon City to look after some ponies. Father did not want to keep it, but the Indian insisted he should do so. He said a very bad Injun wanted it, and he could not leave it with his squaw. Father asked him if the Indian knew he was intending to leave the gun with him, and the Indian said no. Then father agreed to keep it. He stayed so long we thought he would not return at all. But at last he did, and was very pleased over finding it safe. He shook hands with father, shouldered his gun and went almost leaping up the hill and out of sight.

We heard later that he had killed an Indian and got his gun, then ran away and hid the gun by leaving it with father. He went to Oregon City to escape the Indian's friends, and stayed away till they had gone to other hunting grounds. He was a bad Indian and his tribe would not own him as chief. He left his squaw because she was old.

One day an Indian came to father at work. He wanted matches. Father was afraid he would set the woods on fire, but when the Indian promised to be careful he gave him a few. The Indian was glad saying, "Me like fire this cold night."

There was an Indian graveyard not far from our home which was a curiosity to us. When one died, everything belonging to him was put on or near his grave. We would go and look at the place just to see what was left there. One time we saw an umbrella and several baskets and pans.

We found many places of interest on our ranch as we explored it year by year. The ruins of Goliath, as we called them, were a wonder of some note. It was two miles from the house and a rough road to the place which resembled an old tumbledown castle. There were great octagonal columns scattered around and piles of stones here and there as if once a large building had stood near the place. Great trees were growing among them. We wondered what it had been and when. *[More recent residents of the area explained that it was a columnar basalt outcropping. A rock crushing crew worked the basalt up into road rock in the 1930s. Ed.]*

Eugene was now quite a village. Our married brother *[James]* tired of the farm and moved to town to work at his trade. We missed the family very much. Two other brothers went to the gold mines in northern California. Soon after they left home we received word that the Indians in southern Oregon were on the war path. Several families had been killed and houses burned. We did not hear from my brothers for some time. They reported that they had just passed the place of attack and saw the smoke of the burning houses. Volunteers were sent from our area to fight the Indians. One of our dear friends who crossed the plains with us was killed. It was the young man who gave the Indian the ginger.

There were now good schools in Eugene, and I went there to attend during the winter months. How glad I was to get home to see mother and baby sister and all the home folks in the spring. How I enjoyed tramping over the hills to see the little lambs frisking in the sunshine, working in the dairy to make butter into pound patties, hunting eggs in the barn and watching the cute little chicks.

I often saddled my pony and went after the cows when the boys were busy. I was trotting along a hillside one evening when my saddle turned and I fell to the ground in the high grass. I didn't stop to think if I was hurt, but fixed my saddle and mounted the horse quickly to escape any rattlesnakes that might be present. I later discovered my arm and shoulder were sore, but I drove the cows home all right. Of course the boys laughed at my disaster.

We had been on the ranch two or three years, and had located several snake dens. Father prepared some long poles with sharp hooks on them. With those picks the men and boys would go snaking on warm days early in the spring. They would hook the rattlers out from among the rocks and kill them. Some days they would kill hundreds and in this way keep them from leaving their dens and scattering over the valleys. When we once saw a snake we never let it escape if we could prevent it. In this way we cleared them out considerably in a few years.

Another time I was after the cows when my horse jumped and nearly threw me. I heard the dreaded rattle and soon spotted a very large snake in its coil. The horse had heard it and shied from it. I rode to a pile of stones, dismounted and left my horse standing. I got as many stones as I could carry and cautiously walked back and killed that snake. Then I threw the other stones on it and got away quickly, fearing the poison in the air which is bad for the eyes or to breathe. I left it writhing. A few days later I was riding near and looked to see if it was there, and was surprised to see it had got away from the stones in its exertions.

One day brother Frank, always into some mischief, was walking about the yard. He spotted a large old rattler and with a long stick was driving it over a large bare place in the dooryard. He called us to come out and see it. We went. He said, "Pink is afraid of snakes. I want to see how near she will come to this one." She walked up very near it. We were all around her and the snake's head was away from her. We were not anxious about her approaching it in this way. We had startled it, however, and it sprang around toward her and almost to her feet. I snatched her away and Frank killed the snake. Mother told him a rattlesnake was a dangerous thing to play jokes with among the children.

Some of our neighbors collected the rattles of all the snakes they killed, showing how numerous they were. A Mr. Maloney who had a stock ranch near us had secured a string of rattles eight feet long.

The Indians protested against the whites killing them, saying they gave us warning to keep away by rattling. They never killed them when they rattled, as that was the snakes' manner of saluting. If an Indian encountered one that did not rattle, then he felt it his duty to kill that silent enemy because it meant to strike, or it would have warned him.

We found nice strawberries and blackberries on our place and crabapples and cherries. We feared the snakes most in strawberry season. We moved along quietly, picking berries, and often put our hands near them before we noticed them. Then that terrible rattle, and we would jump away and likely encounter another one, as they were seldom alone.

A neighbor called for me to go strawberrying with her and I said I was afraid of snakes. "Well," she said, "I think you could see a snake quick enough when you are looking for a little strawberry."

"Yes, but I don't want to look for snakes. They are pesky things and the bane of my existence." I would go horseback riding after blackberries and, as they grew on tall bushes and logs, I could wear boots and pick them in some degree of safety. But strawberrying was another matter.

Father got a band of sheep and, in a few years, the snakes seemed to change their quarters. As sheep run in flocks they tramp over nearly every inch of ground in their range, and father thought they caused the snakes to go to more quiet places.

Father built us a large old-fashioned farm house, and our log

*"Father built us a large old-fashioned farm house and our log house was pulled down and moved away to the hills to be used as a wool house and to store farm implements in."*

house was pulled down and moved away to the hills to be used as a wool house and to store farm implements in. We had many hay barns and grain barns, sheep shearing houses and shops and a tannery. All together it made quite a village. Father bought land from time to time till he had 2,000 acres under fence.

And now brother Frank had returned from California and was to be married to a young lady near Albany. [*Charles Franklin, second son, married Rebecca Burkhart in Albany, Oregon, May 27, 1858.*] This time brother and I went fifty miles on horseback to attend the wedding. After the wedding we visited old neighbors while the bride and groom went on their wedding trip by horseback to Oregon City. They passed up a river trip because the steamers were not always on time and they were in great haste to escape a noisy serenade—a chivaree. We hurried them off, and threw the slipper after them, and went in to try to comfort Rebecca's mother, as the bride was her youngest daughter.

Sister Mamie's two little girls contracted scarlet fever. They were convalescing and begged to go to grandpapa's. When the parents thought it safe to do so, they brought them to our house. How delighted they were to be there, but alas, they relapsed and both died. We buried them in one grave on a hill near where they had once played. This was our first sorrow and it fell heavily upon us. Dear sister was brokenhearted. How could she go home without her dear little girls?

Mamie came to see us, but how lonely she looked without her girls. She would visit their grave and grieved so much that father advised a change. So John and Mamie planned a visit East. Mamie became interested in the trip. They were gone nearly a year. We knew it was a long and dangerous trip by ocean steamer. [*They traveled across Panama on mule back. Then across the Gulf of Mexico and up the Mississippi by boat. Another daughter was born in 1858. Lane County Historian Vol. VI, p. 28*] How pleased we were when they came safely home with their sunny little baby girl. She was just learning to walk.

Mamie had only been with us a very short time when we received the sad news of the death of brother's little boy in Eugene. He was about a year old. Father said life is made of sunshine and shadows. We buried sweet Willie near his little cousins. [*William Monroe Gay died July 16, 1859. Son of James and Frances.*]

Two other brothers went to the gold mines in Idaho to try their luck in searching for the yellow metal. Six were away and our family not so large. Three were married [*James, Frank and Mamie*] and three were absent *[John, Baker and Evan.]* Six were at home with father and mother. There were several grandchildren now to visit grandma and the years went by. Pink was now a big lady and very fond of music. She played nicely for the little folks when they came home. Her brothers bought her an organ, and it was her delight to get a group of them around her in the parlor and play and sing for them. The children were very fond of her and she made much of them all.

Pink had a very gentle old pony which she often rode about. She began riding horseback when quite young and was a good equestrian. The children liked to ride her pony around the yard.

I was fond of riding myself and often rode ten miles to church on Sunday morning, then stayed to Sabbath School at two o'clock and rode home before dark. Brother and I were fording the Willamette River one morning at a dangerous place, and he got some distance ahead of me. My horse got off the ford by going too far upstream into deep water. I called loudly to brother, but he could not hear me over the noise of the water. Several times my horse stumbled and almost threw me into the rushing current. Brother thought I was following after him all right and was alarmed when he looked around from the shore and saw me so far into deep water. He motioned me to go downstream. At last I made the landing, thoroughly wet, as the water nearly ran over my horse's back. I felt the wetness especially because it was a cold day.

Another time I was riding a large Canadian horse. He was nearsighted and would often see scarecrows where there was nothing to be afraid of. This time I was crossing a stream which had a gravel bar put in just wide enough for a road. On either side, the water was deep and muddy. I had got almost across when he shied at a stump. I tried to urge him onward but he persisted in going backward and was just on the edge of the bar ready to fall into deep water when he changed his tactics and bounded forward again. He had whims of his own. If he did not want us to put a saddle on him, he would snap his teeth at us.

I was invited to go with a party of young people to visit in the Mohawk Valley. We went on horseback. Soon after we arrived at the house of our friend, we were in the sitting room chatting away when the cook came running and told us the house was on fire. A brother-in-law of our hostess ran to the kitchen and located the fire. It was around the flue in the roof. He got up there quickly and called for water. We went off to the creek in the back yard with buckets and soon had a supply of water up in the garret. I was going after a second bucketful when I met the cook coming from the creek with an empty bucket. I asked her why she didn't get water and she thought she had. She was so excited she did not know what she was doing. We saved the cottage.

While some were fighting the fire, others were very busy carrying things out of the house. The girls who went with us amused me by first taking out all our hats and riding habits. When asked why they didn't try to save the lady's things too, one girl answered, "I knew we'd need our hats and habits to wear home if the house burned."

The brother-in-law who had gone there with us rode a lovely race animal. She was trim and spirited. I had often begged him to let me ride her. He said she was not safe for ladies and had always refused to let me on her. After dinner the schoolma'am who was boarding at the place insisted on riding Lista and, while I was interested in the household indoors, he saddled her and let the schoolma'am take a short ride down the lane. I went out just in time to see her returning. Then I told him it was my turn. If Miss Mina could ride her I could too. He thought to reconcile me by saying, "I think too much of you to risk your life on her back."

"Oh, you don't either! I mean to ride her home. Now can't I? Do say yes." He shook his head as I went to get my riding habit as the girls were ready and waiting for me. I called to him to be sure and put my saddle on Lista, but I was disappointed. When I had to ride the same horse I had come on I concluded he knew best. We started on our way home, he riding by my side. I began coaxing him again to please let me ride her just a little while. At last he reluctantly consented, and I was proud to be seated on her back. While he was changing the saddles, the girls had got quite a distance ahead of us. I was just saying to him, "Now don't you see I can ride her?" He said, "I knew you could but I am afraid she is not safe for you." We were talking about our visit and the fire and I was not thinking of danger just then. He said we must overtake the girls for Anna's horse was not safe. Then he threw up his hands and clucked to his horse. That was his signal to Lista to run fast. Off she went like the wind. She almost flew over the ground. I knew he was not trying to keep up with her, or to pass her. She would not stop and he knew it, but he thought I might fall. On we went. I sat firm and steady and did not think of being scared. For a quarter of a mile she carried me like a whirlwind. We passed the girls, circled around and came to a halt. My escort came up to her and reached for the bridle saying, "You had a fine race. How did you like it?"

"Splendid! Isn't she grand?"

"Don't you know she ran away with you? I was afraid for you. Do you want to ride her any farther?"

"Yes, I want to race her to Mamie's." He saw I did not fear her and let me ride on. When Mamie saw me riding Lista she said to him, "Why did you let Amanda ride her? Weren't you afraid she would run away with her?"

"She did run away, but Amanda rides splendidly and did not get hurt. Even so, she can never ride her again with my consent." And I had to give her up.

I was permitted to ride a very nice small race horse one other time, and it ran away with me. I always liked to ride fast, but I certainly did not like to have a horse go faster than I wanted it to. I really could not get either one of those horses to check their rate of speed till they were so inclined of their own free will.

Mamie was sick one time with a fever. In those pioneer days there were no trained nurses to be had. Jane, our hired girl, and Pink and I went to stay with her. We had a great deal to do. I cared for Mamie. Pink looked after her little girls.

One morning just after breakfast Mamie's husband said he had business to look after in Eugene, and left me in charge of all. He said he would return as soon as possible. There were no near neighbors to depend on. We hoped to be all right until he could get back.

I put the baby boy to sleep and laid him on the bed by his mother as she had asked me to do. Jane was in the kitchen busy about the morning work. Sister and the girls were in the yard with the fat lambs. I left them and went to the garden down near the river to get vegetables; then to the wash yard where Jane had left the clothes out the day before. I hurried back to the house fearing the baby might waken and disturb his mother.

As I drew near the kitchen door, I could not hear anyone or see anyone in the yard. I wondered where they had all gone so quickly and why Jane had left her work. I was alarmed to hear a loud voice calling out, cross and fiercely demanding. I rushed into the kitchen and could tell that it was the language and voice of an Indian. Where were Jane and the girls and sister? I ran into the living room and saw Old Fisherman standing in the door of Mamie's bedroom with a sixshooter in his hand. He flourished the gun wildly about demanding pay for his land. Old Fisherman was a bad Indian who lived in the Mohawk country. He was really mean and wild when he got drunk.

I said to the Indian, "What are you doing here? What do you want?" He whirled around when I spoke and watched me going toward a gun which hung nearby. He put his gun in its holster and started his loud talking. I could tell he was drunk.

I stepped to sister's door and saw that she was there as I had left her. Also Pink and the little girls and Jane crouched in the corner behind the bed. They had seen the drunken Indian coming and ran in there, not stopping to close the door against him.

He looked sullen and mad as he said to me, "Give me money! Give me flour." I told him he must talk to the Boston man. He drew a great knife from his belt and went out to the grindstone to sharpen it. He wanted me to turn the grindstone for him, but I refused. He tried the edge of the knife to see if it was sharp enough to suit him, then put in into his belt. I felt relieved then, thinking he meant no mischief; but what did the wretch do but draw another knife from the other side of his belt and grind it. Mamie's little two-year-old went out and stood by him while he ground his knives. We couldn't coax her away and were afraid to go fetch her.

Just then we heard men driving cattle down toward the river. I sent Pink and Jane to tell them to come to our rescue. "Tell them the Indian is drunk and we fear him."

While they were gone he came into the house again and ordered me to give him bread. I went to get it for him, and he called to me to put butter on it. I told him I had no butter. I carried a plate of biscuits to him expecting him to eat them. He snatched his old slouch hat off his head and held it toward me. I turned the bread into it, then gave him a paper to put it in and helped him tie it up. He grunted thanks, grabbed it from me and almost ran out of the house. As he darted around the corner I went to the door and locked it after him, but could not see him anywhere.

In a short time a man rode up to the gate, dismounted and came to the door. "Where is that Indian?" His men did not tell him at first that the girls were afraid of the Indian, and he apologized for not coming sooner. He said he would hunt him up, but Mamie said he was gone now and best leave him go for, if we molested him, others would seek revenge.

Brother Ev, Pink and I went with a party of young people to Albany and Salem to spend the Christmas holidays. We left Eugene early one morning in an old-time stage coach. There being several travelers, an extra wagon was sent along to convey the baggage. The rain was coming down in torrents, and had been doing so for several days. But our plans were made and friends were expecting us, so we couldn't stop because of a little rain.

We had gone only a few miles when we realized that we would

meet with many obstacles on that day's journey. Swollen streams and floating bridges were already in our road. Some thought we should go back, but the majority were inclined to proceed if possible. At noon, we called at a farmhouse and asked for dinner for eight of us and a good feed for the horses. We were shown into a large room where a glowing fire welcomed us. One of our company began speculating about what dinner would be served—sodden bread, burnt bacon and beans?

When we entered the room a number of little girls scampered away and were peeping at us. We coaxed some of them in and told them about Santa Claus. We asked a bright-eyed little one where the rest of the children were, as we only counted seven at home. She said ten had gone to school and their big brother was at the barn feeding our horses. One big sister had gone to a party and the other was in the kitchen helping mamma fix dinner. The sister from the kitchen came in and got a tablecloth from some shelves.

Soon we were invited to the dining room. There we found a feast at a nicely spread table, and how we enjoyed that warm dinner. One of our group learned from the big brother in the barn that there were twenty children in the family.

Our trip during the afternoon was complicated by bridges out or afloat. Darkness soon came and we were miles from Albany. In crossing a ford on a small stream, which was out of its banks, one wheel of the stage slipped off the track in some way and we almost capsized in the cold water. Later we heard a shout from the passenger riding on top of the stage. He had spotted the lights of Albany. Then we reached the door of the hotel where a crowd had collected anxiously awaiting the southern stage.

We were all cold and hungry, and it was late when we retired. The boat for Salem would start out before daylight. A small room, a regular little pen, was assigned to us four girls. The hotel was already crowded when we arrived. One of the girls was carrying a large sum of money and was afraid of being robbed. She asked us, "Where can I put the money?"

"Don't speak so loud!"

"I'll put it under my head." Then she decided I should keep it for her. We were in quite a dilemma when we missed one girl. I found her in the parlor praying for our safety. We were soon asleep and rose early to see the girls and two of the gentlemen off.

After breakfast, a coach called for Sister and me. We went out into the country to spend the holidays with relatives. Brother had gone to Salem.

On the return trip, we all boarded the steamer for Eugene. We had trouble with driftwood and had to tie up at Harrisburg where we were invited to a New Year's Ball. We preferred staying on the steamer where we had a nice New Year's dinner. Then brother said, if we wished, he would take us down and show us the machinery of the steamer. We all went with him to the lower deck and inspected the machinery. He then wanted us to see the cook who had prepared that nice dinner, and he pointed out a great, fat, dirty greasy man laying asleep on some old wool sacks. The girls gave a shriek and ran upstairs. The cook wakened and was shocked to think all those girls had been looking at him in his dirty apron. We had a talk with the captain in his cabin. There was a musician on board who played his guitar and sang for us. We played games and told stories until midnight. Then wished all a Happy New Year, and so to bed.

The next day we arrived at Eugene. We found the folks at home anxious about us, as they had heard of the dangerous boating.

We never failed to attend the Oregon State Fair where we would meet old friends and make new acquaintances. The fairs were well worth going sixty miles to see, even if we did have to go in a wagon and camp out and do our own cooking. Hundreds of others were camped around us, all feeling happy and independent while they enjoyed the fair. The products of this new land were impressive—the fine cattle, horses, sheep, goats, pigs, chickens and turkeys. Then the grains of all kinds, the fruits and garden vegetables, the butter and Oregon cheese. One cake of cheese I remember was as large as a big washtub. And a bar of soap which weighed hundreds of pounds, perhaps a ton; and a fat hog weighing 1,000 pounds. There were magnificent flowers and fine arts and machinery. Everything imaginable from an apple peeler to a locomotive. We were proud to see all this in our new country of Oregon.

A brother who had been absent in Idaho for some years informed us that he would stop a few days in Portland, be married there and then come home. He had met a charming young widow who had a seven-year-old daughter, he explained. This was all very nice, but this brother, two years my senior, had always been my companion, my playmate in childhood and my escort in after years. To think of giving him up to another brought tears to my eyes.

I met the steamer when they arrived in Eugene and accompanied them to our country home. In spite of my misgivings, I found brother's wife very likable and her little Jess was full of fun and very interested in the lambs and chickens when Pink showed her around the place. She raised quite a laugh at dinner when she informed us

that she was married. She had insisted on standing by her mamma
during the ceremony and imagined she was married too if mamma
was.

*[This is all Martha tells us about her brother, Martin, Jr.'s
marriage and family, but Fred Lockley interviewed his widow
many years later and her story was published in the Oregon
Journal, December 10 and 11, 1927. Since her story provides
more fascinating insight into a woman's life on the northwest
frontier, I have included it here. The following portions of that
story are quoted from Mike Helm's book* Conversations With
Pioneer Women, *pages 193-199.]*

My maiden name was Elizabeth Paschal. My father, Isaac
Paschal, was born in Virginia. His people were Hugenots. . .
(They) came in the early days from England to Virginia. My
father moved from Virginia to Ohio where I was born June 5,
1838. I will be 90 years old if I live till next June. My mother's
maiden name was Margaret McVicar. She was also born in
Virginia. Her father was Irish, her mother Scotch. Father and
mother were married in Virginia and the first three of their five
children were born in that state. . .

On December 4, 1859, I married Dr. A.R. Dillon of
Virginia. We were married in Virginia. My husband was a
skillful surgeon and a good doctor when he was sober. We
started for Oregon in the spring of 1862. A widower with two
small children wanted to come to Oregon. He told me that if I
would do the cooking and take care of his two children, he
would bring my husband and myself across the plains for
$200. We paid him $100 down and were to pay the other $100
when we reached the Willamette Valley. He started out with
young cattle. One yoke gave out, so my husband had to buy a
yoke to replace the ones that died. When we got to Fort Hall,
the man announced that he had changed his plans and was going to turn off there for California. This left us stranded.
However we found a bachelor who was headed for Oregon
and arranged to go with him. When we got to Salmon Falls he
sold his outfit and told us he was going to the mines, so we
were stranded once more. I had to throw away my feather bed
and all of our cooking outfit except a frying pan and a teaket-
tle. My husband had to abandon his medical library. Our little
girl, Jessie, was two years old. I paid the man $10 to let Jessie
ride in his wagon. My husband and I struck out on foot with
what food we could carry and, during the next five hundred
miles, I only got to ride three miles. We were without money
and when my husband heard that a town had been started a
few months before at a place called Auburn. . . he decided

there might be a chance to practice his profession there, so we walked to Auburn.

A great many of the emigrants who were on their way from Missouri to the Willamette Valley learned about the new mining camp at Auburn and settled in Auburn or elsewhere in eastern Oregon. When we got there late in September, 1862, there were several stores, a livery stable, blacksmith shops and quite a number of saloons. The houses were all log cabins, as there was no sawmill anywhere in that vicinity. (Late that fall Mr. Leveredge brought some sawmill equipment up from Portland.) We lived next door to a family named Peters. I remember Alice Peters very well. My husband started the practice of medicine in Auburn. Most of his cases were surgical cases caused by accidents. When he was not too drunk he had very good success. He spent all he made in the saloons. I took in washing to pay for our food. Food was high. I charged a dollar to wash and iron a boiled shirt and 50 cents for a woolen one. I remember one day a saloonkeeper's wife gave me a big washing. She had not had any washing done for over three weeks. It took me all of one day to wash it and all of the next day to iron it. It really was worth more but I decided to charge her only five dollars. When I took the washing to her she said, "I'll have my husband credit the five dollars I owe you on the bill your husband owes at the saloon."

I felt terribly bad about it and told her I needed the money. She wouldn't pay me, however, and as we were arguing, her husband who was in the next room said, "Pay the woman the five dollars you owe her. She don't have to take in washing to pay her husband's bar bills. If I was fool enough to trust him, it's my fault, not hers." He made her pay me the five dollars.

You have no idea of the difficulty I had that winter. I had to melt snow in a pan over an open fireplace to do the washing. We had no stove. I boiled the clothes in a brass kettle and strung lines from the rafters all over the house so the clothes would dry. I had to walk through the deep snow to deliver the washing, except for miners, who brought their dirty clothes and called for them.

We spent the fall and winter of 1862-1863 at Auburn. In the spring of 1863 we moved to the mines in Boise Basin. I ran across a family there who were keeping a restaurant at Placerville. The man's wife and I had both taught school in the same district in Iowa. My husband did not earn enough money to feed our baby and myself. The woman who was running the restaurant told me if I would wait on the tables and do the dishes my baby and I could stay there and work for our board.

The miners who boarded at the restaurant would frequently give me a nugget or sometimes a half dollar as a tip.

When my husband. . . was drunk, which was most of the time, he would worry Jessie till she cried and then he would beat her for crying. Life with him was so impossible that I went to The Dalles to get away from him. He really loved me. He followed me to The Dalles and told me that he had had his lesson, that he would never, never touch another drop. I hoped he would keep his promise, so I took him back.

An epidemic of smallpox swept over the mining district and my husband was put in charge of the pesthouse at The Dalles. In those days there were saloons on every corner and the saloonkeepers and gamblers dominated politics and business. Men felt that they had to drink rather than offend the saloonkeepers. My husband said he would not get any practice from the saloonkeepers, gamblers, or their adherents unless he drank with them, so soon he was as bad as ever, being drunk most of the time. My father having been a doctor, and my husband being a doctor, I knew a good deal about nursing, so Reverend Ben Lippincott. . . employed me as a nurse for his wife. . . When Mr. Lippincott was called as pastor of the Taylor Street Methodist Church in Portland in 1865, Mrs. Lippincott wanted me to go with them to Portland to help with the work, as she was not strong. So I went down to Portland and lived at their home till I married my second husband.

When I was waiting on tables at the restaurant in Placerville in the Boise Basin, M.B. Gay, a miner, boarded at the restaurant. From Placerville he went back to his home at Eugene. On his way back to the mines in the winter of '66 he heard I was working at a boarding house at The Dalles, so he came there to board. He boarded there for six weeks. By this time I had found it was hopeless to try to live with my husband. Judge Woods, later governor of Oregon, secured a divorce for me in April, 1865. Mr. Gay and I corresponded after I had come down to Portland and in June, 1866, he came down from the mines and on June 17, 1866, Reverend Ben Lippincott married us in the Methodist parsonage here in Portland.

My husband's brother, John Gay, owned a farm on Albany Prairie, seven miles from Albany. He was a bachelor. He asked us to come to his farm, and he paid my husband to work on the farm while I did the cooking and the housework. We were there two years and would have stayed longer, but John married Helena Pike, the daughter of a neighboring family. We moved to Albany and my husband took a contract to cut 500 cords of cordwood for Perry Spinks. Working on the river bottom my

*"John married Helena Pike, the daughter of a neighboring family. They lived on a farm near Albany." Helena, in later years, and their children.*

husband got a good case of old-fashioned ague, so he had to throw up his contract. My husband's oldest sister had married John Cogswell, who had a place twelve miles from Eugene. We moved to his place and my husband worked for him for some time.

My husband was considered a visionary by his friends. He always thought that the fartherest fields were greenest. On our fourteenth wedding anniversary, we figured that we certainly must be rolling stones, for we had made twenty-one moves in fourteen years.

Martha's story continues.

A younger brother had also been in Idaho three years. We had a letter stating he intended coming home, but did not say when we might expect him. Late one evening in October two men rode up to the gate and asked for directions to the next house. Fearing they might meet with some mishap in the fast-approaching darkness, they asked to stay overnight with us. Father said we could keep them and sent a boy out to take their horses to the barn. One of the men went with him and the other, a tall military-looking gentleman in cap and cloak, walked in and asked for supper for two. He drew the offered chair up near the fire, remarking that it was a cool evening and pulling his cap down over his eyes. We supposed the glare of the light affected them.

Father talked with him and learned that he was from Idaho. He said, "I have a son in Idaho, and when you called I thought perhaps you was my son." The man said, "I likely have met him," as he looked up toward father who was inspecting him very closely. I stepped into the dining room and told Pink I thought that was our brother. "Just see his great whiskers," she said. "It can't be." I said the same to mother and she said, "Why child, if it was your Ev, father would know him." I went back into the room and tried to transfer my thought to father.

Just then the gentleman arose. He took off his cap and cloak and stepped into the hall to hang them on the rack. He then walked out into a back porch to the washstand like he was accustomed to the place. The other man and boy had come in from the barn. We heard a hurrah and a jolly laugh and, now with his cap off, we could see it was our long absent brother. Father commented, "Well, now, I thought it was you, but I didn't know for sure. Those long whiskers! You must cut them off."

Brother Jack had spent some time in Idaho. He told us that one time when he and some mining friends were going from Florence, Idaho, to another camp late one evening, they met three horse thieves who had some very fine horses with them. They hurried along and did not wish to speak or be noticed. Brother and his party soon made camp for the night. Next morning before it was quite light, Jack was preparing breakfast while his men got their pack horses ready for an early start. He was attracted by a sharp click of a gun and looked up in the direction of the sound. There stood a man with drawn gun aimed at him. When brother's face came up the man instantly lowered his gun saying, "I was about to shoot you, Jack, when you raised your head and I recognized you."

"What did you want to shoot me for, Tom? Come have some breakfast and tell me about it." They were old friends. Tom told of stolen horses. He was with a posse after the thieves and had heard they were camped near here. He couldn't see good in the half-light and didn't want them to escape. Jack chided him about nearly shooting an innocent man, then told him they had met the thieves with the horses late the previous evening. He learned later that they had been captured and brought to justice.

A May Festival was held on Skinner's Butte in Eugene in 1864. Quite early the children of our schools were gathering in flowers from hill and garden. A throne for the May Queen was erected under a large oak tree and decorated with evergreens and flowers. A flower crown hung from the boughs overhead. The coronation ceremony included four little maids. There was music, a procession and winding of the Maypole. From base to top it was garlanded with flowers and the stars and stripes floated from its crown. Refreshment booths had been set up here and there. One of those present was a pioneer nearly one hundred years old. The repast had barely concluded when a heavy shower drenched everything. A ball in the evening ended the festivities of that May Day.

We had neighbors from Virginia, a father and mother and their children, Allie and Jack. The father and mother were both in very poor health. They had a good home and enough of this world's goods to keep them safe. The father was the weaker and thought a journey might restore him. He went away. In a few short months a notice of his death was received. The mother sank under the news. We brought her and the two little ones to our own home, where we did all that could be done to help. But in six months, she too passed away leaving the orphans in our care. Allie was seven and Jack a year younger. They asked if we would keep them always. Their mother had told them of an uncle who was a designing man and would not treat them kindly. He would take them only to get their money and property.

He never came while his sister was sick, but he showed up a few days after the funeral and tried to appear deeply distressed. The children would not go with him willingly. He left and returned after some days. He had been appointed their guardian and took them away. He got possession of all their property and money. He made them work for their living and charged them for every article of clothing and for all their school books. By the time they were of age they had nothing at all of their estate left. The uncle, who should have been their counselor and guide, was their worst enemy. I have watched their lives for thirty years, as I promised to do. They are happily settled now.

## Chapter 8

# Family Reunion

W E HAD SPENT FIFTEEN YEARS OF HAPPINESS on our mountain ranch. Our home had been a haven of rest to many. We cared for the sick and aged, and the needy ones. Charity never knocked at my father's door and went away empty handed. Those whose hearts were bowed down with grief found in him a true friend. The wanderer found shelter and food. People loved him for his generosity of soul, for his honesty and true worth, and for his warm-hearted Southern chivalry. Children loved him for his kindness and gentleness toward them.

Father was growing old now. He often spoke of the absent ones and wished to see them. Some were married and some were away. It was ten years since we all met at the dear old home. Father's birthday was drawing near. A younger brother and I thought of a surprise we would give him on that day. We told mother of our plan and she agreed to help. So we prepared for a family reunion. We wrote to all the absent ones, and all agreed to come. We took Pink into our plot and she was delighted. We kept it all from father, because we wanted to give him an agreeable surprise.

We prepared for diversions and festivities. Rooms were ready to receive the guests who were due on a certain day. Some came the night before, then others late the next night. It got dark. Only one family missing now. We lit up the house and kept listening. Soon we heard them calling and there they were—all together at last. We hustled the little ones into the warm, lighted room and removed their wraps. Then they made a rush for grandpapa.

What a housefull! Father looked on the group with pleasure as our oldest brother said, "Here we are, father and mother. All of us." We gathered in mother's large sitting room. Father said, "I am so glad to see you all once more. Who got up this surprise for me?" He

*Martin and Ann Gay, circa 1865*

told us to all stand up in a line. We circled around the large room. We then asked father and mother to stand up with us, as such a long train needed headlights. After supper the children played games in another room while the grownups visited and discussed plans for the following day.

The next morning, we all congratulated father on his birthday. We did not think him old, but his hair had been white for years. We told him we had arranged to have a family picture taken and asked him to go to Eugene with us. He could not refuse. We had engaged an artist *[probably a photographer]* for the day and also for dinner at the hotel for the entire family party.

We started out from home in good shape. We left friends at home to prepare supper for us and care for the home during our absence. It was a happy day. Many friends called in to congratulate father and mother on the reunion of their large family. We got home just in time for the feast awaiting us. What a merry time we had. The little cousins chattered to each other and clambered over grandfather's knees and clustered around Pink.

After breakfast the next morning some prepared to go and father asked if we would ever meet again. They kissed him goodbye and some shadow seemed to pass over the group as they left us behind. In a few days they were all gone to their homes. We missed them.

How still the house seemed. How quietly we moved about. Pink looked sad and father talked but little. He would walk out and return weary. Friends called. He tried to talk, but he seemed too quiet for him. The pictures were brought home. He cheered up to see them and had one sent to each child. We were busy about our work getting ready for winter which was approaching. Already the storm clouds were hovering over the distant mountains. The birds had taken flight toward the sunny south.

Father said he was failing, that his time was about over. We tried to cheer him up. He knew we were distressed about him, but said we had best understand from the first that he was soon to go hence. He said he would never be well again. He did not fear to go, but he would like to stay with us longer. He told me of the improvements he wished to be made about the house and on the place. He grew weak and weaker and took to his bed. We called a physician. We sent for the brothers and sister. They came to see father for the last time. He called us all around his bed, then looked at the family circle and faintly said, "All here but one." We hoped he would soon come, but he did not receive the telegram and we never all gathered in the family circle again.

Father talked to us and told us where to bury him and to take care of mother and our young sister and to live the lives we had been instructed to live and not grieve for him. That his race on earth was run and he was ready to cross over the river of time. So, calmly, he passed away. We thought him only sleeping.

We buried him as requested, then sadly turned toward our lonely home. No more would he greet us there. Mother was disconsolate. She sat by the lonely hearthstone. For forty years he had been her companion in sorrow and danger, in joy and mirth. Now she saw him no more. She often started to meet him when she heard approaching footsteps, but it was not he.

Time moved on. We became more reconciled, but we could not forget him. Our memories of him were pleasant. We were now busy caring for mother.

Pink went away to school. Her homecomings were always a pleasure. Our absent brother Evan came home and told her he was to be married soon. He eulogized his bride-to-be till Pink was really eager to meet her. They were married and went to Walla Walla on a short bridal trip before coming home. The bride he brought home had large expressive black eyes and a smiling face. She was very small. We were all in love with her the first evening, but felt sad too, for it was plain to be seen that she was consumptive and not long for earth.

Pink became very much attached to her. Brother wanted to set up housekeeping, but mother insisted they spend the winter with us at the ranch as we had room to spare and needed them for company. We feared the care of a home would prove too much for her, for we soon realized she was very frail indeed. They had been married in early June. Before the roses bloomed she was fading. Brother was sorely distressed. She tried to convince us that she was not sick or failing. We tried to think she was right, but she grew weaker and kept to her bed and said she was so tired. Yes, tired and could not rest. Her breath came short. We watched over her day and night. One night she sank into a deep sleep, and when I tried to rouse her she opened her eyes and looked at me steadily. I saw she was going and called to brother. He spoke to her but she could not answer. He tried in vain to catch one word, but she sank away and was gone as the Sabbath dawned. She died August 15th, 1869, and we buried her near our other loved ones.

Another shadow was now cast over our home. Brother was desolate. He had worshipped her and could not think she would be taken from him. He went away for a few months but soon returned to visit her grave. He made his home with us. Pink went away to school and we were very lonely.

We had many little surprises waiting for Pink when she came home in the spring. She was pleased to be at home again, but we observed a melancholy sadness in countenance which distressed us.

At first we said nothing to her about it, but when we found her weeping in her room we inquired. She tried to evade a direct answer. She denied being sick. "Just weary. I need to rest after being in school so steadily." We planned to send her to a boarding school, and during vacation we had been preparing her wardrobe. She wanted me to put all sewing aside as she was tired of seeing it. Felt she would never need it as she thought she wouldn't be with us long.

Mamie came to see us and insisted on taking Pink home with her, thinking a change would help her. She came home a week or two later, no better.

A brother who lived near Albany was to be married, and sent us cards of invitation. We declined going, as Pink was too feeble to think of leaving home. We sent a request to him to bring his bride and spend some time with us, hoping a visit from them would interest Pink. They came. We were all fond of brother's bride and were sorry when they had to go.

Brother insisted Pink was sick, and we must call a physician. She was opposed to it, saying again she only needed rest. She didn't seem to care whether she recovered or not, only for our sakes. She lingered along for a month, then took to her bed. We could see she was failing fast, and we changed doctors. The new physician thought he could soon cure her. In a few days she seemed much better and asked for food. Then to sit up. Then she was able to walk about the room. One evening she asked to go into the parlor. We warmed the room and she went to the organ to play. On the way back to her room she begged to look out for a moment at the lovely evening. So I let her just peep for a minute. The next morning she was up and seemed much stronger. We left her alone while we were busy with the morning work.

I was working near a window in the kitchen and saw someone pass. I recognized Pink, although she was wrapped in a shawl. I ran out to her. "Why did you come out? It's so damp in the grass."

"Yes, I found it was, but I did so long to get outdoors. I just thought I would surprise you."

I helped her in quickly and to the fire. She was soon in a chill. That night she was worse. We got the doctor quickly. He thought she had a light cold and some fever, but in a few days he pronounced it typhoid. We knew she was weak. We had little hope. She sank rapidly. We sent for our brothers. Mamie was with us. Mother was to see her youngest child taken first. Pink noted our sorrow-stricken faces and said, "I am still here. I don't want you to grieve when I go."

When the summons came she looked steadily at each one for some moments, then closed her eyes to shut out the world. Her lips moved. We tried to catch a last word. In a short time her spirit was wafted away.

Loving hands prepared the inanimate form for the grave. She was buried near those she loved in life, and within sight of our rural home. Winter days were here. The rain and wailing winds sang a sad refrain to our sad hearts. Our home seemed so dreary now.

But springtime came, and we could get out more now. We tried to keep busy about the farm, garden and dairy. Brother Greene who was at home was to be married. Mother asked him to bring his youthful bride and make their home with us.

We were pleased to have them with us. Brother had a farm joining our home place, and he would build a new house and move to it some day. I went away for a while to see Mamie and visit friends. Home was such a dreary place now. It was just for mother that I stayed there. Friends often came to visit trying to help us forget our sorrow. I taught my young sister-in-law many things about housekeeping, and we made useful articles for her own home which would soon be ready for her. We helped them move and outfit their new house. We missed them in ours and visited often. Our home was so lonely now, I could not be satisfied there any more.

"We told (father) we had arranged to have a family picture taken and asked him to go to Eugene with us."

# Part II
# A Frontier Wife

"The pioneer woman did what she did without fanfare or self-pity. . .
She was sustained and strengthened by the very fact that she was a pioneer,
that she was playing a significant part in a major American ex-
perience—the conquering of the last frontier."
—Westward the Women. Nancy Wilson Ross. San Francisco, California:
North Point Press, 1985. p. 191

A T THE AGE OF THIRTY-THREE, after twenty years on the
family homestead, where she was her mother's mainstay, Martha Gay married J.A. Masterson. Alfred, as he was known, was a
widower with nine children whose wife had died of tuberculosis a
year and a half earlier. Martha stepped into a home where there
were still five children, the youngest being three years old. Within
months she was managing "one of the leading hotels" in Silverton,
Oregon. Despite her rather sheltered domestic life, she proved to be
a mature and competent woman who assisted Alfred in many
businesses, and often carried on alone when he left to scout out new
locations.

Alfred, who was a blacksmith by trade, was never content for
long in any one place. Martha was the stable element in the family.
Alfred seemed to drop his responsibilities to home and business
quite easily. He became ill with what seems to have been inflammatory rheumatism about five years after they were married, when
he was nearly fifty years old. He spent frequent periods of time
away from home "for his health" after that.

While Martha was able to write about her exasperation when a
move they made had disastrous results, she never openly con-
demned Alfred. Neither did she reveal any strong affection or
respect for him as she had for her father. In accounts of the early

91

*"I thought of going to a home of my own."*

years of their marriage, she spoke of missing him when he was gone. But in the story of her son Freddie's critical illness, we don't even know Alfred was away until after the boy's death.

At the end of 20 years, and after Martha declared she had made her "last" move, it appears that she and Alfred separated. There is no further reference to Alfred in Martha's continuing story. Family genealogists have determined that Alfred lived for a time with a son in eastern Oregon. Another record shows that he died in Coeur d'Alene, Idaho, presumably having lived there with, or near, his youngest daughter by his first marriage.

Martha's story graphically illustrates the stamina and adaptability required of women who survived and raised children on the Western frontier. Martha, her mother and her sister were examples of how women were socially and economically tied to the men in their lives during this era. However, they apparently lived full and rather cheerful lives. While most of Martha's stories are positive and focus on the family's many moves and adventures, she occasionally expresses her vexation—and sometimes despair—about being left alone so often to deal with sick children and the problems of closing out her business to make a move.

Her story provides a rich, complex picture of how pioneer women dealt with frontier circumstances and made a rather bleak life bearable. What shines through is Martha's indefatigable spirit and her amazing ability to bring dignity and genuine good cheer into her own life and her children's lives. She was a keen observer and a talented reporter. She was a natural writer with a gift for seeing the humor and drama and the history in her life. In her plain but articulate style, Martha has left a rich account about the pathos and pleasure of one woman's west.

Chapter 9

# A Home of Her Own

I THOUGHT OF GOING TO A HOME OF MY OWN, but how could I tell mother? I was her only company and comfort when the brothers were off on the farm at work. At last I got the courage to tell her. She said, "If you think you will be happier, child, I will try to endure it, but you have shared all my sorrows and also my pleasures of bygone days. I will miss you so much!" It was hard to leave her. I deliberated for days. Finally, I decided to go. On a quiet Sabbath morn, I took the solemn vow to love, honor and respect, and to trust one who might deceive me. Dear old home, fare thee well. *[Martha was married August 27, 1871 at her mother's home to James Alfred Masterson with John Thompson, county judge, officiating.]* I could not say I was a happy bride, for I felt sad to leave them so lonely.

I went with my husband to a new home. There were little children there to welcome me. My husband had been married before. On our way home we called for a girl of three who had been staying with her aunt since her mother's death. She was a lovely little girl with wondering blue eyes and golden curls clustering over her head, and at once found a place in my heart. We were one day going from Eugene to my new home near Salem.

Two girls, who had been keeping house for their father, welcomed us with smiles and kind words. A nice dinner awaited our arrival. They were so pleased to have their baby sister with them again.

*Martha's husband, J.A. Masterson, apparently was called Alfred. He was born October 4, 1827, in Logan County, Kentucky. He married Vilinda H. Campbell April 6, 1854, in Missouri. He has left a handwritten account of his early years.*

93

*The original manuscript is in the Lane County, Oregon,
Museum Library. A transcript follows:*

When I was a young man I left my home in the east with a
company of emigrants who were bound for the gold mines of
California. We had been detained in various ways in our
preparations for the journey and got a late start across the
plains *[in 1850]*. The company traveled very slowly and often
lost time when they should have been moving onward. Hardships and disappointments of various kinds combined with
trouble from Indians all caused us to make but little progress.

It was late in the summer when we reached Salt Lake, and
here a consultation was held by the company as to what was
best to do; winter at the Lake or try to reach California before
winter. Those having families decided to stay where they were
until spring.

However two other young men and myself concluded to
press forward on horseback, hoping to reach the settlements.
Our friends were opposed to this arrangement, fearing we
could not take sufficient provision to last all the way. There
was no chance to buy anything after we left the Lake. They
also feared the Indians would kill us, but we bade them goodbye and started out with little hope of ever seeing any of them
again. We had a tiresome journey and met with much suffering.

After some days we encountered two other men who wished
to join our company. We gladly added them to our little band
and felt much safer, for we were now among the hostile tribes.
We met a party of fifty warriors one day—ten to one. We
thought our chance to escape was very small. They tried to sur-
round us or induce us to attack them when they came too near.
We would draw our guns on them and they would halt. We did
not want to fire on them first and tried to get them to charge us
and fire as our guns were muzzle-loaders and we did not want
to be left with empty guns first. We tried in every way to elude
them and managed to keep them at bay until sunset, when they
dashed off to the river. We then built fires and prepared our
supper and, while the fires were burning brightly, we quietly
moved away and by traveling all night escaped them.

One of the men who had joined our company proved to be a
coward. When he saw the Indians rushing towards us he
became pallid with fear and gave up. We told him not to shoot
at them until they attacked us; then to fight or we would kill
him, and we compelled him to do as we did. We went forward
with more caution after this encounter and the Indians did not
molest us.

We saw death and destruction on every side. The route was marked out by graves, deserted wagons and dead stock. Many times we would see wagons standing by the roadside with the loads in them and no one near. The stock had starved or perished for water. One evening we camped near some emigrant wagons and were pleased to think we had company once more. However, we became very much interested about our supposed neighbors as we could see no one moving about the camp and could see no fires. Curiosity moved us to investigate. We cautiously advanced toward the wagons, fearing the weary ones were either sick or asleep. Imagine our surprise when we discovered there was no one in or about the wagons. They were loaded with emigrant's outfit of clothing and cooking utensils, but no provisions were in sight. We supposed they had lost all their teams and had been taken in by someone more fortunate, or had trudged on foot.

For days we pressed forward, many times ready to fall by the wayside. After weeks of suffering and narrow escapes from Indians, sick and weary, we reached the settlements of white men once more.

I stopped with a friend and with proper care and food was soon strong enough to go to work. Money was easily earned in those days of gold. I remained in California until the next summer. Then with an old schoolmate, I came to Oregon and stopped near Jacksonville a few months, then went on to Lane County. In the fall of 1851, I met a brother and his family who had just crossed the plains. I was glad to see them and to hear from home. After a short stay in Oregon I went to San Francisco by steamer, hence home by way of the Gulf of Mexico. We encountered a fearful storm which, for severity, was pronounced by captain and crew to be the worst ever experienced by them on the Gulf. It lasted three days and nights, and we thought the ship would go down with all on board. But we finally landed safely at New Orleans. We spent a few days in the beautiful Southern city, then boarded a river steamer and went up the great Mississippi to St. Louis and from there by stage to my home near Jefferson City, Missouri. How glad I was to see home and friends once more. After my adventures in the far West, my home folks received me as coming from a foreign land. Even the Negroes were delighted and thought me a most wonderful person. People came to see me from all over the country to hear from the gold mines.

I grew tired of the dull life at home after living in the bustling new countries out West and decided to get married and cross the plains once more.

Early in the spring of 1854 our company for the journey was organized, consisting of my two married sisters and their families, some hired men, a single brother and my wife and I. About twenty persons in all. We had a small band of cattle and some horses besides the oxen we worked on the wagons. We were well equipped for the journey which was a fearful undertaking in those days. Five long weary months we plodded along, day after day, with little change except the change of scenery and also the change of hardships and suffering. We met with some savage tribes of Indians and were often in great danger, as our company was not strong enough for protection if the Indians should attack us.

We treated them in a friendly manner and let them know that we did not want trouble with them. There was a young man in the company named Tom Adams who, much against our wishes, would play pranks on the Indians when they came to our camps. I knew that kind of treatment was not the best policy and told him so, but he would not heed my advice. We had passed the most dangerous tribes and hoped to reach our destination safely.

While we were traveling down Snake River in August, we camped one night near an Indian village. Next morning some of the savages came to our camp to beg for food. Three of them stopped at the fire where Tom Adams and two other men were preparing their breakfast. One of the Indians stepped too near a pan of frying bacon to suit the fastidious taste of Tom Adams and he thoughtlessly and cruelly threw a shovel of hot ashes and fire on the bare feet of the red man. It was a reckless and unkind thing to do, exposed as we were to the barbarous Indians. We were helpless to defend ourselves against even a small number. They are an inhuman race and never leave a wrong unavenged. Women and children are sought as victims of torture. Men are soon disposed of. *[This attitude seemed to prevail among many of the overlanders, usually based on hearsay. Ed.]*

The Indian bore the pain in silence, but there was vengeance in his eyes. He made known to his people how he had been abused by the white man and without cause. They talked excitedly together a few moments and would have killed Tom Adams then, but we prevented them from doing so. They went sullenly to their wigwams and did not return as we fully expected them to, but were seen following after us for several days, watching for an opportunity to kill Adams.

August 19th we camped on Boise River about twenty miles below where Boise City is now situated. We did not see any Indians about. Early next morning my single brother Robert, my wife and I started out from camp first for the day's journey, driving the cattle before us. At noon the rest of the company had not overtaken us. They were four miles back on the road and had stopped for their mid-day rest and to eat dinner. As they were preparing to start on their way they were surprised to see ten Indian warriors, well armed and riding good horses, coming toward them from the brush. Instantly every man ran for his gun and made ready to fight. The women and children hid in the wagons. The Indians halted in their charge and one rode in advance. He drew his gun to shoot Tom Adams who was near him with the oxen, but the white man was too quick for him and the Indian fell from his horse, shot dead by Adams.

The others whirled and dashed away into the brush. The white men ran the wagons into a circle close together and hurried the women and children into the enclosure, and none too soon. A wild yell and war whoop greeted their ears and they saw the enraged savages charging toward them, now sixty strong, in war paint and hideous dress, armed with guns, bows and arrows, war clubs and scalping knives. On they came, yelling like fiends, sending a death stroke to each helpless woman's heart. The warriors made no halt, but circled around their victims like a band of fire and, with an exultant yell, they swooped down upon them from every side. The few men were the first to fall. The savage monsters struck down the women and children until all were moaning in heaps excepting two little children whom they kept as captives. After selecting such articles as they wished to take away with them, they built fires and the bedding and clothing were piled on and burnt. Iron rods were taken from the wagon boxes and laid on the fire. When red hot, the wounded emigrants were pierced with them until death ended their sufferings.

Two boys, aged twelve and fourteen, who were left for dead, revived. While they were feigning death and afraid to move, they heard several words in English as if two white men were speaking together. The younger boy was picked up that evening by a man from another train who was looking after some lost oxen. He could see from a hill nearby the fearful sight of dead lying in heaps. Upon going to the place of death he found the friends from whom he had parted only a few days before, cold in death. He went quickly for help, but it was too late. From indications, the Indians had been gone some hours.

The older boy had been shot thru' the body with an arrow, and he had crawled away to get water and feared to go back to the road. He wandered about six days and nights, subsisting on roots and rose buds and was then found and cared for. The arrow which pierced his body had remained there all those days. He had broken it off, but could not pull it out of his side and his suffering was intense. Mrs. Ward, my oldest sister, her husband and five of her children were found dead. The two boys, who were left for dead and revived, were hers, as were the boy and girl taken captive by the Indians.

My youngest sister and her child, a boy of five years, were killed and all the hired men. In all, there were fifteen persons found dead. The two children who were carried off by the Indians were never found. A squaw told the soldiers who were sent in pursuit that one of them died a natural death, and that the other was too old to keep, and it cried so much they killed it. But we never knew their fate. The Indians very likely kept them or traded them to other tribes . . .

*Signed, Alfred Masterson*

*Alfred and Vilinda settled in Oregon in 1854. The census records identify him as a blacksmith. The 1860 census shows the family living in Eugene City. They had eight children at that time. By 1870, they were living in Waconda near Salem where Vilinda died of tuberculosis in February of that year.*

*A pension claim paper filled out by J.A. Masterson for the Rogue River Indian War of 1855-56 describes him as six feet tall with blue eyes, brown hair and a fair complexion. Now that we know something about the widower Martha married, let's go back to her account.*

Husband's daughters and I were soon good friends. They were industrious and helpful. Little Bess was a pet for us all. She was a happy, prattling little one and filled the house with sunshine. She wanted to know who made the nests for the birds and, when told the birds made them for themselves, she tried to make one. She was disappointed that it was a failure, but we told her that was bird's work.

When her sisters started to school she wanted to go too. When she was four years old, we let her go occasionally. One Friday afternoon, the pupils were having a recitation. As she was such a little girl, the teacher thought to please her by calling on her to recite, not thinking she would try. She disappointed him by stepping out and saying, "I know two pieces. One is the old woman who lived in a shoe and the other one is something else." She then rattled off Little Bo Peep and brought the house down with applause. She laughed too and stamped about and joined in the cheering, creating quite an uproar unconsciously.

*"We had lived in Silverton but a few months when we were offered a good position in a leading hotel." Perhaps the Wolfe Hotel pictured here was the one Martha didn't name.*

To be more convenient to a good school we moved to Silverton. It was a nice little village, and we had a good business. The sunlight of other days was coming back into my life. I was lovingly emplaced. The girls were interesting in many ways and were making rapid progress in their studies.

Bess often wished for a large doll, one that could cry like her playmate's doll did. One morning her sister Genie called her to come in and see a doll we had for her. She opened her big blue eyes and said, "What a cute little baby. Can I have it?" Genie told her she could have it for a little brother. Then she wanted to hold it just a little minute. *[John Balf Masterson was born March 12, 1873].*

When baby was five months old, I made a visit to the old home to see mother. Bess was delighted to go. She had been there before and liked the journey by rail very much. She had a nice time with a little girl her own age who had lost her mother and now lived with her grandmother. *[Evan and his wife had a daughter born in 1869, three months before her mother's death.]* When I was ready to go home, she said she would stay with grandma too if I would leave baby with her. Of course I could not leave her, so she was glad to ride on the cars and see the conductor and get some oranges.

*John David and Iphgenia (Genie) Masterson Smith*

We had lived in Silverton but a few months when we were offered a good position in the leading hotel. We at once moved into it and soon established a flourishing business. We liked the excitement incident to such a life, and were having a prosperous time, when I got a letter from home saying mother was very sick. I hastened to her by stage to Salem and by train to Eugene. A brother was waiting there to take us home. I stayed with mother several days. After she improved, I said goodbye and returned to my home.

Meanwhile, my husband had gone to Canyon City in eastern Oregon to carry on a business for a nephew and liked the country so much that he wanted us to close out our business in Silverton and move to Canyon City. We were very much opposed to the change and deliberated over it some days. When we decided to go, we sold out and packed up for the move.

Genie did not want to go and leave her lover. They decided to be married and stay at home. I wrote to her father and asked his advice in the matter, as she was very young. He said he would meet us in Portland and attend the wedding, but insisted on them postponing their marriage since Genie was only seventeen. They would not consent to do so, and we were obliged to allow the marriage and leave Genie behind.

We prepared her bridal robes and outfit for housekeeping. Her younger sister grieved over the separation and begged her to go. At last, we started on the journey. It was in midwinter. The Columbia was blocked with ice. We waited many days for it to clear out, then we went to Portland and found husband there waiting for us. I engaged the parlor of the Centennial Hotel for the wedding. The landlord said he had it all in trim for such an occasion, as he had two weddings there the previous evening. At the appointed hour we assembled to witness the ceremony. Genie looked modest and sweet in white with orange blossoms in her brown hair. Her husband *[John Smith of Marion County]* was proud of his girl-wife and said he trusted she would live to be a great deal older. We bade them farewell the next day, and they returned to their home.

Chapter 10

# Off to Canyon City

W E PROCEEDED ON OUR PERILOUS WAY. We arrived at
The Dalles all right. From there we went with teams over the
dreary bleak country. The weather was very cold and disagreeable
and Bess and Balf had whooping cough. There was much danger of
their contracting a cold on such a long journey, as we would be
necessarily compelled to camp out since there were few settlers on
the route. The distance was 197 miles.

The cold, bleak wind greeted us as we ascended the hill from The
Dalles, an introduction to much worse. The first day brought us to
Alkalie Frank's station where we stayed all night and fared well.
The next night, however, things were a little more gloomy. The
weather was intensely cold. We crossed the river on a bridge and
slowly ascended a long rugged hill. The road during the day lay
across a high tableland. We suffered with the cold. This day's travel
brought us to Bakeoven, a woe-begone looking place kept by a woe-
begone looking man. We managed to crowd into his hut and kept
warm for the night. He was very kind to us and tried to make us
comfortable.

The next day we encountered snow and had a cold drive which
carried us to Cold Camp where a very pleasant family resided, and
we were royally entertained. From then on we encountered snow
and cold winds and failed to reach the proper station. We had to
camp for the night at a horse station kept by another solitary man
who cared for the stage horses. He had a miserable hut made of
stones, dirt and clapboards, banked up against a hill to keep out
cold and snow. His burrow was only intended for himself. He had a
stable adjoining it for the horses. He told us we could stay in the
hut, as it was better than staying outdoors with the children, and
husband could shelter in the stable with him and the horses, for to

*Sherar's Bridge, one of the stage stations on The Dalles to Canyon City route.*

stay out only meant to freeze to death. May and I made a bed on the bunk for Bess and Balf and kept up a fire all night. We tried to sleep by resting our heads on the bunk. We were dozing and dreaming about our sorrows, when, in the dim light, we saw someone near the fire, wrapped in a blanket. We were alarmed because we thought it was an Indian, but it proved to be my husband who had come in to replenish the fire. As he found it too cold in the stable, he stayed in by the fire thinking we were asleep and would not notice him and get frightened.

Our next alarm was given by an old mule clambering about on the hillside above our hut. He stumbled and fell against our domicile and almost demolished it. We feared he would tumble right into our bed chamber, and we snatched the children out of the bunk quickly, which caused them to set up a wail of dismay at being treated so unceremoniously. We abandoned the idea of sleep and only tried to keep the children warm, as they were having a serious time now with whooping cough. From exposure, they had relapsed. We were glad when the long night was past. We partook of a hasty breakfast and started out on the most difficult drive of the journey. We had to cross a mountain and the snow was deep. During the short afternoon we encountered snow so deep it was almost impossible to get through it. We got lost once and wandered about for some time. At last we got on the right way and proceeded down the mountain side arriving at the station about dark, cold and hungry, as we had fasted since dawn. We enjoyed a nice warm supper, then put Bess and Balf to sleep snug and warm. The rest of us passed a dreary night as the house was crowded when we arrived.

We started out early the next morning and were glad to leave the snow in the distance. The weather was not so cold, and we were a little more cheerful. We made a good drive and stopped for the night with a very kind man and his very profane old uncle. I never met a man who was so profane. He had an oath to almost every word. His nephew said, "Why, Uncle Billy, you promised you would quit swearing." Uncle would reply, "Damn it! I have quit."

We rejoiced that two more days would bring our journey to an end. We moved along all right on this day till we came to a deep muddy stream that had huge boulders hidden in the ford. Persons acquainted with the ford knew how to shun them, but husband had passed there on the stage and knew little about it. He thought he could go through all right and drove fearlessly into the muddy stream. All went well until we were about one third across, then we encountered a huge stone and came to a halt. The front wheels of our wagon had struck it square and solid, and there we were away out in the stream and the horses trying to move on and becoming very restless from standing in the cold water. We feared they would capsize the wagon. We got them unhitched and back to shore. Then husband put a saddle on Black Hawk and conveyed us all back to land. He would lead the horse near the wagon, and we would climb on his back and the faithful creature would take us safely through the deep muddy water. We then went to an old bridge and crossed on foot. It was not safe for the wagon. After some time spent in prying and unloading, the wagon was got across. Then we went happily on our way with good speed, as we were now in a valley and would soon arrive at our nephew's country home. In a little while we were delighted to see him and his wife coming to meet us. They stopped to talk a bit and directed us to their home. They asked May to get in the buggy with them, saying they would go back home and have dinner ready for us, as we could not travel as fast as they did.

We soon arrived and enjoyed a comfortable rest, then went on to Canyon City. We were sadly disappointed. We had hoped to see an inviting place, but instead we saw a little mining camp built in a nar-

*Main Street, Canyon City. "Freight wagons coming in to town had to drive the entire length of the street and out of town to find room to turn around."*

row canyon. There was only room for one street, the houses being built on either side of it. Freight wagons coming into the town had to drive the entire length of the street and out of town to find room to turn around. What a barren-looking place it was to us after living in the verdant Willamette Valley.

On inquiring at the post for our mail, the first letter stated that my dear mother was dead. There was no way I could go over the long road back to have a last look. I felt that such news was a bad omen in our new home.

We went direct to our place and found our household goods all there ready for us. They had been sent on ahead on freight wagons. The house was large and convenient and would have been quite comfortable in a mild climate. The weather being very cold after our arrival, we suffered intensely. We were not accustomed to such a frigid zone. We had just got fairly settled when husband concluded he would rather live on the hill near his place of business. We moved to the hill and settled again.

May went to her cousins in the country to spend the summer, as our nephew was to be absent and his wife wanted her for company. I took care of Bess and baby Balf and kept house. We had a very nice cottage on the hill and some pleasant neighbors. We liked the place some better since becoming accustomed to the wild, weird aspect of the surrounding country. The summer was hot and thunder storms were quite common. Bess and Balf were out playing most of the time in the shade of a great perpendicular bluff and the house. There were no trees in town and no gardens and very few flowers. Bess had a potato growing in the sand by the cellar door which she petted with much care.

Old deaf Jack had a garden out on a hill and sold vegetables about town. His garden was in need of rain. He feared a drouth. He soon had rain enough. One afternoon a storm arose very suddenly. It was a most terrific storm. Thunder pealed and lightning flashed. A fearful clap of thunder caused many to scream with terror. It seemed to strike every house in town. The glare of the electric storm was almost blinding. It had actually struck the courthouse which was on a hill just above the village. The rain poured down—a cloudburst which caused a regular deluge.

*"The electric storm had actually struck the courthouse which was on a hill just above the village."*

Deaf Jack complained because his garden was all washed away. The courthouse was slightly damaged. Court had just been in session, and the aisles had been strewn with sawdust. This was scattered all over the house as evenly as if put through a sieve. A Chinaman who was in jail in the basement made his escape and was never seen again by the authorities. The sheriff said if he was liberated in that way he surely was innocent.

During the intensely hot weather dear little Balf was very sick. I was alarmed about him. For weeks he was an invalid. As the weather changed, he improved and was able to walk about again. Bess was glad to have her playmate once more. They played hide and seek often.

One day while she was at school I missed him and ran all about searching for him, indoors and out. Had he gone to the river or been carried off? I ran back again into the nursery, and he called to me. Still I could not see him in the room. I raised the scarf from a stand, and there he was hid and quietly waiting for me to find him as Bess would often do. Under the stand smiling at me and tossing his curly head. Hid away on the table shelf. I drew him forth and then he wanted me to hide from him, but I told him he must wait for Bess.

Our stay in Canyon City was not a happy one. My husband lost his health there and had to go away. While he was gone, Balf got sick again. I was very anxious about him. I called the doctor who said Balf had pneumonia. I had little hope from the first. Oh, the dreary days and nights of suspense. I saw him failing. His suffering was intense for two weeks, then death relieved him. How could I give my dear child up? I loved him. Bess cried for him. She looked so lonely. I wished we had not come to the place. The climate did not agree with him. I feared we would lose Bess if we stayed there. Husband was sick.

We sold out and prepared to go. Husband went on ahead of us to The Dalles by stage. We went and got a freight wagon. When we were ready to go I almost gave up the idea. It was so hard for me to leave my dear dead child. I tore myself away. May stayed with her cousin and would come later. Bess and her brothers, Clay and Leafe, aged eight and ten years, came with me. We had a dreary cold journey and a tiresome one. When we reached The Dalles husband said we would go to the Valley. I was not opposed to going home, but how I regretted that we went to the mountains. We had lost our time, property and everything we possessed—our home and fine business and more precious than all, our dear child.

Chapter 11

# Back to the
# Willamette Valley

W E WENT TO MY DEAR OLD HOME for a few days, then
to a home of our own. Times were dull and we were dreary.
Husband built up a little business. We were not very well pleased
with the place. I tried to be cheerful in sight of the old home, but
when I looked over toward the once happy place, I saw only the
graves of the loved ones.

Bess and the boys were in school. Friends of other days came to
see me and talked of old times, of our school days. They tried to
cheer my life. Mamie came to visit with her little ones.

The days came and went, and Bess was delighted when told she
had a baby brother. She wanted to name it Balf like the little one
that died. We called him Freddie, and she liked that name. [He was
born May 23, 1875 at Creswell.]

After a year, husband was sick again and we went to the old
home. Doctor came many times and said he would get well. He was
sick four months, all winter. In the spring we went to Eugene where
we found a home, and husband was able to go back to work. Freddie was a year old and a great pleasure to us now.

Bess went to school with Clay and Leafe. She made friends wher-
ever she went. In a few months, husband got sick again. Doctor told
him to go to the mountains. He thought a summer near the mineral
springs on the McKenzie River would restore him. We moved up
there and located on the bank of a rushing stream. Our camp was
under a great old cedar tree in the heavy forest.

We had been there some days and had a pleasant time. Others
were camped near us picking blackberries and rusticating. Then the
berries were all gone and the men grew tired of hunting and fishing.
Our neighbors all left except one family. We needed some groceries,
so husband left us in care of the family and went to Eugene after
supplies.

He had been absent a few days when the family near us received word from home which caused them to leave at once. There was no one else living near our camp and bears and panthers were prowling about. We were unprotected, just under a tree. We had our household goods and two cows and calves to care for and could not leave them. I did not expect my husband for two more days, and the thought of being left there with the children almost drove me frantic. I begged the people to wait, but they could not and could not take us along.

How we did wish someone would come. We dreaded nightfall; with it came fear. We had discovered that we were camped in a trail where the wild animals passed to the river to drink. I had often heard father say animals were afraid of fire. So we collected wood and brush into piles and got them ready for four fires, hoping this way to intimidate the cougar which we were assured were in the woods. We kept the fires burning brightly till a late hour. Then the little boys were too sleepy to stay up any longer.

I went around to rebuild the fires after the children had retired. We had a little shepherd dog, a faithful little animal. I called her to me and told her to keep watch, and I lay down with Bess and Freddie. Not to sleep. I scarcely expected we would be spared till dawn. Oh, the agony of those long hours. I had about given up when the dog barked fiercely and ran across the road. Her barking broke the spell. She raved and snarled as if some animal was very near. I got up and called the boys to help brighten up the fires. The dog came to us trembling with fear. We lay down, and she tore out again and was chased right into camp by a wild animal. We got up again and kept the fires burning brightly till the sun shone through the treetops and the little birds sang to us.

After breakfast we looked after our cows, and the long day wore on. How we did wish for husband to come. We dreaded to see night approaching. Then bad luck befell us. Our cows did not come home. We waited for them till late in the night, then let the calves out to feed and prepared for another night of terror. We expected the animal to pay us another visit. We feared it was after the calves.

The second night was a repetition of the first. The cougar came and chased the dog into camp and under the bed. We screamed with fright, got up and did not try to sleep. Next morning I told the boys we would not stay another night. We could not find the cows. We never did find them. We thought someone killed them for beef. We fixed everything as securely as possible and started out on foot through the wild forest and across a stream on a log to try to reach

*"A baby girl now brightened our home."*

the only house in that part of the wilderness, about three miles away. We saw one bear on the way and came near falling off the log into the rushing river. We reached the place all right, tired and distressed about our cows.

During the afternoon husband arrived after being detained. May was with him and we were delighted to see her. They were surprised to find us so far from camp. We told them what a time we had and about the cougar. We all went back to camp, but soon got tired of it and returned to the valley. May went to stay with Genie, and husband went to eastern Oregon to go into business. The children and I stayed near sister Mamie for the winter, waiting for husband to build up a home and come for us next spring.

Bess and the boys were glad to get out of the mountains and away from the wild animals. Our summer had not been altogether pleasant. Little Freddie had been sick and was still quite feeble. Bess was pleased to have Mamie's little girl her own age for a playmate. We lived very near them for some months, and the girls played together.

Winter was soon gone. A baby girl now brightened our home. *[Frances Hortense was born February 11, 1877.]* Bess was delighted to have a sister. The children saw a dimple in her cheek and Freddie said, "She's dot a dimple." Then the girls called her Dotty Dimple. She was Dotty or Dot till she was quite a large girl. The dimple in her cheek grew too, and many have said she had an appropriate name. She sits near me as I write, nineteen years old, soon to be a graduate, and the treasure and comfort of my old age.

*Mary (May) Masterson and Wilbur Fisk Cauthorn*

*Henry and Viola Presley Masterson*

*Alfred (Leaf) and Clara Rutherford Masterson*

# Chapter 12

# To Eastern Oregon Again

S PRINGTIME CAME with its roses and bright sunshine. We were to go to Eastern Oregon to join husband. First by stage to McKenzie Bridge where husband met us with a team and wagon. We were so glad to see him, and he thought our Dotty very cute. We started out from the Bridge on a lovely day. We had gone about nine miles when a wagon wheel broke. We were in a deep forest, going up hill. There was no possible way to mend a wheel there on the road. Husband had to unload the other wagon and put the broken wheel in it and go back to the Bridge to a shop and mend it. This left the children and me alone in the forest miles from anyone, with wild animals prowling about. I thought we could not stay and begged to go along.

After he had gone a while we seemed to gain courage. I told the boys we would build fires again as we had done before to frighten the cougars away. They gathered wood cheerfully and soon had great fires on every side. I prepared the evening meal with a heavy heart. We were eating and listening for our enemies. They give a fearful yell when in search of prey. We were alarmed to hear a yell echo from crag to crag. How we listened as it came nearer. Now it sounded like someone singing, and we only heard the higher choruses.

At that moment a man came in sight around a rock. He was on horseback coming to the Valley from east of the Cascades. When he came near we recognized a cousin. Never was anyone more welcome. We asked him to come and take supper with us and told him about our accident and about his uncle having to go back and leave us. We told him we were afraid to stay, but wouldn't be, with a big boy that knew how to use a rifle with us. He ate his supper, then walked to his horse. We thought he would remove the saddle and feed him, but he mounted and made ready to go.

111

"Tom," I cried, "you are not intending to leave us here alone? Why, what would your uncle think of you doing anything like that? Do stay with us, for pity sake. We are so afraid of cougars and so unprotected. You know they are around us. Think of your dear little cousins, Bess and these babes." I pled with him to stay. He left us. I thought it a cruel act. He could have stayed with us but would not simply because he wanted to get home to see his lady love. I think she would have discarded him if she had known of this unkind desertion of us.

We rebuilt the fires and a storm arose and put them out. Then another danger arose. We were camped where the trees are very large and tall, and we feared they would blow down on our wagon. We tried to sleep. The boys had a bed under the wagon. Bess, the babies and I had our bed in the wagon, but I could not sleep. I clasped Dot in my arms and tried to keep her perfectly quiet lest her crying might attract the wild animals. Bess and Freddie slept the innocent sleep of childhood which knows no fear.

Oh, the long hours of that dark night, and oh, the Egyptian darkness. I heard a noise. It was near the wagon. My heart seemed to stop. I listened for the stealthy step of the cougar. Now the noise was in the tree over my head. Next it fell to the ground. Then I recognized it as the noise made by small branches falling from the trees. They had been broken off during the storm.

I looked out now and could see the trees. Then I heard the chirp of a bird. The long night was drawing to a close. I fell asleep, and when I woke the sun was shining. It was a glorious June morning. Lovely, lovely is early morn in the mountains.

We got up and fixed breakfast with cheerful hearts and waited the return of husband. It was late in the day when he came, rejoicing to see us all safe. He had met nephew and gave him a deserved reprimand for leaving us. We moved on.

One night we camped near the summit and saw snow hawks. Also the snow-capped mountains called Three Sisters. The next day we crossed the lava beds during a fearful storm. The black lava on every side extended far to the south. To see immense trees growing there was a mystery, as there was no soil visible. I looked down into the deep channel where the molten lava had flowed away and thought of the intense heat on the occasion, and of the long years it would take these miles and miles of burning mountains to cool off. Then for the seeds of trees to be carried there in some way and sprout and grow to such wonderful size in that dry lava bed. All marvelous to behold.

The graded road which leads around on the very brink of the precipice was a frightening place to pass over during a storm. Our wagon near capsized several times in the wind. Rain, hail and snow beset us while crossing the lava. We saw one little conie which darted away into the depths of the black mass.

The grade was narrow, only room for one wagon. To our right was a steep mountain, while on the left was the chasm which was deep, dark and dismal. I hoped we would not meet anyone, for one would be almost compelled to turn back, or be pushed from the precipice into the yawning abyss below. We saw dead horses and cattle down there. Where we crossed, the lava bed was several miles wide.

After leaving that dreary looking place, we had some very good road, and found a wayside cabin to camp in during the night. We were very thankful, for we were cold and wet from the rain. We soon had a bright fire going and all got dry and warm. We prepared our evening meal by the open fire and had a cheery time.

We were soon in bed and all asleep except myself. I was musing over the events of the day and shuddered when I thought of that graded road. Just as I was dropping off to sleep I heard the boards creak just over my head, as if someone was walking on the roof of the cabin. I listened and soon heard it again. My bed was near the door on the floor and the door was ajar. I had Dot in my arms as I lay there. We could not close the door at all. Just then a heavy thud on the ground outside caused me to almost scream out to my husband to know if he heard that noise. He said it roused him from sleep, and he supposed it was one of the horses. I told him I had heard something on the roof just before the heavy thud. He then fastened the door as securely as he could. Next morning we found the tracks of a mountain lion in the mud in the yard. Fortunately, I had heard it on the roof, for it could easily have clawed baby from my arms if I had been asleep.

The morning was very bright, a nice change after the storm of the day before. We were detained several hours as our horses had strayed during the night.

The road lay down the eastern slope, and we made a quick run for Squaw Creek Station where the family lived who had left us in the blackberry patch. We then had rough road up hill and camped on a high table land among the juniper trees and rattlesnakes. We pitched our tent near a grand old tree. The children were playing around camp when little Freddie cried out in pain. He held up his foot for me to see. He was barefoot and said his foot hurt. I feared it was a rattlesnake, but we could find none, so supposed it was a scorpion. He had a bad toe for a few days.

After supper the boys thought it would be fine sport to build a low fire to light up the night. Wood was handy and a brilliant light soon reflected far away over the landscape. All were interested in the great fire when we noticed a hissing, rattling noise, seemingly coming from the fire. "Listen! Rattlesnakes! They are in the old tree. Get away children. Look out for them!"

No need for caution, really. No snake could crawl through that fire and live. It was like a furnace. The fire had been built at the root of the old juniper tree. It was hollow with a hole near the ground, and the hollow in the tree drew the fire into it, serving as a flue. The snakes had made their den in the hollow tree, hiding away from the storms. More wood was piled on, making an immense fire which caught the branches of the tree. Then our tent was in danger and had to be moved back to what we supposed to be a safe distance.

After thoroughly burning out the snake den and watching that none escaped, we retired for the night thinking there was no further danger. We were aroused about midnight by a roaring noise. The fire had burst forth anew. Some of the huge branches were already falling to the ground, and we feared the tree would fall on our tent. We got up and moved it quite far back, thinking now we were safe and could sleep. In a very short time we were once more called forth. A strong wind had sprung up and was driving the fire and smoke directly into our tent and wagons. We had to hurry to save them from the fire. And this was only started up to amuse the children! Behold what a great fire a little spark kindleth. The great tree was a wreck of its former self. There remained only a charred trunk and some bare branches. Its beautiful foliage and bright berries were things of the past.

We were off early the next morning and soon crossed the Deschutes River. It wound its way through the hills and looked like a great ribbon of water as we viewed it from the heights. We had a hard pull up the hill from the river. Then we got along all right for some time. When we reached the Ochoco Valley we were met by a strong wind which blew all day and night. We stopped at Prineville, where husband thought of going into business. He changed his mind, left us in Prineville and went to the mines at Silver Springs. When he returned little Fred was very sick. The winter being so very bad in Prineville, we thought best to go on to Ochoco. We stayed at Ochoco Village three months, then moved to Bridge Creek where we spent the winter at a nephew's country place.

*"We stayed at Ochoco Village three months, then moved to Bridge Creek where we spent the winter at a nephew's country place." Burnt Ranch.*

Ochoco was about ten miles east of Prineville. Bridge Creek was north at the mouth of the creek where it flows into the John Day River. That spring the Indians about our area were inclined to be hostile. Spies ascertained that the Bannocks had laid in a supply of ammunition and had moved their families far into the mountains and were ready to fight. They were only waiting for the willows to leaf out on the creeks to afford them hiding places. Excitement was getting very high in May of 1878, and we thought best to go to The Dalles for safety. We were afraid to sleep at night, as we were near a heavy willow thicket. When the dogs barked at night, I would hug my little Dot close in my arms and listen for a war whoop. At last we got started, Bess, Leafe, Dot and I. Husband had gone on before us to look after a home, and Clay stayed to come with his cousins. We arrived at The Dalles after a week's journey. We had been in The Dalles two weeks when word came that the Bannocks had killed two men and two boys and burned some houses and were on the warpath with their band of warriors.

The neighbors had been forted for protection in the house we had just left, and the Indians were making a raid through that part of the country killing stock and people. Several battles were fought with them and quite a number were killed. The settlers rushed into The Dalles, some on wagons and some on horseback; others on foot. There was a regular panic. One man was so excited to get his family to a place of safety that, in his hurry, he started out with his wagon full of children and left his wife in the back yard getting their clothes from the line. She went screaming after him, not liking the idea of being left in such a dangerous time.

A battle was fought the Fourth of July and dispatches were coming in all day. One of my neighbors had a brother killed. One of our old-time friends, who crossed the plains with us, was killed.

In the Harney Valley, some three or four families were in a stronghold. The men were out after the Indians. The women and children barred the doors and kept quiet. They were alarmed, some hours after the men had left, to see a party of hideous looking monsters approaching their fort. They were Indians dressed in ox hides with the horns on to make them look as much like demons as possible. They came near the house and called out to the women and children to come out and see them. They knew the men were all gone. The women said, "No, we don't want to see you."

"Yes, come and see us. We won't kill you." They were told to go away.

"No, we won't go away. If you don't come out, we will set the big house on fire and burn you all to death." After some time spent in talk, they prepared to apply the torch but changed their minds when they saw the men returning and got away as fast as their cumbersome dress would allow.

Our nephew, Jim Clark, in whose house we lived at Bridge Creek, was one man who fought hard to make it possible for whites to live in eastern Oregon. He had built his first house at the mouth of Bridge Creek more than thirty years ago, and soon after was run into the brush by hostiles, and saw his house go up in flames. He narrowly escaped capture himself.

[Further details about Bridge Creek, Burnt Ranch and Jim Clark can be found in the Works Progress Administration Writer's Project book, Oregon, End of the Trail, pages 449-51: One of the most noted of the stage stations on the route from The Dalles to Canyon City in those days was on the south bank of the John Day River at the extreme western edge of Wheeler County. The name Burnt Ranch was given the station in 1862 after an attack by marauding Indians who burned the buildings and menaced the lives of the occupants. . . . The original ranch was owned by James N. Clark, who, in 1866, settled at the mouth of Bridge Creek and established himself on a stock ranch.

Burnt Ranch became widely known to early-day travelers in eastern Oregon. It comprised a low-roofed house with a covered porch extending across its front; a large barn with stock corrals, and huge stacks of hay for feeding the stock of the stage company. In front of the house, between it and the barn, ran the long dusty road with its parallel, winding lines of ruts where wheels had worn deep into the soil, a fringe of willows and cottonwoods revealing the presence of the stream whose waters gave scanty life to the parched herbage. . . .

How the noted stage station came to be called Burnt Ranch is explained as follows by the *Grant County News* in its issue of August 6, 1885: "In 1866 James Clark was occupying the position of a pioneer settler there and had a very comfortable home. Along in the early fall his wife departed to the Willamette Valley to visit her people. One bright September morning Jim and his brother-in-law, George Masterson, forded the John Day River and were cutting up a lot of driftwood on the opposite bars. Suddenly they discovered a band of Indians rushing down the hill from the Ochoco country. The men had left their rifles at the house and they thought there was a possible show to reach them ahead of the Indians. They unhitched the horses and climbing on bareback, raced for the house. But when they saw the Indians were going to get there first they swerved to the left and struck up Bridge Creek, with the enemy in hot pursuit.

It took but a few miles of hard riding to use up Masterson's work horse and he told Clark to keep on and save himself. Masterson then jumped from his horse and struck into the brush. He jumped into the creek and, swimming down stream a little distance found a deep hole, overhung with thick brush where he 'camped'. The Indians chased Clark a few miles farther and then returned to finish Masterson. But he confined himself to his covered haunt, and after hunting all around for him, the Indians gave up and returned to the house, where they took everything they considered of value. Clark kept on to the nearest ranch, eight miles distant, where he found a number of packers with whom he returned to the scene of action. They yelled for Masterson, and at last taking chances on their being friends, he came out of hiding almost chilled to death.

The party then went on to the house, which was found smouldering in ashes and the Indians gone. The raiders had cut open the feather beds, taking the ticking and scattering feathers abroad, and also doing other acts of destruction. What was a happy home a few hours before was now a scene of desolation, but Providence had ordered the safety of the occupants. Another house was constructed, but ever since that time the place has been called Burnt Ranch.

Some time after his house and other buildings had been destroyed, James Clark, owner of the ranch, engaged with C.W. Lockwood in the operation of a stage line between Canyon City and The Dalles. While driving stage Clark put up one night at Howard Maupin's cabin at Antelope Valley. During the night the Indians tore an opening in the stone corral and drove off a bunch of Maupin's stock. As Clark started to resume his trip next morning Maupin told him if he saw the Indians, to come back and that the two of them would go in pursuit. This Clark agreed to do.

As the stage topped a rise a short distance from Cross Hollows, another station on the stage line, Clark sighted the Indians. Turning the stage around, Clark and his lone passenger returned to Maupin's ranch at Antelope. From there the three men started after the Indians and shortly overtook them. Maupin threw his gun to his shoulder and shot Chief Paulina, breaking his thigh. The other Indians, seeing their chief was down, turned and fled, abandoning the stolen stock. Riding closer to Paulina, Maupin again raised his gun with the intention of finishing him.

At this junction Clark, who had ridden up and recognized the Indian, yelled, "Don't shoot him, Maupin. Don't kill that Indian. Let me finish him! That's the Indian who chased me so far on Bridge Creek and burned my cabin and barn." Maupin is said to have lowered his gun, whereupon Clark emptied his own gun into Paulina.]

Martha's account continues.

In 1878, Jim was out again after the reds. In close quarters he had a horse killed under him, and he was supposed to be killed, but he escaped the Indians in the brush and rejoined the whites in Canyon City a few days later. While hiding from the hostiles, he was three days and nights without food. At last he eluded them and found a shepherd's deserted cabin. In it there was sugar, coffee, bacon and eggs. He said he was so near starved that he cried when he found the food, but did he dare cook it? The smoke might disclose his hiding place. He thought he could endure being shot as easily as he could to starve, so he made a fire and boiled his coffee and broiled his bacon and sat down to eat. When he made the attempt, he could not swallow food at all. He told me he tried and tried, and he could not eat. After a while he was able to swallow some coffee, and then he got so he could chew a small morsel, then able to swallow. The suspense and anxiety, and expecting every moment to be killed, had nearly unstrung his nerves.

One cold March day while we were living at Jim's place, an Indian man and squaw came to our gate and asked to stay in our hay barn for the night. They were on their way to The Dalles to sell deer shoes and gloves. We gave them permission to stop in the barn, telling them to be careful with their matches and fire, to which they agreed. The next morning the squaw came into the kitchen. I was busy about my work and scarcely noticed her. Months later, I was busy at The Dalles when an Indian woman came to the door selling berries. She looked at me and began to laugh. She said, "You don't know me?" I said, "No, I never saw you before, did I?" Then she laughed more heartily and said, "Ah, paleface soon forget. Indian never forget. A long time ago I stay in your barn to keep warm." She told me the Indians were getting ready to fight the whites. Not her tribe, the Warm Spring Indians, but the Bannocks. Three weeks later, there was a war sure enough, and it was the last Indian war in eastern Oregon. Usually an Indian woman told the whites when the men were preparing for war. I think they preferred peace to war.

# Chapter 13

# Life Along the Columbia

W E REMAINED AT THE DALLES DURING THE SUM-
MER, then went to the Lower Cascades and lived in a noted
old building which stands on Phil Sheridan's first battle ground. It
was there that he fought the Indians in early days after the fearful
massacre of the whites. The old blockhouse stood there on the bank
of the Columbia then, but has since fallen down. I picked up an old
style cannon ball for a relic and some Indian arrowheads. I met with
some women who made their escape. They told me about the distressing time.

An Indian woman had come and told them to go quick or they
[my informant] would be killed. She told them when they saw the
canoes coming down the river, and the Indians standing up in them,
that was the time to go, because they had come to kill all the
"Bostons". The old lady told me she looked and saw them. She
snatched a loaf of bread from the oven and then, with one child in
her arms and one by the hand, they ran for their lives. They got to
the boat and across the river to the steamboat just as the Indians
began firing on them. Other hostiles had attacked those on the other
shore and killed a number before help arrived. All night long they
had kept up their war dance.

A man and his wife and their wood chopper lived in the forest
near the river. The woman begged her husband to go seek safety,
telling him she heard them dancing and singing their war songs. He
heeded her not. At dawn they were aroused by fearful yells. The Indians had come to destroy. They hurriedly got a few things together,
but it was too late to go to headquarters. The Indians attacked the
settlers all along the shore and in the woods. At the same time, the
woodchopper and his wife were killed. The hired man got out
through the roof and made his escape to tell the story of how the

*Lower Cascades settlement in 1867, showing blockhouse on point and store on the river. Is this where Martha kept store?*

woman begged to go while they could. This was called the Cascade Massacre. General Sheridan and his men got after the Indians. Their chief was captured and hanged. I often saw his son and his pretty young daughter, Princess Mary. She was a handsome Indian girl and dressed very stylish and was kind and pleasant. Her grandfather was our bitter enemy. She was our friend and would come to see us.

We were walking from the wharf to the hotel one day while we lived at the Lower Cascades. We were on the trestle which was built along the bank of the river. The water was deep, and we had to use great care to make the trip at all with the little ones. I was carrying Dot, and Bess was leading Freddie. One misstep would have sent us into the river below. My attention was on the trestle as I knew it was not train time. I did not imagine any trouble ahead of us. I heard a noise and looked up to see a train of detached box cars tearing down towards us. I whirled around and instantly snatched Freddie up and told Bess to run back to the wharf boat. How we got there we never knew. As we stepped off the trestle the cars swept by us. We had thought it difficult to walk over such a dangerous place when we were careful! After recovering from our fright, we started out once more, and had to almost crawl because we were so unnerved. We had created quite an excitement for several had seen our flight and feared we would be crushed.

The company's lovely new steamer, the R. R. Thompson, had made her trial run. We wanted to go to the Upper Cascades to see her. There was no train due at the time, and husband said we would go on a handcar. We went up all right, but on our return husband lost control of the brake on a downgrade. The car was tearing along, and we were terribly frightened as we were on a high trestle. We flew along. Husband kept telling us to be quiet, and he would stop the car. At last, when we were nearly home, he got it under control. Fortunately, we didn't meet another car.

I always associate the Lower Cascades with many disasters to us. While living there, our house caught on fire three times and narrowly escaped; once by the stove falling down when full of fire and burning coal, once from a lamp, and the last time from the chimney.

*"We were on the trestle which was built along the bank of the river. I heard a noise and looked up to see a train of detached cars tearing down toward us."*

*Main Street, Cascade Locks, Oregon 1894. Before the railroad, the only access was by river.*

My husband got a severe burn accidentally by a careless man who was handling a red hot bar of iron in a shop. He struck one end of it against a post, and in moving it back, ran the other end into husband's arm. It was red hot and cooked his flesh. How painful! It was agony. How much we can bear and live through it. *[This probably happened in a blacksmith shop, an indication that Alfred was working at his trade in the Lower Cascade community.]*

Then we left the Lower Cascades and went to the Upper Cascades. We encountered a wind storm and were nearly swept from the trestle while walking over it. Then we had to cross the Columbia River in the storm in a small boat. The weather was fearfully cold. I begged not to cross, but there was no place to stay. I got in the boat, Bess and the boys with me. I wrapped Bess and Freddie snug as possible and then, with Dot hugged close in my arms, we started across. Two sturdy boatmen pulled at the oars. About half way across, one of the men feared the children would freeze, and he pulled off his great coat and threw it over them. He kept himself warm by hard work. How the boat would roll and plunge.

Dot screamed all the long distance. I could not imagine why. I thought she wanted her face uncovered, but I was fearful she would freeze if I let her see out, and I would hug her closer and she would

*The canal under construction at the Locks, 1895*

scream louder. When we got to the shore one of the men grabbed her out of my arms, and then uncovered her face and found it covered with blood. I was ready to faint. I thought she had bursted a blood vessel by crying so hard and was bleeding to death, but found a great shawl pin had been jagging her face all the way across the river. There was one scar left which she carries on her right cheek yet, to remind us of that fearful crossing when she was two years old.

We moved our grocery and drygoods store to the Upper Cascades, and opened up quite a business there. *[Martha was probably running a store in the Lower Cascades while Alfred worked at blacksmithing.]* The ship canal was just begun, and hundreds of men were employed on it. We had a nice place near the plant and also opened a boarding house. Building the canal and locks was a stupendous undertaking and would require years of hard work to complete. The first work was done in 1878. It is now eighteen years since they were begun, and they are not complete yet.

We met with some very nice people about the Locks and had a pleasant time for a while. Then my dear little Freddie got very sick. We nursed him with tender care and were pleased to see him up once more, but, alas, in a few days he grew much worse. I devoted my entire attention to my darling boy. We had the best doctor in the place. I watched over him day and night.

Husband was away at the time. Friends came and offered their assistance. How pale and sad he looked. I was all alone with him one afternoon. Dot and her nurse were out walking. The boys were out after berries. He opened his eyes and asked for me. Then he called for his papa. I told him papa was away. Just then his little sister came in with her hand full of strawberries and offered them to him. He said, "Put them away, Hortense. I can't eat them." I saw a change and knew he was going. Dot's nurse came in and saw I was crying. She, an Indian girl, said, "Don't cry. Maybe he get well." Then she went to him and laid her hand gently on his head and said, "Poor little boy, he so sick." How lonely I felt there with my dying child, and only this Indian girl there to console me. She was a kind girl and had been with the whites nearly all her life. She ran for a neighbor, then begged me not to cry.

How could I bear to give up this child? He was a lovely bright-eyed boy and ever near me. He said, "I love to follow you, Mama." His last words were, "Don't leave me, Mama." It was on an early summer afternoon that he left us. The flowers he loved were strewn over his grave. We buried him where he had played near our home, and the little birds he loved in life sang their evening songs over his grave. The little children who had been his playmates came loaded with lovely white flowers to cover him over. The name he called Dot [Hortense] when he last spoke to her is the one we called her from then on.

A few days before he was taken sick I cut his curls off. When he looked at them I asked, "What will you do with them, Freddie?" He thought for a moment and then said, "You take one curl, Mama, then I will put the others out by the big tree and the birds can have them to build their nests." He ran out with them and I was so busy I soon forgot all about what he had said. Late in the fall, after the leaves had fallen, the children were out playing near the big tree and Bess found a bird's nest in a bush. She got it and soon saw it was lined with hair. She ran to show it to me. I recognized Freddie's curls woven into the little nest and told Bess we would keep it. I remembered then what the dear little boy had said. I have the nest yet. A friend who lives on our place there cares for his grave. I hope to see it some day. He would now have reached his twenty-first year.

When husband came home he was almost heartbroken to hear his little boy was dead. He had promised to bring him a pet, and he had a little fawn in his arms, a bright-eyed, cute little pet for a child. But the child had gone to the home beyond, and his father knew it not. My letter never reached him. We loved the pet for his sake and nourished it as best we could, but it died.

Next year after Freddie's death, husband had gone to the upper country to rest during the hot weather. We had a few boarders and a good cook and were living very quietly. I tended the store and looked after our affairs. I was aware that there were some light-fingered persons in the vicinity and always made things secure for the night. Our house was a large one. The boarders all slept upstairs; the cook and the children on the lower floor. I was awakened one night by hearing a noise at the side door as if someone was trying to burst it open. I called out to know who was there and received no answer. Again I heard them, and jumped up and called to the men upstairs, saying, "Someone is breaking into the house."

A man heard me and ran out on a front porch. He saw the burglar running away and said, "Shall I shoot him?"

"Oh, no! Don't shoot him. Maybe he is hungry and was trying to steal food." He made many visits after that, always stealing fish from a large barrel which sat in a shed. I just left them there and let him take them, as I thought he must be very hungry or he would not steal. I thought to put a card on and tell him to take the barrel too, as we had others. I think he was a born thief. He was often accused. One of our boarders lost his money and suspected this man as the thief.

We had two Germans just from the old country boarding with us. They were employed on the canal and received good wages, as they were sturdy good workmen. After they had received quite a lot of money, they could not decide how or where to keep it. They had never had money before, and it worried them a great deal. So much that they told several of the men and asked their advice about the matter. A smart little Englishman told them to go out in the woods and bury it by a stump. They waited till almost dark and off they went to bury their money. Then, every evening one of them would go out and see if it was there all right. He had gone so often that he had beaten a path to it, and the Englishman told him someone would track him and find his money. He advised him to move it and then not go near it, but the German said he wanted to know every day if it was there.

We closed out our drygoods and groceries and turned our attention to the boarding business. I employed several to assist me. Husband was with the company and Bess in school. I managed the affairs, buying my supplies in Portland and The Dalles. I did an extensive business for a year, then had to close out on account of impaired health. There were so many boarders I found the work too difficult. Graders were arriving ready to begin work on the Northern Pacific Railroad as soon as the line was located. The old steamer, Idaho, landed and discharged her cargo of one thousand Chinamen. In a few hours a city of tents sprung up as if by magic. I said to my cook, "Just see your cousins." He was a "tony" Chinaman and said, "Not my cousins, either."

In December I made a trip to The Dalles to purchase supplies for my boarding house, and also to look after toys and presents for the Christmas Holiday. The weather was favorable when I left the Locks. On arriving at The Dalles we were met by a fearful storm. It raged in all its fury during my stay there. Fearing a blockade, I returned the next day. We encountered a fearful gale on the river. Although the steamer was one of the Company's best, we had fears for her safety. The snow, sleet and rain were whirled now east, now west. The wind blew a regular cyclone. We made a quick run down to the upper Cascades. The landing was on the Washington shore, and our home was across just opposite in Oregon at Cascade Locks. There was no hotel or boarding house at the landing where one could get either board or lodging. We could stay on the steamer till it was ready to return. After that we could only have shelter in the wharfboat.

Hortense was with me and the superintendent's wife who also lived at the Locks. We wanted to get home, but to attempt crossing

*"The old steamer, Idaho, landed and discharged her cargo of one thousand Chinamen."*

the Columbia River so near the great falls in such a storm was a fearful undertaking and the cold v as intense. We did not know what to do.

The government steam launch was there waiting to take us across. We looked at the boisterous expanse of mad waters. Then viewed the falls. It would be a fearful death to go over them. We tried to take courage. We said, "Oh, let us go." Captain Morrell was willing to make the attempt. We had confidence in his ability to manage the craft. He put her in good trim. He said he would use every precaution, as it was dangerous at best. The anchors were set ready to be hurled overboard if we became disabled in any way and were in danger of going over the falls.

All being ready, we walked bravely on board and were assigned seats near the engine as being the most comfortable. The awnings were all raised and the steamer made to catch as little wind as possible. The white breakers rolled and tumbled. The fearful roaring from the falls and the storm was deafening. The river is about a mile wide.

We saw the brave man at the wheel and felt that our lives were in his hands. He ran upstream half a mile, then struck directly across. We could see the expectant crowd on the opposite shore. We looked in wild dismay toward the falls. We were flying down toward them. We noted the distance yet between us and the home shore. Oh! Save us! We missed the landing and were near the seething whirlpool. Many ran here and there reaching out toward us. We were not lost yet. We struggled against the strong current. We gained a few strokes. Now a little more, and we made the landing. The cable was thrown ashore. Strong hands seized it. We were safe! Husband was there with blankets. They almost carried us up the temporary bridge. We were very cold and ice clung about us.

Blankets were thrown around us, and we were hurried to our homes. We looked back toward the wild expanse we had just crossed and watched the great body of water dash and plunge over the falls and were thankful to be alive. We felt grateful to the brave man who brought us safely across, and we praised the staunch little steamer.

The stone quarry where the great square rocks were obtained to build the canal was just above our place, and the stone cutters had to pass our store going to and fro. They boarded at the government house near the canal. One evening, on their way home, an Italian named Latardo called in the store to get some article. He had often passed, and we had a speaking acquaintance.

The next morning, as the men were on their way to work, I observed there was some excitement among them. They talked hurriedly and had much to say. They were nearly all foreigners. I wondered what had gone amiss, when one called out to me and said Latardo went over the falls. I at once inquired, knowing if he had gone over the falls he was lost. I was told he had been rowing a race the evening before with a friend, and when just above the falls, had broken an oar and lost control of his boat. His friend offered to row to him and bring him ashore, but he refused to take the offered assistance. The strong current soon drew him into its embrace. Then no one could reach him. Efforts were made to send him a rope. When last seen in the spray, he was standing up in the boat pulling off his coat making ready to swim. He was never seen again—went down in the whirlpool.

Two men who lived on the Washington shore had been over at the works and drank heavily before starting home. It was late at night and a heavy gale was blowing downstream. They carried a lantern to light them through the woods to their home. Fears were entertained for them when they left the hotel and watch kept to see if they reached the opposite shore. They had gone two thirds of the way when the light was observed to be going rapidly downstream. Then all hope was lost. The light soon disappeared over the falls, and they were never seen again. Had gone down into that fearful whirlpool, down among the great crags and boulders. Oh, what a fearful death! Many narrow escapes have been chronicled there, and many have lost their lives by venturing too near.

The Indians say that many years ago there was a bridge there, a mountain bridge, and the water ran under it and they could cross over and follow the wild deer. But the Great Spirit frowned on them and made the bridge fall. The mountain fell into the river and made the falls as the water had to run over the great pile of rocks left there. [*A well-known legend speaks of this as the "Bridge of the Gods." Ed.*]

There is a moving mountain on the higher or Oregon side. It is always in motion, moving toward the river. Since the Northern Pacific Railroad was built there it is easily detected. The rail line gets out of plumb about one foot each year. It is an immense mountain and will some day slide into the river, no doubt, and cause an overflow of the country on the Washington shore. It is called Slide Mountain.

Chapter 14

# Life in the
# Northern Pacific Line Camps

W E LIVED AT THE LOCKS TWO YEARS. Then husband's
business led him on with contractors of the Northern Pacific
Railroad as it was being built through eastern Oregon and Washington. We left the Locks and went out on the line of N.P.R.R. and
spent the summer, to be with the business and for my health. We
had several other families along with our company, and we had a
fine time camping along the line on the grand old Columbia River.
We first camped near Shell Rock Mountain by a little mountain
stream and within sight of the river. We had a supply store and traded with the settlers and workmen. We had some exciting times when
the giant powder blasts were set off. They were very dangerous,
throwing rocks, gravel and stumps high in the air, often killing people or anything they would strike. The hours were set for firing the
blasts, and then everybody would seek safe quarters behind trees,
under bridges and in any and every place one could think of.

The signal was given one day for a gravel blast while we were at
Shell Rock. We ran to shelter. A company of Chinamen were
camped near us. They were at dinner. They were terribly excited,
hid behind trees and stumps. Bang went the blast near us. The
gravel flew high. One Chinaman peeped around the tree too soon
and a gravel struck him on the head. He fell like he had been shot.
Others ran to him and set up a loud chattering. They hurried him
into a tent and put a bandage round his head and made quite a
racket over him. If he had been crippled so bad he could not work
they would have left him to die, but he was only stunned and soon
got well.

Our next camp was at a boat landing near where a grade was being cut. One day I saw a company of Chinamen running toward our
camp. When they came near us they called out to me to "fy! fy!"

(meaning to hurry up). I did not run quick enough. A heavy blast rent the air. Rocks flew around. One shot passed my head so near I felt the breeze from it. The Chinamen saw it and saw me dodge, and they set up quite a laugh at me for not running when they told me to. They searched about and found the rock and brought it in and laid it on the scales in the store. It weighed 11 pounds. One of them said to me, "It big enough killed you." I said, "Yes, indeed. Big enough to kill Elephant John."

Our little dog was very cross toward Chinamen and would try to bite them, and we had to keep him tied. He got loose once and bit one. The man cried out to me and told me to give him medicine to cure it. He said, "Your dog bite me. You hab cure me." I told him to keep away and the dog would not bite. Soon after, I was in the store and the dog raved out toward a Chinaman and was shot at. I ran out and told him to stop shooting and go away, but he refused to do so. Then I got my shotgun and he left. He was the boss, and had come to kill the dog for biting his man. He shot into our camp very carelessly.

I needed some potatoes one day for dinner and could not wait to send away for them. I went to borrow some from their cook. He said he could not lend them to me, but said he would give them to me. They neither borrow nor lend. They are peculiar.

When the men were working on the grade they were chained to a tree or stone to prevent them falling. The mountain was very steep. One lost his footing some way and fell and pulled his chain loose and plunged headlong down the precipice and was killed. Building a railroad down the Columbia was no easy task. One blast killed a white man and two Chinamen near us. It had not discharged and the blaster was picking at it with an iron spoon when he struck a spark out of a stone and set off the blast which killed him and two others. Blew the Chinamen into the river. When a tunnel was being cut, an explosion killed one and wounded six. There were many mishaps.

The men in the messhouse were at their noonday meal. A heavy concussion startled them and then the stones fell on the house. One descended through the roof, then through the table and finally struck a man's boot and split it from top to heel.

We were going from our old camp to a new one late one evening when we heard a stump blast. Next moment splinters and dust flew above and around us. The teamster was struck in the back. I hugged Dot close to me in the wagon and dodged behind a board none too soon, as we were enveloped in sand, gravel and dust. It was a hid-

*"We left the Locks and went out on the line of the N.P.R.R., and spent the summer camping along the line."*

den blast and was thought to have exploded at the proper time. Such things happened quite often. However, none of us were hurt.

We witnessed a grand blast. Tons of powder were used. It was necessary to blow off the front of a mountain that ran to the river. Tunnels were dug in some distance from either side and the powder put in. The fuse was set all ready, backed up by an electric apparatus for fear the fuse might not work. All things being ready, parties from Portland, The Dalles and other points were in steamers to witness the tumbling of the mountain. The steamers were anchored about a mile distant for safety, and all persons had hied themselves away. The whistle blew as the signal. We waited and listened in suspense, expecting to hear a terrific roar and feel the earth tremble. A heavy dull thud was all we heard. We waited in hiding thinking something had checked its final racket, but when we saw the Chinamen creeping out, we imagined we had heard the blast. When we walked out where we could see, the sky was overcast as if a cloud obscured the sun. What a shower of sand and dust. The blast was a grand success. The spur of the mountain had turned off into the river, leaving a fine roadway around the point. So suddenly had it all happened that it left no time for the Chinamen to move their tents, and the mountain turning into the river had caused an overflow of the bank and washed the Chinatown away. What a racket they raised about it too.

The Chinamen are fond of games. They gambled a great deal. Some of them were experts and robbed those who worked of their hard earned money. We were in camp at Crates Point below The Dalles. There were about two thousand Chinese and perhaps six hundred whites. It was a large camp. All the forces were finishing that grade before going into winter quarters. The location was a lovely one under the tall pines and on the bank of the river. The Chinamen were mostly down near the river. We were having lovely weather in September. Beautiful moonlight nights, calm and peaceful. About midnight I was roused by such an unearthly yelling, as if from the throats of a thousand wild Comanches. "Where am I? What does it mean? What is it? Indians? Oh, no!"

Husband had grabbed his gun and was at the tent door. I jumped and got another gun and looked out. What shrieks! I saw a thousand or more white-robed figures all coming directly towards the grounds where the whites were camped. They looked like a troop of ghosts, only they were all armed. Here they came, but they passed our tent. I lay my hand on husband's arm and said softly, "Don't shoot. They are passing us and chasing someone." A foreman was near us in his tent door ready to shoot. We asked him what this meant. He waited a moment, and when one of his gang ran near him, he called out to know what the racket was all about. The man answered, "Three bad Chinamen steal all the money, and we catch him and kill him." A large crowd of them had a regular carousal, and in the disturbance three of them had grabbed the money and started for the hills. No one interfered, just let them settle their own disturbance. The next day we heard from the agent that they killed three of them. We were glad to escape them in their mad career. They looked like flying demons in their long loose white pants and blouses, and they made night hideous with their demonic yells. In the moonlight they presented a weird appearance.

There was a little Chinese boy with the company who interested me very much. I often saw him pass carrying tea to the Chinamen who worked a mile away. He many times noticed Hortense and Bess and would smile at them pleasantly as he watched them playing near camp. At last I spoke to him, and he came near me and seemed so pleased because I had noticed him. He was very small. I asked him his age. He said thirteen years. I said, "You are very small to be so old." He was a nice looking little boy. I thought him to be eight, perhaps, but thirteen and so small? He said his father was dead, and he had only been here three months. I asked, "Do you like to be tea boy?"

"No. Me like you keep me." I told him I had no work for him to do. He went away. Next day he came again and said he wanted to be my boy. I told him to ask his boss man. He wanted to let me know how he could work. He picked up the saw and sawed some wood, then he got the bucket and ran to the river after water saying, "Me likee you. Me stay with you and workee." I gave him some bread. He thanked me and begged I would go see his boss man. I told him I would on Sunday at three o'clock. He told me where I could find him.

At the appointed time we all went to see "Billy," a name I had given him, and he was proud of it. He was out from the tents watching for us and ran to meet us. He had told the boss man about wanting to live with me. Billy led me to his tent and told him my errand. The boss told me Billy's history. He was thirteen years old. His father was dead, and Billy had been greatly abused. Billy was the boss's cousin, and he had brought him to America to earn his living. He wanted a home and a family. I told the boss I liked Billy, as he was a pleasant little boy. He wanted to learn to read and write and said he wanted to go with me. I had about concluded to take him, and he was so pleased and seemed to understand what we were saying. He watched us closely. I said, "You are my boy now, Billy." He was so pleased. Then the boss man said, "How much you pay him a day?" I answered, "I was intending to take him as my boy, feed, clothe and teach him and give him a home."

"Oh, no. You can't take him. He is worth a dollar a day." Billy could see I was disappointed, and he walked away. I was sorry for him. He was never so nice toward us any more. I think his boss forbade him talking to us, because he knew Billy wanted to go with us. He was a bright-looking little fellow and dressed in American costume. I was sorry for him. They soon went away and we lost sight of Billy.

One day there was to be some heavy blasting near camp. The foreman sent word for everybody to be on the lookout at six o'clock, as there would be danger. The rocks would fly in every direction. I sent the children away and thought to seek shelter near camp behind a tree, as I had supper on the stove. I did not like to leave everything so long, the goods and provisions. At the signal I ran to the largest tree, and soon found it wasn't as large as I had thought. There were two small trees, one on either side of it, almost touching it. The blasts were going off rapidly now, the rocks falling all around me. I did not dare leave the tree. I crouched near it. Oh, what a cannonade. It was deafening. And oh, how the Chinamen yelled, a thousand of them at once. Mercy! The stones were raining down thick on all sides. One struck the tree to my right, and made a glancing bounce and fell by my side. Another one cut a limb from a tree over my head and dropped into the sand on my other side. I screamed with terror, yet I dared not move.

The dreadful artillery ceased. I waited some moments. I was paralyzed with fear. I could not arise. I looked about me and saw my husband coming toward the camp. He looked for the children. I pointed toward the river. They were coming all right. Bess said the rocks struck the house where they were, and they had fallen thick about our tent. I had often wished to witness a battle, and I thought that surely was very much like an artillery attack.

Chapter 15

# We Move Again

IN OCTOBER the companies all left the road, as the grading was completed. We moved our stores with them by steamer some distance, then on flat cars over our new road as far as the Lower Cascades. It was a very crooked line down the Columbia, and over a new road it was very dangerous, especially with a drunk engineer. We were on the flats with the officials and tried to feel safe. Sometimes the cars would jostle and sway to and fro and pitch us off our seats, and the boxes of goods would tumble down. Our stovepipe rolled overboard. We were on a down grade and going at the rate of fifty miles an hour. We would cling to the posts and cry out in fear. Oh, what a wild ride! At last we rejoiced when, with a great crash, we stopped and were sent falling and tumbling head first from the seats. What a tumult the thousand Chinamen were making on the flats behind us. I suppose they had been yelling all the way down, but we could not hear them for the roaring of the train. They were terribly excited and very badly alarmed. They realized the danger as much as we did. I pitied them. One of their boss men, a very intelligent Chinaman, spoke to an official about running over such a road so fast and endangering the lives of his men and all others. He about got killed for interfering. I thought the Chinaman had a better heart than that white man. At any rate, he had some thought for his people and the white boss had not.

From the cars, the Chinamen went into camp, and the white company went on board steamers for Portland and Vancouver. There were three steamboats. It was near six o'clock. There was grade work on the bluff just along the river bank for a mile or two.

We had rejoiced that we had got away from the blasting alive and were feeling very happy over it when we were startled by a signal. A blast was heard almost over our steamer from the bluff. We looked out and saw the rocks falling, then other blasts were heard. We were amazed to realize we were doomed to witness another storm of blasts. A friend stepped in and said we were in great danger, but not to be alarmed. He said the captain thought it best to remain where he was with his steamer, as the danger was just as great anywhere else along the river. He told us to stand in the doorways, saying if a rock crashed through the upper deck, under the doorways was the safest place.

The lower deck of our steamer was loaded with boxes of Giant powder *[dynamite]*. If a rock had struck one box, the whole cargo would have exploded and blown the steamer into atoms. I clung to Bess and Hortense. Husband had not come on board. I was looking toward a steamer that was lying near us when a great rock as large as a barrel crashed past the steamer and fell in the river, just missing our neighbor.

After the disturbance was all over, a search was made for damage. One stone had crashed the deck of our boat and several scars were found over its sides like it had been through a battle. The captain said he had little of hope of living through the blasting as it was terrific and fearfully dangerous. He stood at his post expecting every moment to hear the Giant powder explode. There was tons of it on board. It was a miraculous escape. We had supper with the captain. He was a jovial, kind-hearted man and rejoiced with us that we were all safe. Husband had arrived. He had witnessed our danger from the shore.

The captain was amused with Hortense as she told her experience of life on the railroad. She said she had been building railroads all summer. He said, "What is your name?" She told him she was named for a queen. Then he playfully asked her, "What is my name?" She looked at him very soberly and said, "Your name is Smith." He was very much amused as his name *was* Smith sure enough. She had very rosy cheeks. Someone asked who painted her cheeks. She said, "God painted them."

We went to Vancouver the next day and secured a pretty little cottage on Main Street and set up housekeeping once more, and we felt very much at home after our summer's outing.

Bess was glad to be in school once more. Husband was well pleased with the place and thought of buying some lots in the grove near town and building up a rural home among the green trees on a grassy glade. Vancouver was a lovely old town, having been settled fifty years or more. The place was beautifully laid out, nice broad streets leading down to the grand old river of which we had a

*"Hortense always wanted to walk very slowly while passing head-quarters. She wanted to look at the pyramids of cannon balls."*

magnificent view. The garrison joined the city and had fine large grounds, well kept, and the buildings were a credit to the place. The officers quarters were very nice, and the headquarters building was a grand structure. General Miles was commander of the post when we were there.

We often walked through the grounds. They were well kept and a more interesting place to walk was not often found. Hortense always wanted to walk very slowly while passing headquarters. She wanted to look at the pyramids of cannon balls stacked in the yard and see the little howitzers set up for ornament. She liked to see the soldiers on dress parade and would listen for the bugle call. She was deeply interested in the sunset gun and would watch to see the flag drop as the cannon fired. She thought General Miles was a wonderful man to take care of so many soldiers.

We had been living in Vancouver but a short time when we received a call from a burglar. Bess was sleeping in a bed room adjoining my own. There was no door between our rooms. The door of each opened into the large room. An old man was sleeping in a room beyond the room Bess occupied. I was asleep and Hortense near me when, about two o'clock, I was aroused by a shot being fired near my head in the large room. Then instantly Bess screamed and jumped on my bed. I heard husband say, "Who shot?" The old man said, "I did. I shot at a burglar."

"Did you hit him?"

"I don't know. I hope I did."

Bess had heard him trying to open the door, and she could not get to my room without coming directly toward the door he was trying to open. She went quietly and told the old man. He said, "You get back to your room, and I will look after the burglar." She followed the old man instead of going to her room, and when he opened the door to shoot, she ran into my room and left him to kill the burglar. He saw the light from his lantern and fired at it. Next morning we found his tracks and saw the bullet holes in the fence but no burglar lay there. He had come to rob us. Fortunately, he would have been disappointed. Husband had just gone to Portland and put his money in the bank.

Our stay in Vancouver was a short, pleasant one of six months. We then went to Dayton in eastern Washington, stopping in the country for a month or two as smallpox had been raging in town, and we feared it. Then we ventured into the nice little town and were very cautious, we thought, in securing a house. I searched for days trying to find one that had not been visited by the dread disease. At last I secured a small house said to be all right. We had got well straightened up and felt quite at home when a little girl who was calling on Bess and Hortense said to me, "Aren't you afraid to live in this house?" I said, "Why so?"

"Oh, the smallpox was here." I was ready at once to move out, but by inquiries we ascertained it had been very thoroughly disinfected and only had a case of varialoid [*a very mild case of smallpox in persons who are partially immune. Ed.*]. We then bought a cottage and soon moved to it.

When school opened Bess and Hortense were pleased to enter with the other little girls. Husband had a good business, and we were well situated and had pleasant times. My brother Frank and his family lived there and were our neighbors. We soon found some old friends there and met with some excellent people in town and country. We were glad to have the little girls in school and also in Sabbath School. They had very pleasant little girls for playmates. Bess was fourteen now, quite a large girl. Hortense was near six. They were all we had as Leafe had gone to eastern Oregon to see his brother and ride after stock.

We had been in Dayton a year when Bess came down with scarlet fever. We thought to send Hortense away to prevent her getting it.

*"We went to Dayton in eastern Washington. My brother Frank and his family lived there and were our neighbors." Dayton, circa 1880.*

She would not go willingly saying, if her sister had scarlet fever, she wanted it too and wanted to stay to help care for her. As it was a light form I let her remain and hoped she would escape it. Bess was quite sick for some days. When she was convalescing, Hortense came down with it. She said she did not want any doctor. She had a strange dislike for the medical fraternity. She was growing worse. I insisted on calling a doctor. She said, "Yes, send for the one that cured my sister." He came a few times and pronounced her well and stopped his visits. She grew much worse. I said I must get the doctor again for her. She said no. She didn't want that doctor. He didn't cure her, and she didn't want him again. Asked me to send for Doctor V.

I did so, and he examined her very closely and took her temperature. She did not like the clinical thermometer, and she got vexed at the doctor and would almost go into convulsions if he came near her ever after. I would give him her symptoms, and he would prescribe for her. After some days, we could note an improvement. Doctor called when she was sleeping. I wanted him to notice her breathing, and I motioned him to enter. He stepped gently near her and was watching her. She opened her eyes, saw him and covered her head. I asked, "Don't you want to see the doctor?" She said, "No, I don't like doctors." After she got well she often ran across the street to avoid him when we were down town or out walking. I always had a high regard for Doctor V, and considered him an eminent young physician.

# Chapter 16

# Gold Fever
# 1884

W E HAD LIVED IN DAYTON two years when there was a great mining excitement in Idaho. The news of rich strikes were very exciting, and many were going from our town and country. At last my husband, who was always ready to go to a new field of labor, got the gold fever and insisted on going. I was very much opposed to leaving our pleasant home and nice surroundings. I insisted that he give up the wild idea, but he could not resist. Brother Frank had gone and three other brothers were there. I told him that I did not want to go, and he had best go and try his luck in the mines for a while and leave us at home.

He went to the lovely Coeur d'Alene Lake to take the steamer for the gold fields. He was enraptured with the lovely place and wrote that he wished us to go to him at once, as he had decided to locate at the lake and not go to the mines. We sold out and went. We boarded the train at Dayton, followed by many friends who went to see us off. I was very sorry, indeed, to leave them and my pleasant home.

We arrived at Rathdrum the next day at noon; a railroad station on the Northern Pacific Railroad. From there we went eight miles by stage to the lake and found it really was a beautiful, grand place. A lovely, level country spread out for miles and the broad expanse of water lay as a front view, with tall mountains beyond it. It set my heart on a home there.

We secured a lot and built a cottage under the shade of some lovely old trees and, from the verandah, we could see the lake for miles and watch the steamers come and go. The girls were in love with the pretty scenery. They called our home Rural Retreat.

Camp Sherman was situated just below Coeur d'Alene City and was one of the finest military posts on the Pacific Coast. It was laid along the lake shore. The grounds were large and commodious and

143

*"We arrived at Rathdrum the next day at noon; a railroad station on the N.P.R.R."*

artistically designed. The lovely forest trees added much to its beauty. The officers quarters were on a line off one side of the large parade ground and were all very much alike, each one having a door yard and also a garden. The cavalry quarters were arranged on another side, the stables in back. The band quarters and mess houses were off beyond the square parade. The different companies were here and there, all in good substantial houses. The church and school house were off in a quiet grove of firs, the theater being opposite across the parade grounds. The seats were placed for comfort 'neath the sighing pines around the music stand. It was altogether a very pleasant military post.

Colonel Wheaton was in command, and the lovely steamer belonging to the post was named the Wheaton. It was often seen out on excursions carrying the happy crowds of stylish ladies and gay young officers in their uniforms. Chatting as the band played sweet music, they glided over the smooth water of the grand old lake.

Coeur d'Alene City was very pleasantly situated for a mile or more along the lake shore. It was a pretty little village and bid fair to be a noted summer resort; it was convenient to the city of Spokane and many other larger places and easily reached by train. The rippling mountain streams and quiet shady groves along the lake called to the weary city folk to come out and rest. Hundreds of neat little cottages were occupied each summer by those who liked the cool and pleasant grottoes in which to rest and recuperate.

We saw hundreds of miners waiting transportation to the mines.

We called the place the white city. Tents were to be seen on every hand.

[*For a historical perspective on the early beginnings of Coeur d'Alene and Fort Sherman I quote here from two other sources, which indicate that the Mastersons, arriving in 1884, were among the earliest settlers. Ed.*]

In a way it was a sawmill—and sabotage—that got the beautiful lake city of Coeur d'Alene going.

In April, 1878, a detachment of cavalry from Fort Lapwai bivouacked on the shores of Lake Coeur d'Alene...The mission of the commander, Col. Henry Clay Merrian, was to build Fort Coeur d'Alene....

Col. Merrian had brought along all the equipment for a sawmill...but he had a problem, as his troopers had not been trained in the operation of the mill. Nevertheless, after doing some fast recruiting of knowledgeable civilians...to serve as bosses, Col. Merrian got the mill going before winter set in.

The soldiers...disliked the non-military labor, and from time to time there was sabotage. So the Colonel hired more civilians to work in the mill, and between 1880 and 1884 they largely made up Coeur d'Alene's non-military population of 20 to 30 persons...*Beckoning the Bold,* Rafe Gibbs, p. 201.

Fort Coeur d'Alene was built in 1878. The name was changed to Fort Sherman in 1891 when General Sherman died.

"*Coeur d'Alene City was very pleasantly situated for a mile or more along the lake shore.*"

The earliest pioneers moved in about as soon as the soldiers came—soldiers' families mostly, who lived in tents on land where the city park now lies. Since some of the wives did washing for men at the fort, this became known as "soap suds row." The first dozen or so settlers who came made their living furnishing wood, meat, and dairy products to the soldiers.

The first major gold rush to Coeur d'Alene was in 1883. Within a few months there were ten thousand miners on Pritchard Creek. The N.P.R.R. was partly responsible for the magnitude this first wild stampede attained. The railroad had been built through this undeveloped country in 1881-1883 at colossal expense and the railroad officials eagerly seized upon the news of the mining strike as a means of stimulating travel over the line. They put out glowing, exaggerated pamphlets which lured people from all over the country to come to Idaho.

Part of these thousands outfitted in Spokane...but other thousands left the train at Rathdrum and bought their supplies there...

During the winter of '83-'84 the town of Coeur d'Alene had filled up with miners waiting for the spring breakup so they could head into the mountains. *Steamboats in the Timber,* Ruby El Hult, pp. 20, 26, 31.

It was a lively place and a noisy one. Some drowned their troubles in the cup. We soon found out even in a beautiful place like this, where everything should be good and nice and harmonious, the demon strong drink came along to mar the beauty.

A few days after our arrival we saw a dead man lying on a porch of a saloon near the lake. It was early morning, and we spoke of it wondering if he had slept out there. We soon saw two men go to him and try to rouse him and could not do so. In a short time others were around him, and one walked rapidly away toward Camp Sherman. There the ambulance came, and we saw them lift the man and put him in the ambulance. He was driven hurriedly to the hospital, but he was dead. He'd been killed during the night. The next day a friend told us it was a soldier, and if we wished we could attend a soldier's funeral. We all went to witness the solemn ceremonies. The band was playing a dirge as they approached the cemetery. The soldiers in uniform marched with their dead comrade to his last resting place. Although his death was not an honorable one, he was buried as a soldier. After the grave was covered over, the last platoon (sic) was fired over it, and all fell in line and marched back to the post and left him to sleep in dishonor.

The Fourth of July was drawing near. The commander had ordered fireworks and was making preparations for a grand celebration. The civilians were all permitted to attend the military display, and the fireworks at night on the parade ground. All were expected to observe good order. The fireworks were on a grand scale. Everything was conducted in true military style and was a success. A ball at night ended the celebration.

Excursions on the lake and picnics on shore were frequent. Sometimes we would go out on the lake and not a ripple could be seen on the beautiful sheen of water. We could float along and gather water lilies and catch speckled trout; when suddenly we would be greeted by a wave dashing against our boat. Then, if we were out a few miles, we would quickly pull for shore, and many times we would encounter a gale before reaching it. Storms arise quickly on the lake, and sometimes boats were swamped and persons drowned. The white caps would roll and dash upon the shore, and one was filled with dismay to look upon the mad waters rushing and roaring where such a little while ago all was calm and smooth as a mirror.

One afternoon we were out rowing, and we were caught in a fearful storm. Our rudder was broken, so we could not guide our boat aright. Bess and Hortense cried out in fear. I called for help. Husband tried to quiet us by saying we would soon be ashore, but it seemed so long. At last we reached shallow water and were not so frightened. Where we had been the last hour the water was deep, so deep that no bottom had ever been reached by lead and line, and those who were drowned in it were seldom found.

We secured a smaller boat, and Bess would take Hortense and me out riding where the water was shallow. It was lovely where we could see the bottom of the lake and see the fish go gliding away from us. If she ventured into deep water we would cry out, "Go back, Bess. We are afraid." She would playfully take us a little further and, if the lake was smooth, a more beautiful place on lake or shore was not often found.

But all things beautiful or otherwise must have an ending. Winter came and we were delighted with the deep snow. It being a new place in the edge of a forest, there were a great many stumps all about over town. The trees had been cut to supply wood for Camp Sherman. These stumps were of various sizes and heights. The snow fell quietly down for several days. Then a bright sunny morning revealed their beauty. They were all crowned with caps of pure white. Those stumps presented a comical appearance. They looked like crowds of people dressed in black wearing tall white hats.

The weather was intensely cold. The lake was soon a sheet of ice strong enough to bear up wagons and teams and afforded a grand place for skating. Snow plows were sent all over town to make roads. Sleighing was splendid, and the merry jingle of bells was heard on every side.

The tents were all gone now. Those who occupied them had either gone to the mines or returned to their homes. Times were dull. No business at all. But for Camp Sherman, life here during the winter would have been very lonely. There were a few families near the lake, and we had made the acquaintance of some soldiers'

*"Bess and Hortense attended the Post school, which was held in the chapel at Fort Sherman."*

families. Bess and Hortense attended the Post School, as there was no other school there.

The school was in a flourishing condition and was an honor to the Post. Our girls made rapid progress in their studies and were well pleased with the strict discipline. They grew to be very fond of their military teacher in his regimentals and learned the officer's salutes and learned to keep step.

In springtime, during target practice, I feared for them to go as they had to cross the target line. One morning, they were on their way to school when the soldiers were out practicing at long and short range target shooting. The officer at the long range stand signaled them to stop. The one on the short range said go forward. They started and were stopped instantly by a shot. It just missed them. They had a narrow escape and a big fright. A soldier was killed while we were there. Accidents will happen. He was turning the target for the boys who were practicing. It failed to move as he wished, and he stepped to adjust it and was shot dead at his post.

There was a splendid hospital in connection and a good surgeon. Sick and wounded soldiers always received good and kind attention. Each company had a nice large garden and had to raise their vegetables. [The gardens] were a mile from the Post. They had immense root houses to store their vegetables for winter use. After enough was stored for them, they were permitted to sell the remainder to civilians.

Some Indians were camped on the hill near us and were very noisy, often making night hideous by their wild carousal. They were notorious gamblers in their savage way and were continually drumming on some distressing kind of a tambourine, keeping time to their discordant music by their never-ending hooah, hooah, hoo, hoo. For hours and hours they kept it up, with an occasional yell, as if they had been suddenly seized by the old Demon himself.

One night they were more boisterous then usual. I could hear a voice crying for help. They had fires in their tents which reflected shadows. I was so worried by their noise, I watched from my window. In a few moments I heard the fearful scream again, and could plainly see a young Indian girl tied to a post. I could also see the braves torturing her with fire brands. She cried out in agony and begged her tormenters to cease their cruel work. I could not endure to see her thus tortured and not try to relieve her. I insisted on someone going to the Post after soldiers.

Husband and a neighbor went first to the interpreter who lived near us and asked him to go after assistance, but the fellow refused to do so, saying they would not kill her. He called out to them, and they stopped torturing her. Two soldiers had come along. While they were standing near the Indian camp talking (they had stopped to listen to the racket), they were saluted by a large knife whizzing past one of their heads and sticking in a tree. They looked around and saw an Indian running away. One of them reached and got the knife, then ran to the post after soldiers. The Indian was aware of the fact, and he and some others skipped the camp. Two hours later when the officer of the night drew up his men in a line at our door and inquired for the Indians, he was told they had cleared out while he was getting ready to come after them.

Some resident Indians told us the next day that the Indian campers on the hill had stolen the girl from another tribe. She had tried to make her escape. They followed and captured her and brought her back and were torturing her for running away. They soon moved their camp. We were glad to see them go.

Winter being over now, the people were on their way to the mines again. Many were anxious to be off. They could not wait for the ice to clear out of the lake. They must hurry to the gold fields and go trudging through snow and slush by land up the lake shore.

Husband was one of the first to start out. He had a serious time of it and blistered feet when he got through. He stopped at the Old Mission which had been located there fifty years ago. He saw the old church which Father Joseph had built there. It is a most wonderful house. There was not a nail used in building it, and it is a fine large church nicely finished off with carved ornaments.

Father Joseph had been there all those long years with the Coeur d'Alene Indians, teaching and civilizing them. He made good farmers of them. They were self-supporting, lived in houses and had good schools and churches. The Indian women used sewing machines, and the men had machinery of various kinds on their farms, rode about in wagons and sleighs, spoke good English and dressed like white people.

Father Joseph said when he first came to live with them, they were at war with other tribes. Quite often, and many times when they were on the war path, he was looked upon as being instrumental in their losses. They said a pale face in the tribe was bad luck. They would hold a council and conclude to kill him. They would, however, give him an opportunity of pleading for his life. He would work on their savage feelings by telling them he had great power, and if they killed him, he would come back and kill all their ponies, cause the fish to die, the berries to wither away and the red deer to go far off. Then they would leave him alone for a while. He said he had to use a great deal of caution till he got them to know he was their friend and was there for their own good. They all love him now. He has taught them and been with them fifty years. He is now a feeble old man and will soon pass beyond. His work will live after him. [He] went to those Indians when they were wild savages, risked his own life for their sake, lived on their fish and wild game, and had to do as they wished many times to save his own life. By years of patience, he got them under control.

The mission is a beautiful place on the Coeur d'Alene River, a pretty little valley surrounded by high mountains and the river flows

*"There was not a nail used in building [the Cataldo Mission] and it is a fine large church nicely finished off with carved ornaments."*

through it. Many people have tried to get possession of it, but failed to do so. It is Father Joseph's by right of law. He has earned it by long years of toil and privation.

[Historical note: Father Pierre-Jean De Smet (a Jesuit priest) visited the Coeur d'Alene Indians in 1840 and outlined plans for missionary activities. Father Nicholas Point selected a mission site on the St. Joe River near Saint Maries during the winter of 1842. Catholic Iroquois trappers had prepared the Coeur d'Alenes for the rituals and procedures of the church. Consequently, the Jesuits experienced some success with the Indians even though Father Point despised the Indians' dirtiness, idolatry, gluttony, gambling and 'moral abandonment.' By 1844, Point claimed to have baptized two-thirds of their number and noted that there was a remarkable change among the tribe. Father Point found that his fields were submerged each spring under the flood waters of the river. In 1846, the entire mission and Indian followers moved some twenty miles from Lake Coeur d'Alene to a site later called Cataldo. Several years later the Indians constructed an impressive church building at Cataldo. *Idaho, A Bicentennial History,* F. Ross Peterson, p. 45.

The mission became commonly known as the 'Cataldo Mission' after Father Joseph Cataldo [a Jesuit priest], a man of great energy and purpose. . . . *Beckoning the Bold,* Rafe Gibbs, p. 36.

Chapter 17

# On to Delta,
# A Placer Camp

HUSBAND WENT ON TO THE MINES and located in Delta, a fine placer camp. *[Delta once had 3,000 people, but less than 300 called for their mail there in 1889.* Coeur d'Alene Diary, *Magnuson, p. 77]* He built a house for his business, fenced a garden patch, rented a dwelling house and sent for us. We did not want to venture into the mines. We heard such doleful accounts about the dangerous roads and deep rivers and many other obstacles to encounter on the way. The journey was to be made part of the way on horseback and few women had ventured in over the almost impassable route. He insisted. We sold our home by Lake Coeur d'Alene, packed our household goods and sent them forward. We then spent some days with friends and said goodbye to our dear home. We went on board the lovely new steamer, Coeur d'Alene, with many others who were bound for the gold fields. We had a pleasant ride up the lake thirty miles, then some distance on the Coeur d'Alene River and landed at the Mission. We went to see the noted old church.

I went to the warehouse to inquire about my freight and was told by a dapper young clerk that it had been sent on up the river by cow boats as the only means of conveyance. He said the boat had capsized into the river. I was sorely distressed, for whatever could we do in such a wild place without our household goods, bedding, clothes and almost everything we possessed in that line. He said he heard they had been partly fished out and were in the store at Kingston seven miles above there. We went by stage, crossing the river on the way in a ferry boat. At Kingston we stopped at a good hotel. It was thirty miles to the mines yet. Half of the route was only a trail. Horsemen wound their way around the steep crags and over rugged mountains.

Next morning when the saddle train of about fifteen horses drew up before the hotel door to take the passengers for the mines, it was sad to see but one lady's saddle. There were four to use it. A widow had it engaged, but she consented to stay till next trip and let my niece use it that day as it was necessary for her to go at once. I said I would stay till next time as I could not ride a man's saddle. I didn't want to go that day anyway. I went to the warehouse and inquired for my water-soaked freight. As it was a scorching hot day, I had the packages all opened and dried and, by this means, saved most of them. I had packed my dishes securely in an ironbound box, then locked and baled it with wire. The box sank to the bottom of the river and was fished out by some boatmen two miles below where the accident occurred. The current had carried it gently along on the smooth river bed and not a dish was broken. When the wire bales were loosened, the box fell to pieces. The men sent the dishes to me.

We spent the day there at Kingston waiting for the train to return. Again I was sorry to see only one side saddle, and soon learned the "tony" [*a slang expression meaning high-toned or stylish*] widow had the promise of it. I would either ride a man's saddle or stay again which I would not do. I was anxious to get to the end of this journey.

I was assigned a sturdy old pony and Hortense sat on behind me. Bess had a pony all to herself. There was an old doctor, a young lawyer, some mining experts, the widow and her son, and the saddle boss. We got started at last, with good wishes from the gaping crowd who had gathered around the door to see us off. We met with many mishaps during the morning ride. At noon we halted for dinner at the half-way house which is kept by a family from Dayton with whom we had the honor of acquaintance. Bess met a young schoolgirl friend. They were pleased to meet and had much to relate after their separation.

We had to hurry forward as the most difficult half of the day's journey was ahead of us. We started out in single file on a narrow trail. In many places if the horse had made a misstep, we would have been hurled down a hundred feet or more into a rushing river or on the rugged crags of the precipice. Fourth of July Canyon. We trembled with fear. I told Hortense to close her eyes and hold fast to me. I feared she would become dizzy and fall from the horse and go plunging into the river below. We went slowly onward for an hour or two.

We had just crossed a small swift stream with much difficulty and all got in line once more when the old doctor said, "What is that I hear? Sounds like the firing of guns." Then we were all attention. Maybe a stone rolling down the bluff into the river. We all heard the reports now. We stopped and listened again and looked. We saw a tree fall on a high hill to our right. Then another one followed. Then they were falling by the dozens. A storm! There was only a gentle breeze where we were, but we knew it would meet us all too soon. We were in a heavy forest of burnt timber. The trees fell on every side. When one fell near us, we would scream with fright and crouch down on our horses. We tried to hurry on, hoping to reach green timber. Some went faster than others, and we were soon scattered and out of sight and hearing of each other. We heard a crash near us and here came a giant of an old tree. It was falling directly toward us. How it whirred as it fell through the air and just missed a man in front of us. He called back saying, "You can't pass there." We waited until others came up. Then the men had us dismount, and we crawled under the tree as it rested on the mountainside across the trail. Our horses arched around above it.

Another tree fell across the trail, but high enough for us to ride under if we hurried before it settled. I told Hortense to lie down as much as she could. I leaned forward and urged the pony to pass under it. I was nearly pulled off by the great limbs clawing at my back.

We soon saw our party ahead of us. We waited there till Bess and the others arrived. They had been detained by a fallen tree, and the widow's horse had given some trouble. We were all together now and would soon reach the mining camp. We were very tired.

I saw a little dog coming toward us and recognized it as our own dog. Then Bess called out, "There is papa sitting by the road waiting

*Delta, circa 1885. "Our home was a short distance from the village."*

for us." He had got alarmed about the storm and feared for our safety. When I was assisted from my pony, I could not stand on my feet. I was completely given out. It was months before I even partially recovered from that journey into the mines, and I never have been so well since. We saw this little mining camp in the rugged mountains was rich in gold, certainly its only redeeming quality.

We could occupy a house of one room for ten dollars a month. I said I positively would not pay any such price. I rented a large tent for five dollars and had partitions put in it. I had a large sitting room, bedroom and a large kitchen. We were pleasantly and comfortably fixed and lived in it till our house was finished.

We had some very nice families around us, some who had come into the mines by another route. A road was opened for wagons and, in a few months, we had quite a town and opened a school for the children. Husband now had a good business. We were interested in the excitement of the camp. Rich ledges were being discovered on every side. Men were wild over the mines. One could spend an hour in the bank looking at the nuggets of gold and the jars of gold dust. The mines were quite rich but were soon worked out.

Our home was a short distance from the village, a pleasant walk. Someone gave it the name of lover's lane, very appropriate too, for several couples who walked in lover's lane have married and several others wished to. On the Fourth of July we had a grand celebration and a ball in the evening.

After a few months times were dull. The miners went to other camps. Winter came on and the village was about deserted. Many lost all they made trying to make more. We stayed and some others stayed with us. The winter was cold and the snow was deep. Many were ready to give up in despair. The winter drug on with little to do and no life in the camp now. What a change! Merchants were disheartened, with goods and groceries and no customers. We saw the place going down. The people tried to be cheerful and make the best of a bad situation.

The "tony" people had some sleigh rides but the roads were not very good. Bess and some "tony" friends started to Murray, a small mining camp seven miles distant. All was merry as such parties should be till the sleigh broke down on a bleak hill two miles from a house. There was a regular smash-up on the down grade, and it scattered the merry party of boys and girls here and there. One went headlong under the horses heels. Another was pitched down hill. They were distressed over the accident but made the best of it. One of the young gallants mounted a horse and went after a conveyance

*"Bess and some 'tony' friends started to Murray, a small mining camp seven miles distant."*

and the rest of the party walked two miles to see a famous mine. The foreman showed them all over the works. The quartz mills were a wonder to them. He had them take dinner with him. His kindness was appreciated, for they surely would have suffered out in the snow all that long while, and been very hungry too. The conveyance arrived, and they all came home and had a merry laugh over their day's adventures.

In spring time they took another ride. A coach-load went to see a young lady friend on board a boat bound for the outside world. The day was warm with not a cloud to be seen. After their visit, they said goodbye and were returning. The driver offered to take them home by a new route and show them some nice scenery. They had gone but a few miles when they were greeted by a low rumbling over the mountains. Then a dark cloud could be seen over the hilltops not far away.

They were aware of the danger. A storm in the mountains is to be dreaded. Now the lightning's glare almost blinded them. They were met by the storm in all its fury. Night dropped its sable mantle when they were still three miles from home. The rain poured down. The wind was almost a tornado. Trees were falling. One had fallen across the road. The vivid electric bolts lighted their way. They could go no farther in the coach. They willingly left it as they could protect themselves better from falling trees. No houses were very near. They were anxious to get home, knowing we would be worried.

At home we were alarmed about Bess. I could not rest. I sent husband to inquire if they had been heard from in any way. We waited and hoped. At last we heard them coming and were surprised to see them on foot. Bess was in a light summer dress, drenched with rain and mud-bespattered, a sight to behold, but alive and laughing merrily. She was sorry to have caused us anxiety. I hurried her to her room and into bed, wrapped in blankets to prevent a chill.

On another occasion, all the girls and boys and several women went to a wonderful berry patch to pick berries all day. They carried a lunch with them. The berries were on a high hill. The bears were also on the hill. All were aware of that fact and were afraid of them. After they had all picked berries till they were tired, they went to a nice shady grove and ate their lunch. A boy who had gone home on an errand was on his way back to the crowd and thought to play a joke on them. He had just passed a man on the road who was leading two pet bears.

The party were all sitting in the shade near the road when he came to them hurriedly and said, "You all had best run. I saw two bears coming. Listen. I hear them now." They listened and could plainly hear growling or grunting as they tramped up the hill. People ran and scrambled up trees and stumps. Just then, old Oloff, the Russian, came in sight around a bush leading Bonapart and Josephine, his two pet bears. The children had all seen them often, but did not know they were coming up the road. Ned had a laugh at them all for running from two old pets.

# Chapter 18

# Moving to Spokane

HUSBAND DECIDED TO LEAVE THE CAMP. He thought of locating in Spokane and had gone to secure a home. We remained to sell our house, a lot in town and also our country home. We settled up all of our business, sold off groceries, cow and calf and chickens. We were sorry to part with our possessions, but did not want to stay longer. If we were to go, we were anxious to be off.

In two weeks we were ready to leave the mine. One of my brothers and his family had gone to Spokane to live, and we would go there too. Husband wrote that he was ready for us, but we had to wait for an opportunity to get a ride as we were thirty miles from the boat landing.

While we were yet in our country home, we were startled early one morning by our dog barking sharply and then running to the door as if he feared some animal or person. I looked out and saw a large wolf at the gate. It had chased him that far and did not dare venture inside.

Soon after, I was again alarmed by his fierce yelps. He was farther away, near a large mountain which stood off some hundred yards in front of our house. I looked for some time before I could see anything to make such a racket over. I then looked higher up the mountain and saw a huge cougar or mountain lion sitting looking toward our house. I told Bess and Hortense to stay in the house and be very quiet while I ran for a man who lived next door to come and shoot it. He got his Winchester rifle and came quickly with me. When it saw our rapid movement, it went off up the mountain. It had been seen several times in the mining district, but was shy enough to make its escape.

One day my niece and her two little children were out getting evergreens. She had an armful and could not carry them and baby too. She left baby sitting in the shade while she and the boy, aged three, went to the house, a short distance, with the evergreens. She hurried back. As baby cried, she got him and went to the house. She had but reached it when she heard a fearful yell. On looking around, she saw the lion standing where she had left baby sitting for a few moments.

My niece called to her husband and father who were working nearby. They could not track the big cat. They considered the place too dangerous for the family to stay longer and sent them into town. The cat often made visits after that, usually by night, and would walk on the roof of the cabin while the miners were sleeping in it. They feared it would break through and kill them; but gold lured them, and they stayed some time longer.

Gold was often found in mine pockets and many pretty little nuggets have been picked up in the Delta Mine. A neighbor called me to the kitchen door early one morning. She was very much excited. She had her hand under her apron. I spoke to her and she answered low, "Come here." I went to her and she showed me a large nugget of gold which she tried to keep hid from others. She said it had just been picked up from a pocket in her husband's mine. Its value in fine gold was $307. She said her husband gave it to her. She was very proud of it and glad to have so much money all her very own. She would now go and visit her son's grave. He had been her only

*Mine headquarters at Delta. "Many pretty little nuggets have been picked up in the Delta mine."*

child and died when he reached manhood. How a mother's love turns toward her child!

We sold our cow and pretty calf and our groceries and many articles that we did not wish to ship to Spokane. But we could not sell our real estate. We were to go with brother Frank. He would take us to the steamer. We sent our household goods with teams. We said goodbye to our friends and started very early, as we had a day's journey ahead of us if we were to catch the steamer. Our road was a very good one except some grades around high mountains. If we should meet a team in such a place, there would be serious trouble for there is not room to pass.

We had a pleasant drive and stopped at noon to eat our dinner. We had the globe for a table and the mountain ferns for a table cloth and a merry time at our feast. We were then near the Bunkerhill Mine and saw the great mountains of quartz where millions of dollars were waiting to be brought to light. We saw the wagons loaded with ore. It was hauled to the boats and shipped to mills in Montana.

A railroad was being build to the mines. Then transportation would be much easier. During the afternoon, we often passed the graders. They were strung out along the line, hurrying it through.

At sunset we were nearing the Mission. Hark! A blast! Someone called out to us to halt there. We did so and got under the wagon. "Oh, no!" I cried out. "We are in the blasts again after five year's silence." Bang! Bang! Bang! Bang! How fast they went. No harm done.

We went to the boat landing and learned we could not stay on the boat during the night. Frank looked out a nice camp ground under some lovely old trees, and we built an old-time campfire and thought of the days when we crossed the plains when Frank was a little boy and I was a little girl. The night being cool, we kept up a bright fire.

Next morning there was a dense fog. Frank had learned the night before that the steamer would move up the river some distance to take on cargo and start from the upper landing. We struck out on foot to find it. Frank went to see us on board, then he would return to his team and go by land to Spokane.

We tramped about for some time, looking and listening for the boat. The fog was so dense we could not see very far. The river was so very crooked that we would sometimes be so near we almost fell in and then, again, it was half a mile away. We were looking for the steamer but could not even see the river. At last Frank thought he spied the boat away off to our right. He said there was a bend in the river, and it was surely above that, as he could see it now. We ran to get there before it left us. The fog cleared away just around the supposed steamer and, behold, it was a straw stack looming up in the fog. How disappointed we were away out there in a hay field, and now we did hear the steamer puffing and ran back and found it in the river where it ought to be and not out wandering in a hay field. We hurried on board. Frank left us and hastened back to his wagon and team. We had a laugh over our dry-land steamer. We waited an hour, impatiently too. Then we had a pleasant ride down the river and lake and stopped to stay with an old neighbor at Coeur d'Alene City. Late at night, we were pleased to see Frank coming. He wanted to know if we had been looking after steamboats out in the hayfield anymore, but we turned the joke on him reminding him that he was the one who saw a boat in the hayfield.

We left Bess to visit with old friends for a few days, and Hortense and I went to Rathdrum by stage, then by train to Spokane. This was the route we had taken when on our way to the mine two years before. We were now returning.

Husband met us at the station in Spokane, and we were whirled to a hotel where we stopped a few days. After looking over this prosperous new town, we secured a nice cottage on Front Street.

"The [Spokane] streets were full of teams dashing in every direction."

*"Mamie, dear sister, we were so glad to see her." John Cogswell in later years.*

When Bess arrived, we went downtown and selected a new outfit for housekeeping. We were soon comfortably settled, and the girls entered school. The town was growing rapidly. Some splendid buildings were being erected. There were indications of a boom. Folders were sent out. Hundreds were rushing into the city-to-be. Lots advanced in value and houses were in demand. Rents were high. Many dwellings were hurriedly built and still the people came. For two years the houses sprang up as if by magic. The lots ran up to fabulous prices, but people kept coming to the City by the Falls.

The girls and I were out shopping one evening. On our way home we stopped at the post office, and received a postal saying for us to call at the station the next day. It said we would meet someone whom we would be glad to see. Of course, we suspected it was sister Mamie as she had put her initials very slyly in one corner. Yes, we would be there to meet her, on time too.

Next morning we were up early and could scarcely wait till train time. It had been nine years since we had met. We looked as the passengers were coming off the cars to catch a glimpse of her. At last I saw her speaking to a coachman. He motioned toward us, then we hurried to her. Mamie, dear sister, we were so glad to see her! We all got into a coach and off we went to our home by the river. We had a nice visit of some weeks, but all too soon, the time to go had come. We went with her to the station. We must say goodbye. Goodbye again as she leaned from the window for one more farewell, and we saw her no more.

Time wore on. Bess, who was now a tall graceful young lady, told me in a sweet blushing way of her own that she was thinking of going to a cozy little cottage that was waiting for her by the lake shore. She had a lover who lived there and was preparing to claim her for his bride. I would be sorry to give her up. She was like my own child. I raised her from a little tot, and now she would leave me. How we would miss her. I was pleased to know she would be near us. If she was happy, we must not complain.

The day arrived. The wedding was an exceedingly quiet one. Only relatives and immediate friends were present. It was as the bride wished. Bess looked sweet in her bride's dress and, when the ring was placed on her finger, a modest blush expressed her heart's true affection for the husband of her choice. She would love, honor and respect this noble-hearted young man who had chosen her for his life-long companion.

I received a letter from a niece at Eugene which bore sad tidings. Mamie was very sick, little hope of recovery. How anxious I was. In a few days, I received the sad news of her death. Oh, was my sister dead and I did not see her for a last word? Mamie gone! She had been so much to me all my life. I had her to look upon as my counselor, my guide. My first memories were of Mamie. She was as dear to me as a sister could be.

We often thought of her last days with us and rejoiced that she came. I was glad that my child met her and loved her. It was a sweet memory.

She was buried by the graves of her children, father, mother and Pink on the hill near our dear old home. Thus life is made up of joys and sorrows, sunshine and shadows. One day we rejoice over some happy event, next we mourn over some departed loved one. I sometimes think we should not mourn at all. Why grieve? We cannot change the progress of time and, with time, all things pass away. Nothing continues here.

The years go by and three had passed since our coming to this thrifty little town. What a change! Magnificent buildings on every side. Business was rushing. Crowded streets. Throngs of people hurrying here and there. Electric cars and city coaches filled with stylish ladies and professional gentlemen looking about them for locations. From 5,000, it now numbered 25,000 inhabitants and still they came. Railroads too were coming in on every side. It was now a center, a city of magic, a beautiful city; but the fell destroyer often visited our beauty here—the fire fiend was at work.

I was aroused one night by the fearful clang clang which always brings terror at the midnight hour. The city was illumined by the destroying blaze. A heavy tramping was heard on the pavement in front. On looking out, we saw a band of fine horses. They were prancing and snorting about in wild delight, rejoicing in their freedom. They had just been rescued from the burning building, and we saw it was a fine livery stable in flames. Here they came again. They ran towards the fire with their heads raised, then away again up the street and soon returned led by a noble black beauty. They pranced and tossed their manes, circled about and off they went. What brave noble-looking animals. They dashed away into the darkness, and the city was once more slumbering.

We must give up our house on Front Street. Lots were in demand on the river bank for mills and factories. We went towards the heights to Lincoln Street. We had a fine view of the city from our upper verandah, and we liked the situation and neighborhood much better. We were near the schools and Hortense had some little friends her own age next door to go with her. They had happy times together coasting downhill, sleigh riding over the city, the merry hundreds of them. Sleigh bells resounded from every side day and night. Dainty little baskets and pretty shallops dashed along with their lovely children in furs and caps of down. Then larger sleighs filled with larger boys and girls, a half dozen couples, singing gaily as they skimmed over the smooth surface.

We had lived a year on Lincoln Street and were being crowded out again by business blocks. A large, three-story cold storage building loomed up at our front door and shut off our nice view. Some of our neighbors moved away, and we thought of going to Pend Orielle Lake in northern Idaho. I was sorry to leave my neighbors. There were some lovely children near us of whom I was very fond. I always liked children and usually had some pets in my circle of juveniles.

I heard a child crying at my gate one day at noon. I went to investigate and found a little tot of three summers. I said, "Why do you cry, little girl?" She said in her baby way, "I tant find my home and I tant find my mamma." I told her I would go with her to find her home if she would not cry. I got my hat and then told her to hold fast to my hand, and we would find her home. The streets were full of teams dashing in every direction, and it was rather dangerous to cross. I told her to lead me, as I thought her baby knowledge would direct her aright. I had no idea which way to go as we passed block after block. I would say, "Is that mamma's house?"

"No. No." At last she saw her home across and on the corner of the next street. She cried out, "Dat's my house," and ran to it. Dear little babe had been playing with other children and wandered away into a strange neighborhood and was lost from mamma and home. She was a doctor's little daughter but could not speak plainly enough to tell his name and couldn't find her home and wailed for mamma.

During the summer vacation, Hortense made a visit to Bess in her new home. How pleased she was when told she could go alone. She felt quite grown up to go on a journey all by herself. The train for Coeur d'Alene City left at five o'clock to make connections with the lake steamers for the mines. I went with her to the station and saw her off, wishing her bon voyage. It was a ride of one and one-fourth hours through a lovely valley, and Bess would meet her at the station. It was her first trip off, and I felt quite lonely without her. Next day brought a note saying she arrived all right.

The weather being intensely hot, I was glad to have her out of the city. There was a great deal of sickness and many deaths. So many children died. The hospital was crowded with fever patients. It was a large, three-story building and could not accommodate all who asked for admittance. An addition was built on as large as the main building and was soon in use. The city was becoming very sickly, occasioned by the bad water. The outlet of the lake was not pure. The smelters were at the headwater of the lake and minerals poisoned the water.

This was Hortense and my first spearation and two weeks seemed a long absence. I enjoyed her letters very much. She wrote of nice times at the lake and her visit to Camp Sherman with Bess to see the soldiers on dress parade. They also saw the little chapel and school house under the pine trees where they had gone to school.

Colonel Wheaton had been promoted, and Colonel Carlin was in command, a kindly disposed officer, very social toward civilians. The dear old lake was just as blue and beautiful as when Hortense lived there as a little child. One day I received glad tidings. She was coming home, and Bess and big Brother were coming with her. Sells Grand Circus and Fore Paws Menagerie were to be in the city on the sixth, and Bess was coming to see the elephant and hear the caliopes too. We were glad they were to come down with her as she came at night. I went to the station to meet them, but the train was late. I waited. At last we heard a train. On the platform, I met the conductor of the Coeur d'Alene train. He knew me and asked if I was looking for my daughters. I said yes, almost afraid to hear his reply, for why was he there? Where was his train? He told me his train had met with an accident. They had to stop at the junction and the Northern picked them up. "Our train is behind the Northern. Go back and you will find the girls all right." I ran the length of that long train, and the girls had gone home and were coming back to meet me. I rejoiced to see them safe. Their locomotive had been disabled. No one was hurt, however.

We had a lovely visit with Bess and Roy, and the great show arrived six hours late. It had met with an accident on Northern Pacific Railroad and been detained, and everybody was anxiously awaiting the circus parade which was indeed a wonderful display. Ten bands of music, two caliopes, hundreds of animals and a long line of chariots. There were cute little Shetland ponies, beautiful Arab horses, elephants, lions, camels and all kinds of caged animals. The small boys had a glorious time. Is there anything more to a boy's complete happiness than a full-fledged circus? After the circus, men had all got drunk and engaged in a general row, as is usual on such occasions. The weary beasts were hurried on board the train and departed at midnight.

Bess and Roy spent a day or two looking over the magic city, then said goodbye and hied away to their cozy home by the lake. We settled down to everyday life. The whir and bang of the saw and hammer and click-click of the drill were heard on every hand. Building and grading were rapidly carried on. Some heavy blasting in many places was necessary. I was going down Post Street one day, and I heard someone call out, "Get out of the way there!" I ran as others did into a building near by and none too soon. Bang! Bang! And down came the stone rattling on the roof. I seemed doomed to encounter blasts even here in the city.

A fire alarm. The cry of *Fire* rang out on the night wind. Fire! Fire! And we saw the planing mills on the avenue were in flames. The departments were soon at the scene and extinguished the devastating element. This fire had a tragedy to follow it. There was a large vat full of boiling water in connection with the machinery which was on the outside of the mill and on a level with the sidewalk. The frame around the vat had been demolished by the fire, leaving it exposed. Sawdust and shavings had settled over it. Late in the evening, a little boy unconsciously walked into the vat of scalding water. A man who was near instantly snatched him out. He called for his mother, knowing full well he would die, but wanted first to see his mother. He told a little friend who came to him to run for his mother, and he would give him twenty dollars. She arrived to see him. His last words were, "Mamma, give Ned twenty dollars." He was an only child, the idol of his mother's heart, a noble-hearted little boy, as his last words testified.

Chapter 19

# Off to Idaho Again
# 1889

T HE WINTER had been a cold one. Spring came to cheer us once more. The buttercups were blooming on the sunny hillsides. Many changes were being made. We accepted a position with the Northern Pacific Railroad at the great lake Pend Oreille and would soon bid goodbye to the city with its noise and sickness.

Hortense was now twelve years old, quite a large girl. She had been almost constantly in school for three years and needed a rest. Husband came home one evening and said he would go next day to his position at the lake. We would soon go. We hurriedly packed up as we were anxious for a journey. Early one morning in March, we stepped into a lovely coach of a Northern Pacific train and went for a spring and summer outing.

We passed through some very nice country. After leaving Rathdrum, we went over a route new to us. We passed the logging camp which belonged to the railroad company. Millions of feet of fine logs were cut and sent by train to Spokane mills to be sawed into lumber. Soon we saw the granite quarries where the fine stones were obtained which were used in constructing those fireproof blocks in Spokane. After some hours, we saw the company's ice houses at Cocolalo Lake where tons of ice were stored every winter. Then the great train of living freight went thundering on, around crags and across canyons till Sand Point was reached. There on the lake shore, the company got the sand which was shipped to various points to be used on the track.

What stores of wealth Nature has bestowed along this line for those enterprising men who had courage to build a railroad through this wild expanse of country composed of mountains, lakes, rivers, canyons and heavy forest.

At sunset we reached our new home, the lake, where we were to spend a few months at least. We had been running up the lake for

171

*"We watched the train as it left our door and approached the mile and a half long bridge which spans an arm of the lake."*

some hours and, at this point, it widened to a grand size. We saw steamers in the distance as we stepped upon the long verandah of our new home and looked out upon the broad expanse of blue water spread out from our door as far as we could see. It was surpassingly beautiful; the great mountains reaching skyward from the water's brink. We were enraptured with this scene away off from the busy world.

We watched the train as it left our door and approached the mile-and-a-half-long bridge which spans an arm of the lake. Oh, what a grand structure thirty feet above the water. The immense locomotive and long train went whirling and roaring over the high trestle causing it to sink and sway under the great weight till I feared it would go down, but on they went. We could see them running up the lake shore five miles to Hope where they were met by the Rocky Mountain division. We fain would linger and gaze longer, but we would also like to see our mansion.

We first entered a large room and looked about us. The ceiling was very high, so high that we felt lost in space. There were other rooms, but none so immense. We could be comfortable here, at least, and have room to spare and more scenery than our eyes could devour in a year. Our freight was all here. Next morning we were up early.

Husband must go to his place of business. A man asked for work and something to eat. We employed him. He assisted us to unpack and settle in our great room first. We had no very near neighbors. The family who lived nearest us had spent the winter in Spokane and had not returned to their summer home yet. Our help worked with a will, but I did not like to see him about his work armed as if he was ready for combat at any moment. I was very anxious about him, fearing he was a burglar or a convict. I was quite suspicious of him and felt nervous if he came near us while about his work. When husband came home, I told him I feared the man as he had the countenance of a thief. He said he would not leave us alone with him again. He stayed two days, performed his work well, and seemed anxious to please us. After he was gone, word came that he was a convict, a very bad man.

We were soon settled and delighted with the change for the summer. It was a cozy cool retreat, and we soon ascertained it was a grand summer resort. Many tourists came here from the East to fish. We soon had company. Our neighbor family came home from Spokane. Hortense was pleased to see a young miss her own age. They were soon fast friends and had merry times rambling over the hillsides, culling wild flowers, searching by the shore for ferns, then rowing over the grand old lake. This was all a glorious change from the dust, heat and tumult of the city.

Hortense soon became an expert at rowing and would take me out for a glide over the water occasionally. This lake was like the Coeur d'Alene lake, deep and treacherous. Lead and line had been dropped 26 feet and no bottom reached.

Hortense and her friend Jess rode horseback after the cows. Jess had a brother ten years old, a nice pleasant boy. They were glad when Ned could go with them on walks, rides or out rowing. The girls were afraid of Indians and Ned was not at all. He went hunting and fishing with them, much to the displeasure of his fair companions. We were out walking one afternoon and had left the girls and

Ned at our house. We soon heard them calling to us. We then heard a strange voice crying out in cross, threatening words. On coming near, we saw three Indians approaching the door where the children were standing calling to us. The Indians were drunk and had been in a row with others in a canoe on the lake, who were abusing those on land, telling them they would kill them.

The three at the door walked up to Ned to shake hands. They were glad to see him as they were old friends. They insisted on shaking hands with the girls also, much to their dismay. We often saw Indians at the lake. They came there to fish. We were often frightened by them too, as they were wild, savage-looking fellows up there in the mountains and always armed.

We planned a camping trip up the river. How lovely is everything in nature. We were camped on a grassy plot at the foot of an immense mountain. Far, far away we could see the Rockies which we crossed forty years ago on our way to Oregon. The evening was calm and peaceful. No human abode near us. The bear, deer and cougar roamed around us. Lovely songsters were heard overhead as they sought shelter for the night in the topmost branches of the great forest trees. Then, in the distance, we heard the tinkle of a bell. Some Indian pony wore that and had wandered far from its herd. Our campfire reflected ghost-like shadows.

Night drew her sable curtains earthward, and slowly we saw the myriads of brilliant stars step forth and take positions as it were for the night. An owl on a crag far above our heads hooted his melancholy screech, and a whippoorwill was heard in the heather beyond. The little cuckoo bird, not to be outdone, kept up a continued cuckooing long after all reasonable birds had bid goodnight. Then we heard a wild cat's cry as it came near our camp, lured by the smell of roasting meat or boiled fish. It was late when we retired. Our tent was cozy and we were in dreamland very soon.

However, we were soon aroused by the fierce barking of our dog. Husband rose and brightened up the fire as some wild beast was surely near us. Then we heard a bear clambering about on the mountain almost over our heads. We feared it would loosen a stone and send it rolling down over our tent. At dawn, husband took his gun and dog and went to a stand half a mile away to shoot a deer as it came to drink. (Seems cruel.) Hortense and I were nervous to be alone, and we were glad when we heard a shot, hoping he would soon return. And he did. We were glad the deer escaped. We ate breakfast, then went rowing down the river several miles and across the lake to our home.

We had been at Pend Oreille a month when Hortense met with an accident. She had been out rowing on the lake, and in attempting to land, she missed the wharf when she thought to jump ashore. Her shoe heel caught in the rim of the boat and threw her headlong on the shore. She fell on her elbow and dislocated the joint, sprained her ankle, knocked a tooth loose and twisted her left thumb. The passenger train to Spokane had just passed. There was no doctor near us. We tried to set the joint of the arm, made her as comfortable as possible and got ready to board the first train to Spokane. A local freight was due in an hour which carried passengers. We waited many hours, but no train arrived from the east. Only a local from the west. We were sure there had been a train accident.

Four o'clock the next evening, we saw a passenger train coming down the lake bound for Spokane. We flagged it, and it stopped to take us on board. We learned a bridge had been burned, which had caused the delay of a day and a night. Seeing Hortense was in need of a physician at once, dispatches were sent ahead from the first station by the kind-hearted conductor. We had the best of attention and everything possible was done to alleviate the pain which had become very severe. Her arm was badly swollen. She suffered intensely but bore it bravely.

We reached Spokane at eleven and a coach was ready to convey us to brother Frank's home. We sent for a doctor, and before midnight the arm was in splints and feeling much better. The doctor hoped she would sleep. He feared the arm was fractured and said she would need to stay in the city two weeks.

The girls planned a May Day picnic across the lake. They must go to Garfield Bay, Jess said. Ned said he just could not go, for if he did the sheep and horses and cows would be sure to get on the track around the bend and be killed. It was his work to herd them away from the tracks. His fine mules and several cows and sheep had been killed, and he feared others would be if left alone all day.

Lunches had been prepared. The girls were ready to go quite early. Husband was to go with us in the big row boat. We started for the long pull of four miles across the arm of the lake to Garfield Bay. The girls sang "A Life on the Ocean Wave." Not a ripple disturbed the waters. We had a jolly ride and landed at the foot of a rugged mountain where great old trees drooped their arms near the earth and cast a lovely shade all around. A fine place for our picnic. The lunch baskets, rugs and cushions were all carried ashore. We built a fire, made tea, boiled eggs and fried fish. Jess said we must catch fish at a lake-side picnic, because we could see them darting about in the water at our camp door.

We could see the bay to our left. It was a lovely stretch of smooth blue, almost hemmed in by tall green mountains. We did not care to go on the bay, so husband went fishing alone. We could see him some distance, then he went out of our sight around a point to Battle Bay. The girls ran about quite merrily for some time getting ferns and flowers to make wreaths. After weaving their garlands and crowning each other queens, they insisted on crowning me, saying I was the mother queen. Then we heard a brush snap as if some animal had stepped on it. We looked about and imagined we could see a bear on the hill above us and hear it growling. We called to husband. He did not answer. Then we fairly yelled for him and rejoiced to hear oars and splashes. He soon came in sight around the bend, pulling for dear life. He feared one of us had fallen into the lake and were calling for help. He was amused when we told him we were afraid of bears. He wanted to know where they were. We said, "We have not seen them, only feared we would."

After he rested a while, the cargo was taken on board and we set out on the homeward pull. We were alarmed to see a few ripples disturbing the quiet lake and how we did wish we were at home. We could see the green hill and our houses across the deep waters, but they did seem a long way off. The girls sang "Homeward Bound," and I sat at the rudder with an anxious heart, for a strong breeze had set waves rolling and our boat was leaking so rapidly that we deemed it necessary to bail out the water quite often. We pulled for the nearest point of land on the home shore and soon reached shallow water. We were not afraid now as we could see the water was very shallow, and we could get ashore very easily.

Now we were near the landing and the girls sang "Home Again from a Foreign Shore" and Ned was there to help us up the hill, and we were safe in our homes once more.

*Frances Hortense at sixteen*   *Frances H. Masterson*

# Chapter 20

# A Visitor

WHEN PASSENGER TRAIN No. 2 stopped at our place one pleasant evening in June, two passengers stepped down and walked toward our door. One was a venerable-looking old gentleman dressed as an eastern well-to-do farmer whose long white beard and noble bearing attracted our attention at once; the other, a tall handsome young girl of perhaps twenty summers. She was pale and sad of countenance drawing every heart toward her. She leaned on the old gentleman as they walked to the door. They introduced themselves. We asked them to be seated and assisted her in removing her wraps, then led her gently to a couch and told her to rest. The father explained that he had come there with his invalid daughter hoping the pure mountain air would restore her shattered health. She seemed to be in the last stage of consumption. When they asked to stay, we gladly gave them a home. In a few days the father, seeing how tenderly Laura was cared for, said he would go away for a week, as important business called him. The girls searched for the sweetest berries and the prettiest flowers for her. They sang and played for her. They read and talked to her, and she was so pleased with her surroundings and seemed so much better that she asked to go walking to the lake, then out rowing. When her father returned, he was delighted to see her so improved and asked for her to stay longer. We told him we claimed Laura as our daughter and wanted her to stay all summer.

The girls called her sister. She was soon strong enough to ramble over the hills with them. Health brought a rosy hue to her cheeks, and we saw a beautiful, queenly young lady instead of a pale invalid. We found her to be a fine scholar from an eastern college. She sent for her pony and was soon charging over the sandy beach or running races with the dusky braves, much to their wild delight. She was a fine equestriene. The old man rejoiced to see his Laura romping about once more and wrote to her mother and sisters in their far away eastern home about the wonderful change. They could scarcely realize that Laura was strong enough to take walks over hills and go horseback riding.

A letter came saying Bess and her little babe were coming to see us. The day of Bess' arrival rolled around. We anxiously awaited the local train which was to bring her and that precious baby. A long shrill whistle, then three toots, saying the train was to stop. We saw a tall lady walking toward us carrying a babe in her arms. We ran to her and folded mother and child in our embrace, for we loved Bess and baby too. Oh, the sweet bright-eyed darling! We almost smothered it with caresses while it looked with wondering eyes at the new surroundings. They were to stay two weeks and Roy would come after them. Happy two weeks. Bess was pleased to see us all and to be at home once more. She admired the lovely scenery. The mountains are so much higher and the lake so much larger than Coeur d'Alene and the mountains there. She left baby with me and strolled over hills with the girls and went sailing and rowing and had a joyous time. An old friend was stopping with us who was a good sailor, and he delighted to have them go with him and laughed heartily when they became timid if the wind blew.

The local was late one evening, and when it arrived, Roy was a passenger. He spent several days with us and enjoyed the fishing and hunting and the rest from business. Their visit being over, Bess and Roy prepared to go and we said goodbye to them and baby.

Our summer by the lake had surely passed. There was frost in the air. The pretty flowers were were all gone. The hay on the beach was all ready to be shipped. The crowds of people who came to spend the hot months were departing for their Eastern homes.

We heard happy voices one fine day in late summertime, and on looking lakeward, we saw a pretty little sail boat speeding before the breeze. We heard later it was the Vanderbilt party who had come to this lovely summer resort and were enjoying a sail on the grand old lake of the mountains. Many others from far away Eastern homes spent the hot summer months here.

The sweet summer was gone, and Laura said she was so well now she thought of going home. Her father was very anxious to have her go before the winter storms set in. She loved the old mountains and the lake and hesitated, often saying, "Let me stay a little longer, Father. We can soon go home." Her mother waited to see her.

Laura's trunk was packed. All things were ready for her departure. How we would miss her. She asked to come to us again, and we were glad to even hope to see her come back. "Yes, yes!" we all said. "Do come again." We had an evening entertainment before she left us and had a gay time. Laura herself seemed to be the joy of the happy company. They all said goodbye to her and wished her bon voyage.

The early passenger stopped while it was yet dark. The lights flashed around about, and the cross porter tumbled the trunk on board. We said goodbye. "All aboard!," called out a sharp voice, and they were hurrying away.

We were lonely now. The great room we found too large for cold weather. We kept the stove glowing hot and yet ice formed in our vases. We feared our lovely houseplants would freeze, and they were such a comfort. Winter was fast approaching. We did not fancy the idea of staying here during the long cold season. The scene had changed. Autumn was lovely in its varied hues of gold and red and russet brown. Hunters and trappers now took the place of tourists, and the days grew short and crisp. The great trains sped by over the frozen rails, roaring like thunder or a mighty tramp of cavalry.

One morning, a long freight had run on the side track in front of our door. The train was an immense one, too long for the side track. The overland passenger from the east was seen coming. The freight ran back on the main line to let the passenger come on, and then slowly moved up till each was safe. I was watching the approaching train and was shocked to see it did not check its speed as it came off the bridge. I instantly saw there would be a wreck. On it came at full speed, crashing into the freight as it stood partly on the main line and knocking some flats, box cars and the caboose down an embankment. The locomotive tender and baggage car of the passenger train tore up a long piece of the track and created a panic among the passengers. In a moment's time, hundreds were out looking about them to see what had happened. Fortunately no one was killed or seriously injured. The air brakes were not adjusted on the passenger before leaving Hope; hence, the accident.

All day long we had company enough. How they enjoyed rowing on the lake and rambling over the hills while waiting to be transferred. They thought the mountains grew tall out west, as the trees also did. Some were foreigners and marveled at the wonders of the great West. They were very much surprised to see steamboats away off here on the lake, so far away from New York—the only place in America they had ever heard of in the old country.

At five o'clock the passengers were transferred. A temporary line had been laid to move them and their baggage. All night and the next day a gang of men worked steadily to get the track ready for the many trains which were waiting to pass, going east and west. We were glad when we saw the passengers coming down from Hope and things moving on in the same old channel.

The wild goose croaked farewell as it flew high, going south to spend the winter. Then we witnessed a storm on the lake. Hortense was spending the afternoon with Jess. I was alarmed when a strong gale struck the house. I looked out and saw a black cloud hanging over the lake. The breakers were beginning to roll. A low rumbling was heard, then another sounded over the deep water. The sky was overcast with darkness and the wind blew. Electric bolts shot seemingly into the turbulent deep which had now become a rolling mass of whitecaps. I stood at my casement alone and viewed it all in its grandeur. Husband was on the high trestle. I could see him coming and feared for his safety as the wind was now a terrific gale. I could hear trees crashing down on the hill near Jess's house. I could see someone in the breakers struggling for life. Now they rose, now sunk again. No help could go to them. At last husband, who had almost crawled across the high bridge, arrived. He was safe. After the storm ceased, Jess and Hortense came in all excited, saying a tree had fallen on the house, but no one was hurt.

# Chapter 21

# A Trip to the City

HORTENSE AND I were on our way to Spokane one day. We did not wish to go on the early passenger train so we boarded a later freight which would arrive in Spokane during the afternoon. There were two other passengers on board; one was a gentleman on his way to the granite quarry and the other an Italian (a land pirate if there was one on earth). He had a seat in front of us. I noticed him as we entered. He turned and gave us a scowling look from his black snakish eye, then settled himself as before. We were going at lightning speed on a downgrade, passing some grand scenery. The gentleman went to the lookout on top of the car with the conductor.

Soon after they left us, the "pirate" gave us another staring, searching gaze from his black orbs. He was a dark, vicious-looking person. I told Hortense in mute language that I feared he meant to rob us. We were going to the city shopping and each carried a small handbag containing our money. We were in the car alone with him. The train was long and tearing along at breakneck speed, and if he did attempt to molest us, no one could hear our cry for help. We knew we were in the power of a villian. The train slackened speed. It stopped. The pirate left the car. We hoped he had gone and felt relieved. Imagine our terror when we saw him peeping at us through the half-open door. When he saw me watching him, he moved quickly away. A brakeman came in, and I spoke to him about the dark man. He said he would be on the watch for him as he was a bad-looking fellow. We had started on our way. The gentleman had come in, and we now felt safe. We halted again. Before the train had fairly stopped, the "pirate" rushed out and jumped off and went running away into the deep forest. We all had a talk about him and concluded he was an escaped convict.

We spent a few days in the city. It was a wreck of its former self. We saw the ruins of the great fire. The charred piles of the many

181

homes were scattered about. We were lost in the debris. With the landmarks gone, we were strangers in our old home.

We were glad to return to our icebound lake shore. The holidays were near. Husband took a run down to Spokane Falls to lay in supplies and get Christmas presents. The snow was deep now and icicles hung to the wall. We had stored our house plants in a warm cozy corner to rest till the winter had gone by, and how we missed them.

The girls were preparing for the holidays. Ned had made some nice sleds, and they all went coasting. They invented many ways to divert themselves. No more rowing now. Too cold and bleak out on the stormy old lake.

We took much interest in watching the long trains pass by our door. The faces of the engineers and conductors were now familiar as they went whirling on toward the city every day. Others, who were eastward bound, often threw a bundle of late papers and magazines at our door as they rolled on. We eagerly gathered them up and read them all.

Many times I watched the sturdy engineers as they sat at their posts in the dark nights of winter, their eyes set on the watch for danger. Talk about brave men in battle. I hold that those brave railroad men, who ran on overland trains during the winter nights through mountain gorges, dark forests, rivers, canyons and lakes, were the bravest men on earth. The tracks were covered with snow and ice. The lives of thousands were at their mercy, and we seldom heard of an accident. They had so many obstacles to encounter. Snow plows and flangers and rotary plows kept the track scraped clear, or in a measure so; but there were bridges, stones, fallen trees, broken rails, rotted ties and so many things to cause accidents. They were brave and courageous men and should be reckoned as of next importance to our standing army.

The holidays were observed by all in our little neighborhood. We partook of a fine Christmas dinner with a dear friend and neighbor of whom we were very fond. They were far from their childhood homes. The lady was English. Her home was in London.

Winter was passing away. Some splendid northern swans came to stay near us. We often saw them swimming on the lake. They croaked a doleful cry, not musical at all. The swan sings his sweetest song just before he dies, according to an old saying.

February 1889, was here, the month of Jess' and Hortense' birthdays. They were the same age, or nearly so. I baked them a large cake and put thirteen small candles on it as that was their age. They

*"One evening just after dark a carpenter of the gang borrowed my husband's velocipede and started to Hope."*

met in our large room with all the neighbors and spent the evening playing games, telling stories and watching the night trains as they passed by. Then all said goodnight. Some went home in boats, others on velocipedes and some on foot through the deep snow.

February was a changeable month. The snow was melting. The sun shone brightly. Carpenters arrived. They had much work to do on the high trestle. The winter had almost demolished it. There was great danger now when heavy trains were crossing.

One evening just after dark, a carpenter of the gang borrowed my husband's velocipede and started to Hope. As he was crossing the high trestle, a long freight train dashed by our door following him. Instantly, we all ran out to try to see if he got run over. He carried no light, and they could not see him till almost upon him. Fortunately, he heard the train in time to jump and save his life. As he jumped from the velocipede, the breeze from the train struck him. He fell on the snow twenty feet below. The velocipede was knocked to pieces and went tumbling after him.

I watched the train for a mile or more. I could see that it had stopped. I saw lights moving along on the snow under the bridge, and we feared the man was killed. The lights then returned to the train, and it proceeded on its way. After an hour or so, he walked in, much to our delight. He was bruised and stunned by the fall, but no bones broken. The water being very low in the winter, the beach along the lake was frozen solid, and the snow had covered it over deep, soft and white.

# Chapter 22

# We Move to Coeur d'Alene

HORTENSE WAS WISHING TO BE IN SCHOOL. We planned to go to Coeur d'Alene to see Bess and be convenient to school. Our stay by the lake had extended through summer and winter. We would go to Bess and stay till school closed. Our neighbors were going away, and it would be too lonely here for us any longer. It is a lovely summer resort and a fine healthy place, but we were soon ready to be off. Were folks ever so glad to get out of the wilderness?

We boarded the early passenger train to Coeur d'Alene. The weather was cold and the snow deep. We ran down to Sand Point, then on toward Granite, Cocolalo and Rathdrum. Soon after leaving Sand Point, we were met by a windstorm which banked the snow deep on the tracks. As the road lay around a steep mountain, the snow drifted down faster than the men could shovel it off, and we could not move a foot. A flagman was sent back to warn the other trains coming behind us. The snow was so blinding that the next train failed to see the flag and ran up to us before halting. Fortunately, it also stuck in the snow or there would have been a terrible wreck. After shoveling snow for hours, then dividing the train, the old "loco" pulled us through. We called on the following train for help, but we received no aid as the engineers were at variance. We reached Hansen, and there we wished to go on the junction to Coeur d'Alene. The road was blocked, and we proceeded to Spokane and then went from there on the Coeur d'Alene train. We started out with two locomotives, a snow plow and forty men to shovel snow. The train was crowded to suffocation. The night was the coldest I ever experienced, being 36 degrees below zero. We spent four hours going 30 miles and got there at midnight. Roy met us, and we were soon in Bess's cozy house, but we nearly froze to death getting there. The weather continued cold some days. After the storm was over, Hortense entered school and was well pleased with her new teacher.

We left husband at the lake to look after our affairs there. We had preceded him for once to a new home. He wrote that the weather there was extremely cold, being yet farther north than Coeur d'Alene Lake. When we left the Pend Oreille, there was but little ice. We had been in Coeur d'Alene only a few days when the lake afforded fine skating and wagons and teams crossed on the ice.

Hortense had gone with some friends to Camp Sherman one evening to attend the theater. I was rather anxious about her as the weather was very cold. During my anxiety I heard the clang clang of the fire bell. We saw at once the fire was at the Post a mile away. I said, "I do believe it is the theater." Bess and Roy tried to console me by saying it was too far to one side of the parade grounds to be. They thought it was the guard house. The fire was soon subdued, and all was quiet again. When Hortense came home, she told us about the fire alarm and said it really was the theater. There came near being a panic, but strict military discipline kept the people under control. Some jumped from the windows, and all arose to leave. The officers of the day commanded them to be seated and remain there as there was no danger yet, and if there should be, he would march them down stairs safely. They obeyed him and no one was hurt. They sat quietly and watched the play through. A flue had burned out and did no harm.

How glad we were to see the ice clear out of the lake and the snow melt away. Soon the buttercups and spring flowers came to brighten hill and dale after a long cold winter. Soon the days were pleasant and many little boats could be seen sliding over the waters filled with happy people. Excursions were planned and great crowds went on steamers to haunts above the lake shore.

Roy and Bess insisted on taking Hortense with them on excursion one afternoon. I consented and watched the little steamer bearing the happy crowd as it sped away off up the lake and around a point to Beauty Bay where they were going ashore. Wild flowers grew in profusion there. They stepped from the steamer onto a great old log which extended from the shore to the boat. As Hortense attempted to go ashore, she slipped and fell into the lake and received a very cold and unexpected bath, much to her displeasure and dismay of others.

And now husband wished me to return to Pend Oreille to make a last visit before our final departure. We were to leave Idaho. He had decided to go to Grays Harbor. I made a flying trip, stayed a few days and returned by way of Spokane to visit relatives and old friends there. The days were very warm now in May. When I bade adieu to brother Frank's family, I walked to the station as I wished to do some shopping on my way. Arriving at the station, I stepped to the office to get my ticket and was told the train for Coeur d'Alene would start from Howard Street. It was near train time. I hurried forward and became very much exhausted and was near falling from sunstroke. I was assisted on board and, with proper restorative, I soon revived. There were several passengers on the little train going for an outing by the cool lake shore. There was also an old lady who resided in Coeur d'Alene City. She had been down to meet her boy whom she expected from the East. As she passed the junction, she was told he had gone on to Spokane. When she got to Spokane, she was told he had gone back to the junction. He was her only child, a boy of twelve. Her anxiety for him was distressing to witness. She feared he had met with misfortunes in some way as he was traveling alone. Everyone hoped she would find him at the junction. Before we reached that station, she was on top of the car in the lookout trying to see him. When the whistle blew to stop, she clambered down hurriedly and before the train had stopped she tried to get off to search for him. While she was on the platform trying to find him, a nice looking boy carrying a bundle and lunch basket stepped into the car from the other side. I saw him immediately and asked him if he was Jim McLooney. He said, "Yes, Ma'am." I called to her saying Jim was on board. She heard me and came quickly.

The meeting of that mother and child was the most affecting and loving I ever witnessed. There were few dry eyes on that car. The dear child! He had to remain in the East till his widowed mother could earn money to send for him. She would clasp him in her arms and say, "Jim, you shall never be parted from me again till death parts us. Oh, my dear boy, my own dear poor little Jim. Did you get hungry, my child, on the long road?" When he told her the passengers were very good to him all the way through, she called down a blessing from heaven over them and prayed they would never be hungry or friendless. "Now, Jimmie, my boy, I have a nice home for you. We will be happy there, Jim, in a new country. We will live near a great lake, and you shall have a boat and go fishing. Oh, Jimmie, my boy, I am so glad you are here."

# Chapter 23

# On to Washington

I N A FEW DAYS, husband came and we prepared to go to Puget Sound. This time, he went first and failed to get the position he expected in Tacoma. He went to Grays Harbor down near the sea and wrote for us to come at once. We did not like to leave Bess and her family. Would we ever meet again?

We sent our household goods forward, then went by way of Spokane and took the Northern Pacific for Tacoma. It was near four hundred miles. We had to travel all night. We passed through the Cascade Mountains this time and not over them as I had often done before. We hoped to pass through the tunnel during the day, as we wished to see the mountains on either side, but we did not see them. We arrived in Tacoma early next morning and were sadly disappointed when told the steamer for Grays Harbor had already started out. We then boarded a street car and ran up to a hotel. We stayed for a few days looking over the city which was beautifully situated on terrace after terrace till the upper portion was on a mountain. It was very wonderful to see the electric cars climb the hills. We ascended to Washing (sic) College and had a lovely view of the Harbor and could see many ships at anchor. Some very large ocean steamers were in port. One from Alaska, I remember. I think it was the Ocean Queen. I saw about twenty in port, some from South America, loading with lumber. We boarded the Multnomah with many others who were on their way to the new Eldorado. We had a very pleasant run down the Sound. We stopped at Olympia, the capital of Washington, thence on to a little port where we were all transferred to the most insignificant little train of cars it was ever my misfortune to look upon. However, we were jostled along a few miles through the woods till we reached Moutesance, a lovely little burg on the Chehalis river at the head of tide.

It was plain to be seen the town was in a boom. We stopped at the principal hotel of the place where husband was boarding. After searching for three days, we secured a cottage and set up housekeeping once more.

We were very much displeased with the place but tried to be reconciled. We had some excellent neighbors, and their four cultured daughters were pleasant company for Hortense. They called to have her go with them to church, Sabbath school and to picnics. She soon became interested and felt at home. The eldest daughter was a fine music teacher. Hortense was at once installed as a pupil. The father and mother were from the sunny South. Their three sons were the pride of the happy home. We could endure our dislike for the place with such lovely neighbors near us.

Husband had a place of business and hoped to do well, although indications for a collapse were plainly visible. Booms are ruinous to any place and surely would be to this one. He went with a party of excursionists down to the beach one day and had much to tell us about on his return. The ocean was calm, and he saw some steamers on their way to Seattle. He saw one whale spouting, and one was dead on the beach. The Indians were having a feast. "Great Spirit was well pleased with his children and had sent them a whale," the chief said.

Hortense came in one day in wild delight. She had just received a letter from Laura saying she was sick and asking if we thought the coast a good place for an invalid. We did, of course, and sent an invitation to her to come immediately. When she arrived, she was a shadow of the rosy-cheeked happy girl who left us ten months ago. I feared this time death had set his seal on that fair brow. We petted and nurtured her. A week, then two weeks passed. She was still pale and feeble. Before the third one was gone, she said she was rested now and felt stronger, and we rejoiced as we were so anxious about her. Then she went out walking. Gradually she improved. Then we saw our Laura once more.

The nicest books were hers to read. Her hammock hung in the coolest and most shady places. When, later on, she saw Hortense and the girls going to school, she wanted to go too. After some coaxing, we permitted her to go to the academy and have a talk with the professor. He feared she was not strong enough as yet to tax her mind with study. He offered to give her instruction in one or two branches and left the choice to her decision. She took up Latin and was to go every day to recite. She made rapid progress in her studies and was now a happy schoolgirl once more.

Autumn passed. The winter was approaching. The girls went in search of autumn leaves and took long walks. Laura tripped along as lively as any of them, much to their delight. A friend offered a pony that she might ride. She was so pleased and went away out into the country two or three miles and stayed so long we became alarmed. When she returned, she laughed as she dismounted and said, "I just wanted to keep going. I had such a nice ride."

What a joyous time they all had preparing for the holidays. So much whispering as suspicious looking bundles were brought in and hurriedly secreted. To make the day more precious, it was Laura's birthday and we must each give her some little token in memory of that too. Then the Christmas tree at the church for the little tots, that was fun too. We rested a few days and were greeted by a storm of great severity. The wind was blowing a perfect gale. Trees were falling by hundreds. Even houses were threatened. We heard a crash and our house swayed and receded. It was night and the darkness was more appalling when linked with danger. We all jumped from our beds. The house was surely going over. Oh! Oh! Let us get out! The rain came down in torrents. Husband said we would be drenched, and the wind might blow us away. He tried to console us. I could endure it no longer. I ran downstairs and found a door blown open. Then I feared to venture out and went back and tried to calm myself. As day was now approaching, we could see the sad havoc. Trees, barns and fences laid low, but no houses demolished in our neighborhood. After the storm was over, Hortense wrote about it to an Eastern paper, as it was so dreadful. She received a reprimand for comparing it to an Eastern storm in severity.

Laura received an invitation from a millionare cousin in Tacoma to go and make her home with them for a time. She had often told us about that cousin, and now she was to make a visit to her magnificent home. We assisted her with preparing an elaborate wardrobe telling her we could only permit her to go on a visit and not to stay.

One snowy morning in February, we said goodbye to her. In a few hours she would be at her cousins. She wrote to tell us of the splendor and that she would much rather be with us. The style of such wealth was irksome. They kept late hours. Fashionable balls and theaters soon brushed the hue of health from her cheeks. She tired of it all and left them. She went to the home of another relative who lived more in the bounds of reason and then off to the beach. And there we leave her.

With the winter over, we hoped for better times. But alas the boom was a thing of the past. Times were fearfully dull; no business, no life. Even the ocean steamers were seldom seen in port. We were discouraged and knew not what to do. Many went away hoping to better their condition. We spent another summer there. The schools were very good. The people took an interest in education. Excursion parties to the beach and picnics in the woods kept up some excitement.

I was quite busy in my kitchen one morning when I heard a conveyance drive up to my gate and stop. I looked out to see who had called and was shocked to see a man assisting my husband to our door. I ran out to know what had happened, as he had just left home as well as usual. He was suffering intensely, evidently struck down helpless with inflammatory rheumatism. We got him to a couch and I quickly went for a doctor. He came with a battery and tried to relieve him, but only made him worse. At last, he slowly recovered.

Later on while out hunting birds, he fell through a bridge and sustained a severe injury. Before he was well, he had another misfortune when a horse kicked him and fractured two ribs. He was never well after that. He became discouraged and went to Centralia, a railroad town in Chehalis County.

Misfortune never comes singly. Hortense was now sick and could not attend school. Our dear neighbors were so kind to us. They came and sat with her nights and let me sleep and rest. They sent flowers and books and did many things to cheer her. How glad I was to see her well once more.

Now summer was gone and we were to go away too. Husband wrote that he had a position. We must leave those dear friends and go find others. After many days, we were ready to say goodbye. How we did miss husband.

We must go in a few days. A little girl came in and said their baby was very sick. I went to see it and stayed some hours as Hortense was away with the girls. When at a late hour I returned, she was yet absent. I went to our neighbors, and they had not returned. She had gone with them. I could hear them at the Hall loudly cheering a political meeting where ladies could go. How nice it will be when women can help make our laws. Now I heard them coming. They were saying, "I wonder if your mama has got back yet." I called to them and said, "Yes, long ago and tired of waiting."

Next day, we sent our freight to the station to be shipped. The distance was short, only forty miles. We went direct by rail. Our last evening in the harbor town was made pleasant by a family concert at our dear neighbors. They were a musical family and favored us with some lovely songs and sweet selections of music. We went on an early train. Many friends were there to see us off. The parting was a sad one.

We passed some very fine country and had a nice view of Mount Rainier. We sped on through some pretty little villages, including Satsop, Elma, Oakdale, and Gate City where we boarded the Northern Pacific train on the main line. We had been on a branch road. In an hour or two, we were in Centralia, a railroad town, and a very pretty place nicely situated on the Chehalis River and just now sinking from a boom. As we stepped to the platform, husband met us. We were soon wafted away to a hotel where he was boarding. We went at once to select a house. There were so many vancant ones, it was rather difficult to make a choice. I was at once impressed with the idea that we had made a mistake in coming to this place which was more dead than the town we had just left. But with husband out of business and dissatisfied, we concluded to make the best of a bad bargain. He went to the station to look after our household goods, and they had not arrived owing to some delay in the freight trains. We selected a neat little cottage and boarded at the hotel several days waiting for our cargo. Then we were delighted to get settled. The place we selected belonged to a widow who resided near us with her mother, also a widow. We soon made their acquaintance. They had a lovely home, fine gardens and an orchard. The old lady was a florist. Her two grown sons lived at home with her, and the young widow had a dear little boy who was the household pet. It was a pleasure to go there and see the thousands of beautiful flowers and plants which filled every porch, window and hot bed. They were smiling from every corner of house, garden and yard. "They grow to please her because she loves them so," the little boy said. Many lovely bouquets were sent to the city from her flower garden.

We were settled in our little cottage and prepared for winter none too soon as the rains now descended in true western style. The people were seen on the street under a canopy of umbrellas. The place had once been in a flourishing state with all modern conveniences. Electric lights. Street cars. Fine schools had been an attraction. Grace Seminary was a magnificent building on the hill, and the ascent to it was made very easily by a convenient stairway. The attendance had once been large and interesting. It was now distressingly small and depressing.

The public school was doing nicely, also the music class. There were many large business blocks on Tower Avenue, entirely vacant now, where at one time a flourishing trade was carried on. A peep at the empty shelves caused one to shudder. There was an impression of rats and ghosts, and we hurried along toward inhabited blocks and reflected on the past glory of the place and the future depression which was surely coming. There were some grand structures only partly completed looming up. The owners, seeing the boom was over, had stopped further expense. Splendid houses could be had to live in just for the care of them. This was Centralia, a pretty place, but a distressingly dull one.

I made the acquaintance of another old lady who was also a florist and lived in our neighborhood. She had a grand, magnificent home, but no family with her. An old uncle made his home there. Her husband was dead and her only son married. She had a splendid array of flowers and plants, some very choice plants which my first florist did not have. She was rather jealous of Mrs. G. and would say to me, "Are her flowers as nice as mine and has she as many?" I did not wish to say, as I liked them both and did not want to tattle.

I received a letter from my brother Jack whom I had not seen for twenty-three years. He was coming on a visit. He would leave Portland early in the evening and arrive in Centralia about ten at night. We had sent a coach to meet him and anxiously awaited his coming. Yes, the coach stopped at our door. A tall old gentleman, rather clerical looking, was left with us. Was that my brother? What a change time had wrought. I did not recognize the old man with gray hair and long white beard, but when he spoke I remembered the voice. I would know it in any land. We had a happy, joyous visit talking over our childhood days and life at the old home. When I could close my eyes and talk to or listen to him talk, it was my brother; but when I saw him, he was a stranger of near three score years and ten. His life had been spent in a happy, prosperous home on a large farm near Albany. His charming little wife, son and daughter were the true home treasure of that life. My own pathway on life's rugged road had been a winding and an eventful one. I seldom loved a friend or flower but that it was sure to fade and die. I often had prosperous homes and pleasant surroundings, but some unexpected event would call for a move to other parts. Sometimes we would better our conditions and surroundings financially, but oft times it was worse for us. Such was this move. We had left a good home and friends expecting to find better, but we were sadly disappointed.

Brother found us in a very pretty little home, but in a place of no importance in a business sense. He looked over the quiet town and decided that it had seen its best days and would not revive. He thought we would feel more at home in Oregon. After twenty years of wandering, we were very much inclined toward our old home. We almost promised to go there, and he said goodbye expecting to see us before many years.

The winter was nearly over. Springtime brought a new season, but no change in times. The people put in gardens and changed homes just to have employment. We had no garden in connection with our cottage. We moved to get a garden patch for employment and also a larger house. Bess and her dear little son, who was now four years old, were coming on a visit. We got nicely settled, put in a fine garden and worked with a will. We were anxiously expecting her, and then we heard she was delayed in her coming for a short time. How slowly the days passed by. Hortense found many ways to amuse herself, making use of time by reading, studying and driving with a little friend who had a nice horse and buggy of her own. She was delighted to go out in the country and see the harvest fields and the machinery. The great steam threshers were wonders to her. Then the fine orchards loaded down with luscious fruit. The country was more alive than the town. God made the country, man made the town.

Now the glorious Fourth of July was here again. The people were very patriotic and prepared for a grand celebration and a real old-style picnic in South Park. This, however, was disturbed by rain which pattered down unmindful of summer wear and white dresses. The crowd rushed into town and to the church to complete their ceremonies. At night, a ball concluded the program and the festive firecracker was silenced till next Fourth.

Bess would soon come now. We were awakened by a knock at midnight and I heard voices. When I opened the door, there I saw her holding the hand of a lovely, curly-headed boy *[Lloyd]* of four summers who was her very image when at that age. I called to husband and Hortense who soon came clattering in. After greetings were over, they hied *[hastened]* away to slumberland. Lloyd had wished to get to Grandma's house so he could go to bed right as he did not fancy the idea of sleeping on the railroad cars.

Next morning he came down early to make our acquaintance and amused us all by selecting Hortense for a playfellow. He treated his Grandpa and I with great respect in every way, assuming we expected it from him, then romped with her and had a jolly time.

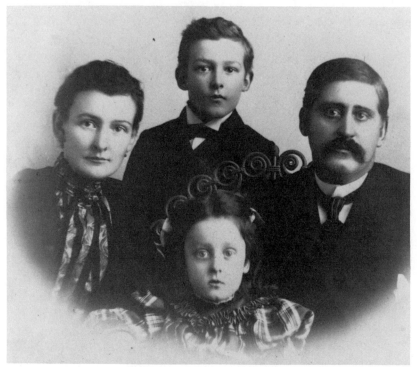

*Bess and Robert (Roy) Mann and their children.*

In a few days his grandfather took him for a walk on the hill to the park, and they were soon very fond of each other and took walks every day. He was pleased to see the fruit on the trees. Being from a cold country, he had not been accustomed to it.

Meanwhile, Bess was enjoying the lovely flower gardens and selecting choice plants for her own garden and packing some of the nice fruit to take home to Roy. Only too soon, the time for them to go had come and we were sorry to see them off.

Our garden was a great comfort to us. We spent many pleasant hours caring for it and were well repaid. The summer was gone again. The leaves had turned red. The hills near town were very pretty in their varicolored foliage. The crickets warbled a lonely song. The wild goose soared away to southern climate. The fruit was all gathered. The days were short and frost was in the air.

# Chapter 24

# The "Last" Move

HUSBAND DECIDED TO GO TO OREGON. A cousin in Eugene wrote to Hortense about the fine schools. The University of Oregon was located there and doing splendid work. She was very anxious to go. It was decided that I would go to Eugene with her where she might receive the benefit of a good school while husband visited with his daughters, Genie and May, who lived in Portland.

A man is soon ready for a journey. Packs his grip, gets his ticket and is off before a woman can decide on the color of her traveling dress. So it was in this case. He was at Genie's in a few hours. We remained to sell out and pack up, as usual, and say goodbye to our neighbors.

It was two months before we were ready to sally forth. We stayed for the holidays and to see the New Year (1892) enter the wheel of old time. Then we started for the home of my childhood.

We had time enough to pack up, consider our move and decide that this, at last, should end our traveling over this mundane sphere. We said we would go on certain conditions, which where that we should stay there in Eugene. It was a settled fact and we prepared to go.

I engaged a drayman to come after our freight. He had a big boy come along with him to assist in handling the boxes and furniture which were already packed in the different rooms.

Hortense had put her rings, watch and keepsakes in a hand bag and hung it in her room under her cloak. Soon after the man and boy left the house with our freight, I stepped into her room and saw the hand bag. I called to her saying, "You were careless to leave your purse so exposed."

She said, "Mama, I certainly did not. I covered it up nicely." I told her how it was and she cried out, "I just know that boy has stolen

197

my rings." I opened the bag and sure enough he *had* stolen her birthday ring, a pin I valued very highly and other articles. I went in search of him at once. I met the marshall and told him about the boy and our loss. He said he knew where to find the boy and was satisfied he was the thief, as he had lately been in jail for stealing. He told me to wait in the courtroom till he came back. I waited two hours and at last saw him coming and the boy with him. He asked me if that was the boy. I told him it was. Then the boy said, "What do you want with me?" I told him I had no use for him. I only wanted the articles he had taken from the handbag while he was in my home. He said he had not taken anything from a handbag. The marshall searched him and found the ring. I told him he could go if he would give up all the articles he had stolen while in my house. But the marshall said, "No, we can't let him go. We will go in and have a trial." I was in a great hurry. It was nearly train time. I insisted on going, but I had to wait and go next day. I had to appear against him and he was put in jail where he had room and board and time to reflect.

We then boarded the Northern for Portland on a cold, crisp evening in January. We had a lovely run down to the Columbia, and we crossed the grand old river once more. The whole line of coaches and two locomotives were conveyed across that great river on flat boats in some wonderful way. It being dark, I could not see the performance as I wished to. We were permitted to walk out and see the boats and the engines, but we could not see the wonderful construction of the boats well enough to explain. I only know it is a grand thing to ferry a long train across a stream like the Columbia River. I think it is two miles wide where we crossed. We were soon speeding on our way again and were pleased to see the thousands of lights sparkling from the city homes. We could only see the lights in the distance as it was near midnight. They reminded me of so many fireflies, as the trees and housetops would hide them from our view. They were seemingly darting about as fireflies are wont to do.

Then as we were nearing the station, we gathered up our big box, little box, band box and grip sack and prepared to go. We were soon seated in a bus with several others and dashed away to one of the principal hotels. Just as we were climbing into the bus, I heard a weak voice saying, "I am alive yet. Did think I would die before we got here." I saw an old man who seemed to be in the last stages of consumption. He was alone. When we arrived at the hotel, I stepped to the desk to register and, as I turned away, I saw the sick man across the room. He looked as if he was dying. I went to him

*"The whole line of coaches and two locomotives were conveyed across that great river on flat boats. . . It is a grand thing to do, to ferry a long train across a stream like the Columbia River."*

and asked if we could do anything for him. He said he had a friend who had gone to telephone a relative who lived near the city. We stayed near him till his friend returned. He assisted him to the elevator and got a room for him where he could be quiet. The poor feeble one had come all the long distance from his home in sunny France to see his relative and had been very sick on the way. This kind young man had met with him on the way and, seeing his need of a friend, had volunteered his assistance. I met him in the hall later, and he told me he had heard from the relative but feared the sick man would not live to see him. I heard no more from them as I left the hotel that night.

We went by streetcar to a sister-in-law who lived up on Washington Street. We were misdirected by the conductor and had some trouble in finding her home. After climbing stairs and rousing people, we at last found her cozy retreat. When she met us, she was a stranger. I had not seen her for nineteen years and was not prepared for the change Old Time had wrought. We were soon snugly ensconced and had a quiet rest. Next morning, we started out to take a streetcar for the hotel in search of our baggage but, when we reached the street, ascertained the weather was cold and the car could not run owing to ice on the rails. We went on foot. We once thought the blocks were small in Portland, but we admitted they were large enough when we had to walk thirty-three blocks to reach our hotel. We waited till the ice cleared, then took a car to her house again. She escorted us about over the city, as she was an old resident and knew all the places of note.

Being very tired after sight-seeing, we wandered home and had a good appetite for dinner. Early next morning, a dear friend of my childhood days called and wafted us away to her lovely home to spend the day. We had a happy time looking over her stately mansion and talking of other days. A sister and brother-in-law and their charming little girl occupied the same house.

Late in the afternoon, we returned to our hotel. Our friend went with us to spend the evening since we were to leave the city on an early train the next morning. We reluctantly said goodbye to her. She is just the same dear friend as in long years ago when we crossed the dreary plains together and later on during our school days. One person over whom time or absence did not cast a chilling blight. Friendship's memories were warm in her heart.

Next morning we were off to catch the train for Eugene. We had long been accustomed to the Northern Pacific. Its coaches were so nice and large. It had such long trains and was so full of passengers that we were amused when we were directed to the little train composed of only two little coaches and a baggage car or two. And then to see a tender filled with wood! We had long been accustomed to coal. At last, we started out very slowly and kept going slowly. I thought they would surely get under headway after while, but I finally concluded they could not run any faster and settled myself to take a nap. However, I soon discovered it was a good chance to view my dear old country and became deeply interested in the places along the route. I had not seen them for twenty years—Canamah, Oregon City and the falls there. Then Aurora—the same quiet little place—Woodburn, and Gervais where husband and a grandson met us.

We had a short visit, then said goodbye and went on toward Salem. We passed the Chemewah Indian School and stopped to let a girl get off who was a pupil there. We then saw the state fair grounds where I had often been in bygone days. Then on to Salem, the capital city. We only stopped for a few moments, then went slowly on up the valley to Jefferson. I saw quite an improvement in that place. We soon came near the butte where we had rolled the stone downhill forty years ago demolishing the pig pen and setting the pig free. The hill was there yet, but the pig was not.

In an hour or two, we reached Albany. Many houses looked just the same. I saw the house where brother Frank was married. The trees are larger than they were forty years ago, but the house had not changed.

Who would meet us in Eugene? Friends of other days had passed away. None of my brothers were near the old home. My sisters lay with my parents on the hill. Would my old home be a happy place to me now? What memories the old-time haunts would revive, days when we all gathered in the dear home.

*James Alfred Masterson in later years.*

Chapter 25

# Martha's Final Years

M ARTHA'S hand-written account ended in 1892. She and Alfred went their separate ways from that time on. From visiting his daughters in Gervais, he went to Juntura in eastern Oregon and lived with his son Alfred (Leaf) for a time. He then ended his years in Coeur d'Alene with Bess and Robert Mann. Alfred spent three short periods of time in the Veteran's Hospital in Roseburg, Oregon between June, 1905 and October, 1907. The hospital records list his disease as rheumatism and a hernia. He died in Coeur d'Alene September 11, 1908.

Martha wrote a letter in 1903 to T.A. Wood in Portland seeking to establish her husband, James Alfred's claim to a pension for his service in the Rogue River Indian War of 1855-1856. In that letter, she stated, "I write in behalf of my husband. . ."

Frances earned a teacher's certificate after they came to Eugene and taught the Lone Pine School on River Road north of Eugene for a couple of years. Undoubtedly, she met Louis Vitus while teaching there since the school was located in the same neighborhood as the Vitus farms. No record has been found of where Martha lived during those years.

Martha's last decade was spent in the home of this daughter, Frances Hortense, who had married Louis Vitus June 8, 1898 in Eugene. The following news items appeared on page one of the *Daily Eugene Guard* of that date:

> At noon today the wedding of Mr. Louis Charles Vitus and Miss Frances H. Masterson was celebrated at the residence of I.L. Campbell in this city. The Ceremony was performed by Rev. R.C. Brooks, pastor of the Congregational Church. About thirty relatives were present and witnessed the wedding and partook of the dinner specially prepared for the occasion. The rooms of the house were elegantly decorated with roses and ivy. The couple will reside on their farm near Irving.
>
> Quite a large number of presents were received by the couple. The *Guard* tenders the happy couple its heartiest congratulations. May they have a long and pleasant matrimonial life.

*Frances Hortense in her wedding dress, 1898.*

Louis built a house for his bride which still stands on a place known as Thistledown Farm on River Road north of Eugene, Oregon. It was here that Martha spent her last years. Daily diaries covering the last five years of her life (1911-1916) have been preserved by her descendants. Whether she kept a record of the intervening years (1892-1910) is not clear, but a detailed picture of Oregon farm life from 1911 through 1916 emerges in her daily entries about churning, baking, laundry and other household chores. She told of farm work, letters from family and friends and visits from the neighbors and relatives. She wrote that her step-son Givens Masterson "came early this morning *[April 3, 1911]* by way of Irving. We were delighted to see him, a fine large-looking, healthy Montana man."

Frances seems to have had very poor health during those last years of Martha's life. Her mother helped regularly with the house-work, always washing the breakfast dishes, milk pans and pails. In 1912, Frances spent the month of February in California because her doctor thought a change of climate might improve her health. Aunt Lizzie Gay *[brother Martin's widow]* came from Portland to stay with Martha while Frances was away. That was the year they got word by phone that brother John Gay had died near Albany February 1.

On August 17, 1911 Martha went to Portland on the train and spent ten days visiting with relatives and "doing the town." As far as the record in the diaries reports, that was her last visit at any distance from home, although she went to Eugene once or twice a year to attend to business, see her dressmaker and visit relatives and friends.

She suffered intensely the last few years with rheumatism, and she wrote that her doctor advised treating the pain with vinegar packs. In 1913, she was moved to a downstairs bedroom.

All through those last years, Martha followed current events with great interest. Her diary entries often mentioned that she would "now get the papers and read about world news."

*Louis Vitus built this house for his bride. It still stands at Thistledown Farm on River Road north of Eugene, Oregon.*

> **Auction Sale—**
> At my place 7 miles north of Eugene on the
> River Road, known as L.C. Vitus place, Tuesday,
> Oct. 24, beginning at 9:30 o'clock. Will sell my
> entire stock of farm machinery, household fur-
> niture, sheep, cattle, and horses as advertised in
> bills.
> L.C. Vitus                                            023

*From Eugene Daily Guard, Tuesday evening, October 17, 1916*

Louis got tired of farming and began to sell off tracts of land. One purchaser was an elderly Mr. Day who worked several months of the year for Louis as a hired hand. Martha reported that Day died in 1915.

In 1916, the family decided to sell the farm and move to Idaho for their health. Frances was sick in bed for six weeks in the midst of harvest season that summer, and Martha cooked, washed dishes and baked for harvest hands even though she wrote, "I am feeling old and feeble. I am trying to do the work alone. It is very tiresome for me, as I am so weak." Another time she wrote, "I am cooking for the crowd, and I don't feel at all well enough to cook, or even be up, but then it is necessary I do all I can stand. I have such a poor appetite, I can't eat enough to give me strength."

During October of that year the family crated their canned goods and furniture, posted auction notices all around the county and made preparations to move to Idaho. Martha wrote of seeing the family, who were to take over the farm when Vituses left, camped by the barn. In her last diary entry she wrote that her trunk was all packed and Louis had gone to Eugene with a wagon load of fur-niture to be shipped. Perhaps her diary got packed the day of the auction and never unpacked, because she made no further entries in it. Martha didn't make the move to Idaho. She died in Eugene six weeks after the auction.

To use a phrase she used to describe others, Martha was a "noble-hearted woman." She was a compassionate, optimistic person who was touched by the beauty of the frontier wilderness. She continued to observe the ups and downs of national affairs in her later years. Scarcely a day passed that she didn't make some comment on politi-cal events, storms, floods, heat or drought. She identified closely with the seasonal farm work, and the daily pressures on her family. She continued to carry responsibilities for chores and in the kitchen into the last weeks of her life in spite of illness and fatigue. Anger and discouragement finally crept into some of her later entries. But she also wrote about the release and refreshment she got from reading a good book.

It was a moving experience to read those last diary entries with the realization that Martha Gay Masterson's life would end shortly afterward. The obituary notice in the *Daily Guard* read as follows:

DIED—MASTERSON—IN EUGENE
On Tuesday, December 12, 1916
Mrs. M.A. Masterson, aged 79 years
Mrs. Masterson leaves one daughter, Mrs. Louis Vitus, of Eugene and three brothers, Evans S. Gay, E.W. Gay and L.W. Gay, all of Coeur d'Alene mines, Idaho. The remains are at the Gordon and Veatch Chapel and funeral arrangements will be announced later.

Martha was buried in the cemetery on the old homestead south of Eugene with her parents and sisters.

It seems appropriate for Martha to have the last word in this, her story, through a few selected diary entries.

**Sunday, January 1, 1911.** A very pleasant day. Not at all cold. A shower in the afternoon. We had a bouquet of roses on the dinner table picked out in the yard. We also have chrysanthemums and carnations, pansies and violets blooming out doors. Cogswell *[a nephew]* came out on Christmas day and stayed all week with us. He went home this afternoon. The New Year finds Oregon very prosperous. Health quite good. Some fever in Eugene. MM *[Each entry is signed with her initials or name.]*
**Thursday, January 19, 1911.** . . . No trains last night from North. Tracks washed out this side of Salem and high waters below here. . . . Louis went to the river, then looked after the stock and churned 9½ lbs. of butter. Made 16 pounds this week. Got 10 eggs today. They are 35 cents in Eugene. MM
**Sunday, February 11, 1911.** . . . *[Brother]* Green stayed with us today. He likes this part of the valley. Been rather a blue day for us all. Frances was sick all day. We talked over old times and wondered at the great changes sixty years have brought about. Seems like a dream. . . . Louis brought in 19 eggs this evening and they are 30 cents if we don't eat them. MM
**Saturday, March 4, 1911.** A veritable spring day. Taft has filled the

chair 2 years. 2 years more. Then Teddy takes the Presidential seat again, to hold for 8 years I guess. Uncle Joe and family came to Hazel's today. An auto passed here. The men plowed. We were busy all day. Frances churned and baked and scrubbed. I baked bread, lots of it, and did little things all day. Read the papers. Got the Housewife [A *magazine?*]. MM

**Sunday, March 12, 1911.** This was Celeste's birthday. A lovely sunny day and she is a lovely little girl. Frances is having a distressing headache. A very quiet Sunday. Very little travel, only 2 or 3 automobiles passed. A few buggies and other vehicles. Ed Reapp called to get the gun. Louis brought in 7 dozen and 2 eggs today. Hens are doing fine. Eggs are 18 cts. now. Good night. MM

**Wednesday, April 5, 1911.** Foggy this morning. Clear this afternoon. The ex-president, (Roosevelt) stopped 12 minutes in Eugene and addressed the school children and high school students. His time is *very* precious. Louis cleaned wheat and worked in the garden. Perry harrowed. Frances helped set out strawberry plants. I called on the Brown family. First time I had been there. They have a lovely home and view. Frances got 17 eggs at the park [*hen yard*]. MM

**Saturday, May 6, 1911.** A very pleasant day. Louis went after Frances. She had a nice visit and a lovely time at the reception. Met many old friends and the Lady and Gentleman from India. She says they look quite foreign and are pleasant people. Singer machine agent called. Gave me an almanac. It is a very instructive little book. A man called asking for help. Said he had rheumatism. I got 22 eggs at the Park. Frances carried Ida a great cluster of Pansies for the reception. They were wonders they were so large. MM

**Monday, June 5, 1911.** Automobile procession passed this morning on the way to Portland to attend the Rose Carnival, decorated with Pennants and streamers. Lovely weather for roses. Nice and sunny. Mrs. Foster cleaned the guest chamber today and both halls. Mr. Earhard called to get a drink of buttermilk. Mr. Day chopped wood. Louis, Stanley and Ed worked on new road. Frances helped Mrs. Foster. F. got 15 eggs at Park. MM

**Tuesday, July 4, 1911.** The *Fourth*. The 135th 4th of July for *us*, a *free* nation. The Star Spangled Banner, long may it wave. Louis cut hay. Cogs helped make ice cream. I dressed the chicken for dinner and Frances made the cake and salad. We had a fine dinner and a fine time. Merton and his cousin Frank from Bakersfield, California, came to eat cherries. Cogs helped Mr. Day on his barn in afternoon. Frances got 15 eggs at Park. MM

**Thursday, July 13, 1911.** 92° in the shade. Finished picking this morning at 10 o'clock. Had 2670 lbs. nice Royal Ann Cherries. Louis took the last load to Eugene at 11 o'clock. Cogswell went home today as Louis went to Eugene. He wants to see his new bicycle and ride out on it if it has come. Grandmother Brown called. We had thunderstorms while she was here. . . . Merton came to return my rubbers. I got 11 eggs at Park, 13 at barn. The lightning struck 2 or 3 trees near Joe Luckeys new house, also several telephone poles. Burnt out lots of phone batteries and demoralized conversation all along the lines. MM

**Saturday, July 15, 1911.** . . . Louis took our phone to get remodeled. . . . It was ruined by electric storm. 160 are burnt out. . . .

**Sunday, July 16, 1911.** . . . 100° for 5 hours. Our phone is no good. I am sure they gave Louis another phone. It is a little rickety old arrangement and we cannot call up the central office one time in a dozen. . . .

**Friday, July 21, 1911.** Our phone is yet in trouble. Got new batteries. Louis will put them in and perhaps it will do better. . . .

**Sunday, July 30, 1911.** . . . Louis went over the phone line looking for the trouble. Found it in an old can someone had attached for a receiver. . . .

**Wednesday, August 9, 1911.** Rather cool this morning for August. Louis and Mr. Day are labouring with the wheat. I hear the whistle of the busy threshing machine and 'tis now the Merrie Harvest Time. Every farmer in the County is running here and there, getting and calling up to get help to garner the grain before the fall rains descend on Mother Earth. And hop picking will soon be here and the prunes too. Got 7 eggs. MM

**Wednesday, November 1, 1911.** . . . Halloween passed off very quietly. Just put a barricade against our barn gate. . . .

**Friday, November 3, 1911.** . . . I made a scarecrow and put it in the pansy bed to keep the chickens away. . . .

**Wednesday, November 8, 1911.** . . . This was my 74th birthday. Frances gave me a lovely book, *The Secret Garden*, and a nice lamp. Alice sent me a book to read. . . .

**March 11, 1912.** . . . A hobo called to get a cup of coffee. He wore lovely new buff gloves, and was very sedate. Pulled his hat down over his eyes. . .

**May, 9, 1912.** . . . The men worked in the shrubbery and cut my pet rose bush nearly all down and *I am mad*. . . .

**May, 25, 1912.** . . . I have rheumatism something tirable *[She always spelled terrible thusly]* this week.

**June 8, 1912.** . . . Green came out to make a little visit. He is on his way to the Pioneer Picnic in Linn County. . . .

**June 21, 1912.** . . . I read *Lavendar and Old Lace.* . . .

**June 29, 1912.** Cool and cloudy and quite blustry for June. Jack ran up home this morning on his wheel. Louis cultivated woods gardens. Old man chopped wood. *[Mr. Day was the hired man who Martha called "the old man" and seemed very disgusted with him but never explained why.]* Frances is indisposed. I did up the work and then ironed and prepared dinner, baked bread and rolls, and had to wait dinner and all was ruined and not fit to eat. I was *just mad* (is all there was about it) and, after this, the one who caused the delay will wait. Morris Coon called to see Louis. *I* fed the hens and got 20 eggs. MM

**April 26, 1913.** . . . I read the papers and sat by the fire and talked by phone. . . *[Almost every day during the next two months she mentioned having a vinegar pack on one or both arms, sometimes on a "limb" as well.]*

**July 18, 1913.** . . . Frances and Esther sat with me. Frances is very kind to me. She stays with me a great deal. . . .

**July 23, 1913.** . . . I can only read. Not well enough to work, I am sorry to say. . . .

**September 15, 1913.** . . . Brother Evans came this afternoon. Been to the Pendleton Roundup. It was fine. We had a talk about old times and crossing the plains.

**Sunday, September 21, 1913.** . . . Louis and Frances went to Eugene to church. Jack and I had a fine dinner, all alone, then looked at pictures of Idaho, told stories, ate melon, had a lunch, then at 5 o'clock Jack went home. *[Jack was Cogswell's brother, son of her niece.]*

**October, 13, 1913.** . . . I prepared a lot of tomatoes for catsup and a basin of pears to bake for dinner, then pared the potatoes and fought against a pest of red ants in the pantry. . . .

**April 22, 1915.** . . . Zona is helping Frances. The girls are here too as there is no school. The teachers are having a three day's play to go to Junction City to a children's contest. Oh, what nonsense and loss of time. The men are plowing and harrowing and drilling. 4 men at work this afternoon. I baked bread and buns and prepared dinner for all, then Zona and I washed dishes. . . .

**May 25, 1915.** . . . Italy is now at war. Austrian aeroplanes attacked Italian towns and attempted destruction of arsenals at Venice. . . .

**June 3, 1915.** . . . I am now getting ready to go to Eugene on the

Jitney bus to stay a few hours. Yes, we are off for a ride. We got home at half past 4 P.M. Had a fine sunny day for our ride. Saw several friends and also saw the new summer goods. Everything was just grand along the way to Eugene, orchards, gardens and flowers. . . .

**June 15, 1915.** . . . Louis went to Eugene to set on the jury (again). He is getting tired of the business; would rather work on his farm. People ought to act right and behave themselves, then the farmers would not have to leave home and their work to act as jurymen. . . .

**June 22, 1915.** . . . A man came to tune our piano. . . .

**July 14, 1915.** . . . I made a bonnet for Velma's doll. . . .

**August 13, 1915.** . . . I will get the papers and read about the Mexican war. I remember one war we had with them in '46 and '47, remember it well. My uncles and cousins were in it. One of them had a company of soldiers. He was Col. Evans.

**Sunday, August 15, 1915.** . . . I stayed by my *lonesome* as I have done many long days . . .

**August 18, 1915.** . . . We *never* go on pleasure trips. Frances is sick. (I am cook) . . .

**September, 17, 1915.** . . . I will get the papers and read about loaning a billion dollars to England. *I* would not. . . . *I* am opposed to that as I do not think it right to carry on the war. It's too severe. . . .

**December, December 20, 1915.** . . . The President *[Wilson]* married a very distant relative of ours—the Bolling family of Virginia. . . .

**Saturday, January 1, 1916.** 28° above to begin the year. New Year came to us with a light snow, three inches deep, this morning. Very nice to see all Nature clothed in pure white. The trees and shrubbery are beautiful and the boys delight in the sport of snowballing. Louis and Jack have gone to Eugene. Frances and I are doing the housework and attending to the fires, reading Christmas books. No mail today—legal holiday. Louis came at 4 P.M., fed the cows, got in wood. Frances brought in 3 eggs. MAM

**February 3, 1916.** . . . We are experiencing a very severe winter for the Willamette Valley, but it seems to be universal from newspaper accounts. Deep snows and floods and cold weather all over the world. And war and starvation in Europe and Mexico. We of the United States have our hands full to settle all controversies and feed the starving. Silver thaw extending from Albany to Seattle. 13 eggs. MAM

**February 12, 1916.** Lincoln's birthday. This morning is very spring-like. The birds are singing and the sun is shining and the frogs chirped all night and the daffodils are putting forth buds ready to blossom. . . . I am baking the various kinds of bread we use in this household, white bread, brown bread and coffee cake. I will prepare lunch for Frances and myself. . . .

**February 22, 1916.** . . I crocheted on red lace doily. . . .

**March 30, 1916.** . . . I finished stitching red doily. . . .

**March 31, 1916.** . . . I am doing the morning work now at 8 A.M. Frances went to Eugene on the Jitney. I will get the papers and read about the Bandetts (sic), then prepare our lunch. Afternoon, I read and made tatting. . . .

**April 2, 1916.** Clear and bright. A fine day for automobiles and they were on the go early. Louis is off to the fields and far away about the stock and to see the grass. We are about the work. The birds are singing on bush and tree, selecting good places for nesting. Frances is an invalid today, and I am just as tired as I can very well be to walk about. Hundreds of autos passed and not one stopped. Louis fed the hens, got 34 eggs. Our mail comes now in an automobile. . . quite an improvement on an OX wagon of 65 years ago. . . .

**April 8, 1916.** . . . Frances did the scrubbing and I sewed the tatting on the Christmas towel. . . .

**June 2, 1916.** . . . I will get the papers and find out if our soldiers down in Mexico have captured Villa yet. He is a sharp one and the soldiers are too slow. . . .

**June 8, 1916.** . . . I have finished the dishes and will get the papers and read about the tirable disasters, about Earl Kitchner and his staff. Too bad to have such men sent down into the deep, briny, surging sea. . . .

**June 21, 1916.** . . . Oregon Militia are ordered to the Border. War seems inevitable. Mexicans are saucy. Rather exciting times for war is tirable. . . .

**July 30, 1916.** . . . Frances is worse. I am baking bread as Louis is here to lift the great loaves and bread pans for me. I will bake enough to do a week. It is lovely bread and we are proud of it. I will put on the roast and shell peas, peel potatoes and wash the M.B. berries for Louis. I don't care for them only in jelly. . . .

**Friday, August 25, 1916.** . . . A kind of mist in the air. I saw the crescent moon in the eastern sky near a brilliant planet. It was a beautiful sight in the early morning *blue* sky. . . .

**Wednesday, September 20, 1916.** Foggy. Oh, the fog! How we wish we were in sunny Idaho. . . .

*Louis Vitus*

**September 29, 1916.** A very nice day. Louis went to Eugene. Frances had headache. I have a tirable cough and sore throat. Walter mended the rake and he is picking apples this afternoon to take to Idaho for winter. I am so sorry we are not feeling well. Not even able to pick up things ready for packing and there *is so much* to do. My throat is *no* better. I will now get our evening meal. . . .

**September 30, 1916.** . . . only got 11 eggs today. Nauty, *nauty* hens.

**October 4, 1916.** 29 above zero and we are near freezing. How sorry we are to see the tomatoes laid low. Quite a snow yesterday round about Spencer's Butte. . . Louis and Walter are cold. Choring is all they have to do now. Plenty of work in the house however. Just the same amount of cooking or even more. . . .

**October 6, 1916.** . . . Louis packed books and magazines. Frances helped him. . . .

**October 9, 1916.** . . . I am reading old letters and burning the refused ones. We cleaned out boxes and stand drawers, disposed of all useless articles. We will have a car load or more after sifting out the things to be left. . . .

**October 11, 1916.** . . . Louis has gone out all over the county to scatter the auction bills. . . .

**October 15, 1916.** . . . I am quite weak today. Get weaker all the while. I see the Howards have pulled into our barn lot with the cooking outfit to begin work on *our* farm. Frances has gone to see Grandma Brown as we are going away soon to Idaho to try and find *health*. . . .

**October 17, 1916.** . . . Frances and Zona packed the fruit and jam and jelly, and the empty jars. Louis nailed the lids on. . . .

**October 18, 1916.** . . . I am sorting out things to take and others to leave. They all packed. I watched and rested as *I* am old. . . .

# Bibliography

**BOOKS**

Dark, Harris & Phyllis. *Springfield of the Ozarks: An Illustrated History.* Woodland Hills, California: Windsor Publications, Inc., 1981.

Escott, George S. *History and Directory of Springfield and North Springfield.* Springfield, Missouri: Printed at the office of the *Patriot-Advisor,* 1878.

Farmer, Frank. *Willard: From Prairie to Present, A Centennial Story.* Willard, Missouri: Willard Bicentennial Heritage Committee, 1976.

Fischer, Christiane, Editor. *Let Them Speak for Themselves, Women in the American West, 1849-1900.* New York: Dutton, 1978.

French, Giles. *The Golden Land.* Portland, Oregon: Oregon Historical Society, 1958.

——— *Homesteads & Heritage.* Portland, Oregon: Binfords & Mort, 1 9 7 1 .

Gibbs, Rafe. *Beckoning the Bold, Story of the Dawning of Idaho.* Moscow, Idaho: Moscow University Press of Idaho, 1976.

Halcombe. *History of Greene County, Missouri.* St. Louis: Western Historical Company, 1883.

Helm, Mike. *Conversations with Pioneer Women.* Eugene, Oregon: Rainy Day Press, 1981.

Hult, Ruby El. *Steamboats in the Timber.* Caldwell, Idaho: The Caxton Printers, Ltd., 1952.

Magnuson, Richard G. *Coeur d'Alene Diary.* Portland, Oregon: Metropolitan Press, 1968.

McArthur, Lewis A. *Oregon Geographic Names* (Fifth Edition). Portland, Oregon: Western Imprints, 1982.

Potter, Miles F. *Oregon's Golden Years.* Caldwell, Idaho: The Caxton Printers, Ltd., 1976.

Ross, Nancy Wilson. *Westward the Women.* San Francisco, California: North Point Press, 1985.

Schlissel, Lillian. *Women's Diaries of the Westward Journey.* New York: Schocken Books, 1982.

Seton, Ernest Thompson. *Lives of Game Animals.* Vol. I. New York: Doubleday, Doran & Company, Inc., 1929.

*Spokane City Directory,* 1889-1909.

Warren, Esther. *The Columbia Gorge Story.* Dallas, Oregon: *Itemizer-Observer* Press, 1977.

Winther, Oscar O. *The Great Northwest,* 2nd Edition. New York: Alfred A. Knopf, 1955.

Wood, John V. *Railroads Through the Coeur d'Alenes.* Caldwell, Idaho: The Caxton Printers, Ltd., 1983.

Writer's Project. *Oregon: End of the Trail.* Portland, Oregon: Binfords & Mort, 1940. Reprinted 1951.

PERIODICALS

*Eugene Daily Guard,* October 17, 1916. "Auction Sale."
*Eugene Daily Guard,* December 12, 1916, p. 3. "Died-Masterson-Eugene."
*Eugene Daily Guard,* June 8, 1898, p. 1. "Married."
*Morning Oregonian,* January 1, 1895, pp. 8-9. "To Pass the Cascades."
Menefee, Leah C. *Lane County Historian,* Vol. VI, p. 21. June, 1961. "First Hundred Lane County Marriages."
Mitchell, Charlotte. *Lane County Historian,* Vol. VI, June, 1961, pp. 27-31. "John Cogswell."
Ozark Genealogical Society, Springfield, Missouri. *Ozar'kin,* Vol. I, No. 1.

DOCUMENTS

Briggs, Ethel. *A History & Genealogy of Gilmore Callison & His Descendants.* Eugene, Oregon; Lane County Museum Library, Mimeographed, 1960.
Ellsbarry, Elizabeth Prather. *Greene County, Missouri 1850 Federal Census.* Springfield, Missouri: Ozarks Genealogical Society Library, No date.
Gay, James Woods. "Unpublished diary, 1851-1854." Eugene, Oregon: Arthur Sperling.
Masterson, James Alfred. "Personal Letter of March 31, 1903," Portland, Oregon: Oregon Historical Library.
———— "The Ward Massacre." Unpublished handwritten account. No date. Eugene, Oregon: Lane County Museum Library.
Masterson, Martha. "Recollections—1896." Three unpublished handwritten tablets made available to the editor by Claire O'Callaughan. Tualatin, Oregon.
———— "Daily Diaries, 1911-1916." Unpublished diaries made available to editor by Claire O'Callaughan. Tualatin, Oregon.
Ransome, Frederick Leslie and Calkins, Frank Cathcart. "The Geology and Ore Deposits of the Coeur d'Alene District, Idaho." Washington, D.C.: Government Printing Office, 1908.
Ozarks Genealogical Society. "Springfield Land Office Abstracts, 1835-1846." Springfield, Missouri.
St. Louis Public Library. "Greene County, Missouri Plat map." St. Louis, Missouri: Circa 1930.
Lane County Courthouse. "Lane County, Oregon Marriage Records." Eugene, Oregon: Book A, Lane County Court House Records.
Montana Historical Society. "Northern Pacific Guide Book, 1886-1887, Idaho Division." Helena, Montana.

CORRESPONDENCE

Bennett, Earl. Idaho Bureau of Mines, Moscow, Idaho. September 9, 1983.
Bonner County Historical Society. Sandpoint, Idaho. September 7, 1983.

Fisher, Raymond. Eastern Washington Genealogical Society, Spokane, Washington. November 13, 1983.

Foster, Evelyn. Clark County Historical Museum, Vancouver, Washington. October 27, 1983.

Genealogical Forum of Portland. Portland, Oregon. September 11, 1983.

Idaho State Historical Society. Boise, Idaho. March 3, 1983.

Koentopp, Susan. Spokane, Washington. July 13, 1983.

Mason, Glenn. Eastern Washington State Historical Society, Spokane, Washington. March 24, 1983.

Minnesota Historical Society. St. Paul, Minnesota. April 6, 1983.

Nelson, Donna. Silverton Country Historical Society. Silverton, Oregon.

Nolan, Ed. Montana Historical Society. Helena, Montana. February 23, 1983.

Olson, Douglas. Eastern Washington State Historical Society. Spokane, Washington. November 26, 1983.

Stephens, Thomas and Eva. Mitchell, Oregon. July 23, 1983.

Stevenson Washington Museum. February 14, 1984.

Vorhis, Hazel. Ozark Genealogical Society, Springfield, Missouri. April 14, 1983.

Wood, John V. Philomath, Oregon. August 3, 1983.

# List of Illustrations

# Genealogies

HUSBAND: Martin Baker Gay
Born __10-24-1803__ Place __on the James River, Virginia__
Married __3-7-1827__ Place __McCreary Co. Kentucky__
Occupation __farmer, cabinet maker__ Resided at __Virginia, Kentucky, Tennessee, Missouri (Boone Co.), Arkansas, Missouri (Greene Co.), Oregon (Albany, Lane County)__
Died __11-17-1867__ Place __on homestead south of Eugene, OR__
Buried _____ Place __Mary Gay Cogswell Cemetery__ Sheet submitted by:
Other wives _____
Father _____
Mother (maiden name) _____

Relationship to

WIFE __Johann (Ann) Evans Stewart__ Husb.: _____
Born __2-23-1808__ Place _____ Relationship to
Church Affil. _____ Occupation _____ Wife: _____
Died __January, 1874__ Place __Gay homestead__
Buried _____ Place __Mary Gay Cogswell Cemetery__ Place sources of information and
Other husb. _____ additional information on
Father _____ reverse side.
Mother (maiden name) _____

| CHILDREN | BORN When Where | DIED When Where | MARRIED To whom When Where |
|---|---|---|---|
| 1 James Woods Gay | 2-5-1828 McCreary Co. KY Kentucky | 1-13-1903 buried in Union Cem. Linn Co. | Frances Jane Gott 10-10-1850 Greene Co. MO |
| 2 Charles Franklin Gay | 9-14-1831 Tennessee | 6-17-1908 Spokane, WA | Rebecca Burkhart 5-27-1858 Albany, OR |
| 3 Mary Frances Gay | 9-21-1831 Boone County Missouri | 10-8-1887 Eugene, OR | John Cogswell 10-28-1852 Lane Co. Ore. Terr. |
| 4 John Walker Gay | 12-25-1833 Boone County Missouri | 2-1-1912 Near Rickreal bur. Etna Cem. | Helena Choate Pike 9-29-1870 Linn Co. Oregon |
| 5 Martin Baker Gay, Jr. | 10-15-1835 Boone County Missouri | 9-18-1899 | Elizabeth Pascell 5-17-1866 Dillon Portland, OR |
| 6 Martha Ann Gay | 11-8-1837 Arkansas | 12-12-1916 Eugene, OR bur. Gay Cem. | James A. Masterson 8-27-1871 on Gay homestead |
| 7 Evans Stewart Gay | 10-21-1839 Greene County Missouri | 11-27-1920 | 1 Mary Melissa Davis Ptld. 6-7-1868 Sarah C. Wilsey 1-27-7C |
| 8 David Green Gay | 9-14-1841 Greene County Missouri | 10-21-1920 buried in Gay Cemetery | 1 Charlotte Linder Eugene 5-4-1871 2 Keturah Isham 1895 |
| 9 Daniel Goode Gay | 4-13-1844 Springfield Missouri | 1930 | Ella Richardson |
| 10 William Kelly Gay (mentally retarded) | 4-12-1846 Springfield Missouri | 4-30-1909 buried in Gay | |
| 11 Lodowick Wadlow Gay | 8-28-1848 Springfield Missouri | 1-30-1926 | |
| 12 Sarah Julia Gay | 6-14-1851 Nebr. Terr | 1870 Gay homestead | |

HUSBAND __James Alfred Masterson__
Born __October 24, 1827__ Place __Logan County, Kentucky__
Married __April 6, 1854__ Place _____ __Missouri__
Occupation __Blacksmith,Farmer__ Resided at __Ky.Mo.Cal.Ore.Wash. Idaho__
Church Affil. __Cumberland Presbyterian__ War Serv. __Rogue River Indian War 1855-'56__
Died __September 11,1908__ Place __Coeur d'Alene, Idaho. Kootenai Co.__
Buried _____ Place __Forest Cem. Coeur d'Alene__    Sheet submitted by:
Other wives __Martha Ann Gay, August 27,1871 Lane Co. Ore.__   __James Mortensen__
Father __Lazarus Masterson b.1782, N.C. d. 1859, Mo.__   __118 S. Fairview__
Mother (maiden name) __Elizabeth Givens  ca 1791 Ky, 1865 MO.__   __Burns, OR 97720__
                                                        Relationship to
WIFE __Vilinda Harriet Campbell__                        Husb.: __g.g.grandson__
Born __August 10, 1837__ Place __Lafayette County, Missouri__   Relationship to
Church Affil. __Cumberland Presbyterian__ Occupation __Housewife__   Wife: __g.g.grandson__
Died __February 20, 1870__ Place __Waconda, Marion Co. Oregon__
Buried _____ Place __Bell Passi Cem. Woodburn__    Place sources of information and
Other husb._____                                    additional information on
Father __Henry Campbell  b. 1799 Va. d. 1873 Mo.__    reverse side.
Mother (maiden name) __Nancy W. Ashburn  b. 1797 Va.  d. 1880 Mo.__

| CHILDREN | BORN When Where | DIED When Where | MARRIED To whom When Where |
|---|---|---|---|
| 1 Gilkey | May 25, 1855 Lane Co. Oregon | May 6, 1876 Oregon bur. Canyon City | |
| 2 Iphigenia (Genie) (Lusiana) | Dec. 7, 1856 Lane Co. Oregon | April 11, 1941 Woodburn, OR Bell Passi | John David Smith Feb. 4, 1874 Portland,OR |
| 3 Mary W. (May) | Feb. 7, 1858 Lane Co. Oregon | May 17, 1934 Salem, OR Bell Passi | Wilbur Fisk Cauthorn Nov. 18, 1891 Marion Co. OR |
| 4 Henry H. | ca 1860 Lane Co. Oregon | March 25, 1902 Harney Co. Drewsey Cem. | Viola Presley Nov. 20, 1891 Burns, OR |
| 5 Givens Montgomery (Dink) | ca 1862 Gervais Oregon | May 18, 1947 Absarokee Co. Montana | 1.Alice Griffith 6-22-92 Saratoga,Wy. 2.Grace Borland-Mont. |
| 6 Claiborn (Clay) | Oct. 20, 1864 Polk Co. Oregon | Oct. 25, 1886 Oregon? Bell Passi | |
| 7 Alfred J. (Leafe) | Nov. 11, 1866 Lafayette, Yamhill Co. OR | Mar. 1, 1938 Juntura, OR Bur. Ontario,OR | Clara E. Rutherford Dec. 30, 1902 Burns, OR |
| 8 Elizabeth (Bess) | ca 1869 Marion Co. Oregon | Aug. 10, 1937 Coeur d'Alene Forest Cem. | Robert Render Mann Nov. 23, 1887 Spokane, WA |
| 9 | | | |
| 10 John Balf | Mar. 12, 1873 Silverton, OR Marion Co. | October 27, 1874 Canyon City Grant Co., OR | |
| 11 Freddie Eugene | May 23, 1875 Creswell, OR Lane C. | ca. 1879 Upper Cascades Wasco Co. OR | |
| 12 Frances Hortense (Dot) | Feb. 11, 1877 Cogswell res. Lane Co. OR | Nov. 8, 1951 Eugene, Or Cremated, bur? | Louis Vitus June 8, 1898 Eugene, Lane Co. |

*Oregon Genealogical Society, Eugene, Oregon*